LIVING IN A
D.A.I.S.Y. AGE

LIVING IN A D.A.I.S.Y. AGE

The Music, Culture, and World De La Soul Made

Austin McCoy

JOHN MURRAY

First published in the United States in 2026 by One Signal Publishers/Atria Books,
an imprint of Simon & Schuster, LLC
First published in Great Britain in 2026 by John Murray (Publishers)

1

Copyright © Austin McCoy 2026

The right of Austin McCoy to be identified as the Author of the Work has been asserted by him in accordance with the Copyright, Designs and Patents Act 1988.

Interior design by Davina Mock-Maniscalco

All rights reserved. No part of this publication may be reproduced, stored in a retrieval system, or transmitted, in any form or by any means without the prior written permission of the publisher, nor be otherwise circulated in any form of binding or cover other than that in which it is published and without a similar condition being imposed on the subsequent purchaser.

A CIP catalogue record for this title is available from the British Library

Hardback ISBN 9781399814669
Trade Paperback ISBN 9781399814676
ebook ISBN 9781399814683

Typeset in Adobe Garamond Pro

Printed and bound in Great Britain by Clays Ltd, Elcograf S.p.A.

John Murray policy is to use papers that are natural, renewable and recyclable products and made from wood grown in sustainable forests. The logging and manufacturing processes are expected to conform to the environmental regulations of the country of origin.

Carmelite House
50 Victoria Embankment
London EC4Y 0DZ

www.johnmurraypress.co.uk

John Murray Press, part of Hodder & Stoughton Limited
An Hachette UK company

The authorised representative in the EEA is Hachette Ireland,
8 Castlecourt Centre, Dublin 15, D15 XTP3, Ireland (email: info@hbgi.ie)

This book is dedicated to Angelith and Melvin McCoy, my parents, who laid the foundation for my love of music and pursuit of understanding.

CONTENTS

PREFACE: What Does It All Mean?	1
CHAPTER 1: *Ain't Hip to be Labelled a Hippie*	9
CHAPTER 2: *De La Soul Is Dead*	50
CHAPTER 3: We Might Blow Up: The Theory of *Buhloone Mindstate*	77
CHAPTER 4: *Stakes Is High*	114
CHAPTER 5: Guidance for Change	154
CHAPTER 6: We're Still Here	191
EPILOGUE: The Future	231
APPENDIX: De La Soul: A Listening Guide	237
ACKNOWLEDGMENTS	247
NOTES	251
INDEX	279

PREFACE

What Does It All Mean?

In 2019, I finally got to teach one of my dream courses—The History of Hip-Hop Culture in America—while working as a professor at Auburn University. I scheduled a class discussion about the Native Tongues and prepared to talk about them, one of my favorite rap collectives, and a couple of my all-time favorite rap groups that were also members—A Tribe Called Quest and De La Soul. I'd start with Queen Latifah and Monie Love's "Ladies First," then follow that with the Native Tongues segment from the Netflix documentary series *Hip-Hop Evolution*.

As students watched the documentary's footage of Maseo, Posdnuos, and Trugoy rapping "Me Myself and I," I could see their faces light up.

"So," I asked, "what did y'all think?"

"Oh my God! I love how weird De La Soul is!" one student said.

"Why haven't I heard of them before?" another asked.

My students' reactions to De La Soul interested me because the group looked and sounded much different than many of the class's stated favorites—maybe except for Odd Future—Drake, Kendrick Lamar, Travis Scott, Young Thug, Future, Migos, 21 Savage, Juice WRLD, and Cardi B.

More than the other groups and artists profiled in the *Hip-Hop Evolution* episode, my students were drawn to De La Soul's aesthetic. They were colorful. My students appreciated Posdnuos's, Maseo's, and Trugoy's willingness to dress differently and be themselves, qualities they had not always seen in some contemporary rap artists.

Unfortunately, the students could not leave the classroom invigorated and jump on to their phones to listen to their newly discovered favorite artists. De La Soul's catalog on Tommy Boy Records, which had reacquired their entire discography, was not available on streaming services at the time of the class.

"What?!" one student exclaimed.

I explained to them how De La Soul's music sampling techniques on their first three albums, along with the group's ongoing disputes with Warner Music and Tommy Boy Records, had put them in a heap of legal trouble. The students came from a generation that has grown up listening to artists sample music from all genres, including old-school rap, so the class sympathized with De La Soul's position as artists. It was a pattern I've seen in every hip-hop class I've taught, with students tending to argue that sampling is in itself a legitimate art.

But despite their lack of direct access to De La Soul's music, the conversation seemed to register with the class anyway. I organized a "draft" of classic music for the students later that week where they got to choose a notable rap album and make a case for why it deserved selection. One student picked De La Soul's *3 Feet High and Rising* second. (OutKast's stellar third album, *Aquemini*, went first.) Another desired to focus on De La Soul for their final project, informing me, "I'll see if I can find their music some other way."

Bug Out

Before De La Soul won the rights to their catalog back in 2023, it was frustrating to have these conversations with students about the erasure of one of the genre's most influential groups. How could I

WHAT DOES IT ALL MEAN?

explain the importance of the group's production techniques, skits, and non-single tracks when the albums themselves were inaccessible? I tried to get around the limitations by showing available music videos and documentaries on the group, and outside of the classroom, I shared the material on social media and included De La Soul songs on mix CDs I gave to friends.

Try as I might, the inability of younger generations to stream or buy De La Soul's Tommy Boy catalog left a gaping hole in the history of hip-hop culture. It is not as if I am talking about missing out on grainy, pirated video of early Grandmaster Flash DJ parties from the 1970s. De La Soul released six albums owned by Tommy Boy (not counting compilations and singles), and, poof, they were gone. *Some* of us knew they existed because we still owned physical copies, those relics of a time before iTunes and Spotify. But with a rare few exceptions, like *Hip-Hop Evolution* or the 2011 documentary *Beats, Rhymes & Life: The Travels of A Tribe Called Quest*, young folks rarely got to experience the wonders of *3 Feet High and Rising* and *De La Soul Is Dead* in all of their sprawling glory. Most importantly, De La Soul's absence on streaming platforms prevented younger listeners from seeing the historical connections between their music and that of contemporaries like Tyler, The Creator and Earl Sweatshirt.

De La Soul, along with other Native Tongues artists, helped establish an iconic aesthetic, sonic, and creative lineage in rap music and hip-hop culture. Along with Public Enemy's *It Takes a Nation of Millions to Hold Us Back* and the Beastie Boys' *Paul's Boutique*, De La Soul's first two albums, *3 Feet High and Rising* and *De La Soul Is Dead*, paved the way for the pastiche sampling techniques of artists today like The Alchemist. Critics have praised Kanye West and Pharrell for their ability to incorporate different genres into their hip-hop production. Well, De La Soul pioneered that, too. De La Soul's incorporation of comical skits—Prince Paul calls them "bug out pieces"—inspired groups like N.W.A, Dr. Dre, and Wu-Tang Clan to infuse some levity into their albums. And it is hard to talk about "cinematic" musical storytelling by the likes of Kendrick Lamar without discussing *De La Soul Is Dead*.

But most importantly, De La Soul was willing to be *weird*—a quality that paved the way for nineties' iconoclasts like OutKast and Missy Elliott.

"Me Myself and I"

I am an eighties baby, born in 1980 in Panama City, Florida, to Angelith and Melvin McCoy. Both of my parents, however, were born in Ohio. Dad was Mansfield through and through, but Mom was born in Cincinnati. She and her family moved and settled in Mansfield at some point in her youth. Mansfield sits in north central Ohio, about an hour north of Columbus and almost an hour and a half south of Cleveland. Mansfield is a rust belt town. It featured a diverse manufacturing sector—rubber, steel, auto parts, and appliances—and a robust working-class community until factories shut down in the early 1970s.

Nevertheless, Mom got fed up with Mansfield's dwindling opportunities for Black women, so she enlisted in the Air Force. Dad followed her as manufacturing jobs started drying up. My parents, but especially Mom, loved music. I only saw Dad's head nodding and foot tapping, but Mom loved to sing along. This makes sense because, according to Dad, Mom sang with a band that played in local bars as a teenager. They appreciated a lot of music that I assumed many Black thirtysomethings enjoyed—Earth, Wind & Fire, Stevie Wonder, The Spinners, The Brothers Johnson, Prince, and The Jackson 5.

Interestingly enough, I do not hold fond memories of my first encounters with music. The early eighties were full of good yet lightly sinister-sounding pop music. Think Michael Jackson's "Thriller," Rockwell's "Somebody's Watching Me," and Jermaine Jackson's 1984 self-titled album, *Jermaine Jackson (Dynamite)*. I shrank with fear when I heard the booming bass thundering from my parents' standing

WHAT DOES IT ALL MEAN?

speakers. I yelled because the overwhelming rhythmic thumps overwhelmed my senses. And when I realized I could not hear my own voice over the commotion, I cried. I covered my ears and begged my parents to turn the music down. Suffice to say, I was afraid of the bass and the funk.

Over time, I shed my fears as I marveled at Michael Jackson's moonwalking while watching the Motown 25 anniversary concert. A year later, my sister, Brandenn, was born early. We took a short trip from Panama City to stay in the Ronald McDonald House in Pensacola as she recovered from complications of her premature birth. In these years, I developed an appreciation for what my parents listened to; I started bopping to their classics before it all led me to this other musical genre called rap.

Then, in 1989, my life as a music listener changed. I watched De La Soul's "Me Myself and I" video for the first time and decided I liked what I was seeing.

Posdnuos, Trugoy, and Maseo's technicolor presentation, their weird haircuts, the catchy beat sampling Parliament's "Knee Deep," and an unforgettable chorus caught my attention. You could hear me repeat right after Posdnuos and Trugoy ended their verses, "It's just me, myself, and I."

I did not understand the specifics of "Me Myself and I" at the time. I could only gather that they spoke to what it meant to be different from their peers. And that I understood, since I was one of the "new kids" who'd arrived at school at the beginning of the year. Outside of playing a little basketball, soccer, and baseball, I was a quiet and shy nerd. Posdnuos wore his glasses proudly, and soon after watching "Me Myself and I" for the first time, I added a pair of my own because my eyesight had gone bad. (If you asked Mom, this was because I stayed up too late trying to read in the dark.)

That song, "Me Myself and I," and De La Soul's debut album, *3 Feet High and Rising*, arrived in music stores at a watershed moment in my life. Mom's service in the Air Force at the end of the

Cold War introduced me to the politics of the time at a very early age. My mother explained to me the history of the conflict, and the centrality of nuclear weapons in US foreign policy. I lived with a fear of ultimate destruction after Mom explained the effects of such weaponry. My anxiety drove me to read encyclopedia entries about the world wars and the booklets mom brought home demonstrating the horrific impacts any campaign of chemical or nuclear weapons would have on my world.

3 Feet High and Rising reflected a countercultural spirit flowing through Black culture and global politics. As many listened to De La Soul's record, as well as other, more explicitly political rap groups like Public Enemy, Polish workers sought independence from the Soviet Union, Black South Africans pushed off racial apartheid, Chinese people stood in front of tanks while protesting authoritarian rule, and East Germans knocked down the Berlin Wall and began crossing into West Germany without consequence. I watched this history unfold on TV with my parents.

Two of my earliest political memories involving my parents are related to Jesse Jackson and Nelson Mandela. While African Americans successfully protested colleges' and universities' business relationships with apartheid South Africa, Black activists and politicians struggled to defend civil rights gains in the era of Reaganomics. Reverend Jesse Jackson ran for the Democratic Party's nomination for president in 1984 and 1988 but lost, dashing my parents' hopes for something brighter ahead.

"Jesse would have won if white folks would have marched with him," Mom told Dad.

"I know," Dad said in response.

De La Soul offered an antidote to a dark decade, especially for Black folks living in cities. Posdnuos, Trugoy, Maseo, and their producer, Prince Paul, showed fans, rappers, and other hip-hop practitioners the importance of collective imagination and creativity in the face of a violent time. US intervention abroad, reckless policing,

WHAT DOES IT ALL MEAN?

incarceration, the crack cocaine crisis, and the HIV-AIDS epidemic had all come to the fore. De La Soul filled the need for something bright for me, demonstrating the importance of forging one's path and identity in a moment when traditional institutions, like the church, no longer retained the same type of appeal they had for previous generations. In 1992, Francis Fukuyama wrote an analysis of the Cold War that triumphantly declared that the coming fall of the Soviet Union represented the end of the battle between capitalism and communism and, in essence, the "end of history." That has proven wrong. But with the arrival of De La Soul, my history, at least as a rap fan, was just beginning.

CHAPTER 1

Ain't Hip to be Labelled a Hippie

"Yo, I see you got a whole lot of ideas. I got this group called De La Soul and if you want to try these ideas with us, we'd be down."

—Maseo

If nothing else, Kelvin "Posdnuos" Mercer, David "Trugoy" Jolicoeur, and Vincent "Maseo" Mason desired to be free—creatively, existentially, individually. They also wanted this freedom for everyone. Posdnuos told Johnny Dee in a 1989 interview in *Record Mirror*, "De La Soul, of the soul and from the soul. Everything we do is from here. Be yourself, that's our message. Me myself and I."

The trio (and we cannot forget their producer-mentor Paul "Prince Paul" Huston) were touring to promote their genre-bending and revolutionary debut album, *3 Feet High and Rising*. The group's sprawling twenty-four–track album revolutionized the genre and elevated the rap album to a high-concept art form. Using much of modern recorded music as their inspiration, De La Soul pioneered a collage approach to sampling, which entailed synthesizing and juxtaposing bits and pieces of music and sounds from various sources—psychedelic pop, funk, R&B, doo-wop, soul, and even television.

3 Feet High and Rising is an example of what historian Robin D. G. Kelley called "freedom dreaming." De La Soul's debut is a utopian rap album. They were among a cohort of rap artists that produced rap albums seemingly with few limits. Kelley argues about the Black radical tradition, "The idea that we could possibly go somewhere that exists only in our imaginations—that is, 'nowhere'—is the classic definition of utopia." Yet, on *3 Feet High and Rising*, De La Soul took listeners somewhere. They used their collective imagination to transport listeners to a place just beyond the realities of Reagan's America—the war on drugs, HIV/AIDS, police violence, and economic and racial inequality—to a newly wacky sonic world, complete with a revolutionary soundscape, quirky use of language, comical skits, and fantastical stories. All listeners had to do was place the vinyl plate on a record player, or put a tape in a Walkman or boombox or a compact disc in a CD player, and press play.

On *3 Feet High and Rising*, De La Soul developed and presented an ethos grounded in the belief of creative individualism, positivity, and a self-proclaimed authenticity that could only be derived from one's inventive spirit. They aspired to be different and desired to operate with little creative restrictions. Posdnuos said in 1989, "Different was always important. We never wanted to be in any way reminiscent of what was happening or what had been done before." They created and articulated their language and aesthetic. De La Soul also challenged dominant expressions of (Black) masculinity in rap. They made it okay for young Black men, and young men of color, to be weird, quirky, and vulnerable.

The group's dreamy psychedelic production and vibe on the album; their playfully innocent, whimsical, and positive lyrics; and the group's Day-Glo D.A.I.S.Y. aesthetic recalled the 1960s and 1970s counterculture to the point where Robert Hilburn of the *Los Angeles Times* famously declared that the album "may well be the 'Sgt. Pepper' of rap." Yet, their presentation and Tommy Boy Records' marketing strategy frustrated De La Soul as they resisted misinterpretations of their D.A.I.S.Y. idea, which means "Da Inner Soul, Y'all." Fears of being pigeonholed as happy-go-lucky hippies then pushed the group to reject Tommy Boy's and the rap industry's expectations that they remain the same stylistically. De La Soul's creative individualism would fuel the group's anti-corporate critique of the rap industry. As they grew up in the late 1980s and early 1990s, they learned to add a little hardness, via rap criticism, into their stylistic repertoire.

"I Can't Breathe Without It"

In a 1955 essay in *High Fidelity* magazine, novelist, literary critic, and essayist Ralph Ellison wrote about the struggles of writing while consumed by the neighborhood's incessant noises, "In those days it was either live with music or die with noise, and we chose rather desperately to live." Ellison then proceeded to complain about "preaching drunks," the jazz vocalist whose singing annoyed him, and the "howling cats and barking dogs." Then, Ellison pivots toward talking about his experiences trying to learn to play trumpet and how his practicing "terrorized" his neighborhood.

The point of Ellison's essay was to demonstrate how individual jazz musicians were able to synthesize what seemed to be discordant sounds into "a fluid style that reduced the chaos of living to form." While rappers share the craft of writing with essayists like Ellison, many hip-hop artists are similar to the jazz musicians he wrote about because they train themselves to engage in similar forms of audio synthesis. However, what distinguishes rap artists from the jazz musicians of Ellison's time is their ability to take all the noises around them and make use of them musically. This is especially true with Posdnuos, Maseo, Trugoy, and Prince Paul. In Ellison's day, one can imagine them as kids who disturb others with trumpets, trombones, or singing. But in the 1980s, they took turntables, microphones, sampling machines, their parents' record collections, television shows and movies, and other noises and created life-giving art with their other artistic inspirations such as comics and fashion. They sampled everything, from Liberace to, yes, barking dogs. I will talk about them sampling dogs in a later chapter.

Posdnuos, Trugoy, and Maseo not only lived with the music, but they seemed to be born into it. Music was part of their DNA. For

Posdnuos, the albums from his father's record collection captured his attention more than playing with toys. "Music called out to me at an early age," Posdnuos told LL Cool J in a 2023 interview. "I don't remember a moment in my life being introduced to music. I was always part of it. It's like air." Posdnuos was an avid reader, which inspired him to write and eventually drew him closer to rap music. "Comic books were my life," Posdnuos explains. "I used to actually try to create comic books. That's why when hip-hop came along, the act of storytelling, it meant a lot to me."

Maseo concurred. "[Music is] oxygen. I can't breathe without it. I can't live without it. If I don't have it, I got problems. I got to have music. It's my drug." Maseo was six years old when he first started playing with turntables. "When I was able to conceive what was happening with turntables, I was on it," he told LL Cool J. Before moving to Long Island, according to Maseo, a babysitter's boyfriend first introduced him to using turntables as an instrument. Over time, Maseo saw old discarded stereo gear as potential instruments. "I was that kid walking the streets, seeing old equipment, taking it home, and trying to add fuses to amps and things like that."

Trugoy added extra flavor. He expressed his creativity linguistically and visually through fashion and visual art. He derived inspiration from his Haitian background when naming the group. Trugoy also took his dad's old clothing and turned it into fresh outfits that distinguished him from other young Black men inspired by rappers like Run-D.M.C. and Rakim. But there also seemed to be something intrinsic regarding Trugoy's approach to music. He might have had synesthesia, giving him the capacity to experience music audibly and visually. Posdnuos later remembered, "Dave was very colorful with his words. Very vivid . . . When he hears music, he starts seeing colors."

Although Posdnuos, Trugoy, and Maseo found each other while living on Long Island, none of them, including DJ Prince Paul, were born there. Their families, like many, migrated from New York City's boroughs in the 1970s and 1980s. Kelvin Mercer was born in the Bronx, while David Jolicoeur and Vincent Mason, Jr., were born in Brooklyn. Maseo was the last of the group to move to Long Island, in 1984, and he explained why his new surroundings were the perfect place for cultural experimentation. "Long Island was a bit more multicultural. Black, White, and Hispanics lived amongst each other instead of across town. On Long Island, there was a mix of everything as one community. They had grass, trees, houses, NBC, ABC, WBLS radio, and then we eventually picked up Kiss FM," Maseo told *Wax Poetics* in 2013.

While the future members of De La Soul did not come of age in New York City's five boroughs, they all admit the Long Island community nurtured their artistry. Posdnuos explained to journalist Brian Coleman, "In LI you had your own four walls that weren't attached to anyone else's four walls. There wasn't the city congestion." Dave concurred, "Hip-hop was something we had the opportunity to digest from afar. If we had all grown up for all our years in the Bronx, De La Soul definitely wouldn't have been the same."

Paul Huston was born in 1967 in Queens, but his family migrated to Amityville in the early 1970s. Exposed to a burgeoning hip-hop culture at an early age, he developed into a DJ prodigy. Huston was the first member of the group to get into hip-hop (or rap), even before the culture had a name. In an interview with Ethan Brown for *The Source* magazine, Paul recalled, "I was going to block parties and backyard parties in Long Island and in Brooklyn. . . . That's how I got exposed to different styles. I would sit in front of the DJ from the time I rode my bike to the block party until they loaded the equipment back up." Over time, Paul learned the most popular records DJs spun and eventually started DJing once he reached the fifth grade. He worked with fellow Long Island rapper Biz Markie in eighth grade and joined the rap group Stetsasonic as the DJ and youngest member in 1984. Maseo says he saw Paul at a party he attended within the first month of arriving on Long Island. But another two years passed before they encountered each other as artists.

LIVING IN A D.A.I.S.Y. AGE

De La Soul was not the only rap act to draw inspiration from growing up on Long Island. Public Enemy, Rakim, and Biz Markie illustrated how rappers' musical styles reflected their suburban experiences. These artists developed distinct rap styles, sounds, and outlooks. Rakim introduced a new rap style with slower verbal delivery and more complex rhyme schemes. Biz Markie might have appeared goofy, but he could do it all—beatbox, rap, sing, and entertain. Of course, Public Enemy, like De La Soul, brought a new sound to hip-hop—one that was more urgent, noisy, and intense.

Developing a hip-hop scene on what became known as "Strong Island" complicates early hip-hop's urban history. Rap was not just limited to the dilapidated landscape of the South Bronx, nor the projects in Queens. The ascent of Strong Island also reminds us of the complicated racial history of suburbia. Of course, Long Island was home to Levittown, the suburb developed by William Levitt's company, Levitt & Sons, which mandated residents abide by racial covenants excluding African Americans and Jewish people. Yet, Long Island boasted its share of predominately Black suburbs and neighborhoods. For example, Rakim grew up in mostly Black Wyandanch. Posdnuos and Trugoy grew up in East Massapequa.

"This is where it all starts, yo," Luck, Posdnuos's brother, said about Amityville High School. Hip-hop entered the schools as more Black and Brown youth took to the genre in the 1970s and 1980s. Thus, like many young people, hip-hop artists, fans, and critics often found their community and honed their talents in high school in the 1980s. Future Native Tongues brethren Q-Tip and Ali Shaheed Muhammad of A Tribe Called Quest and Afrika Baby Bam and Mike Gee of the Jungle Brothers met at Murry Bergtraum High School; Busta Rhymes attended George Westinghouse Career and Technical Education High School, the same school as The Notorious B.I.G.; and Posdnuos, Maseo, and Trugoy connected while attending Amityville High.

Posdnuos, Trugoy, and Maseo took the art form seriously early on.

Posdnuos claimed the creative environment encouraged him to engage with hip-hop culture. He told LL Cool J, "Everyone in the neighborhood, whether you was trying to breakdance, you were involved in this culture that was evolving that would become hip-hop." Posdnuos then explained, "Just like-minded individuals start, like, boosting the creativity to a level like, 'Yo, I can do this. I can do this for a job.'"

Posdnuos and Trugoy began their artistic relationship in 1985 when they joined a rap group called Easy Street. Like scores of music bands forming in and around New York City at the time, the outfit did not last. Trugoy said the other members took music less seriously than he and Posdnuos. "Pos and I really clicked personally. . . . So we broke with Easy Street and got down with Charlie Rock, who was a good friend of mine. We didn't have a name—we were starting to put music and concepts together." Maseo then joined the group at the behest of Rock.

The new group needed a name. Charlie Rock left the group, and Posdnuos floated calling themselves "The Threesome" since they were left with three members. Trugoy and Maseo shot that down. Years later, Posdnuos would recount the origins of the group's name, which translates to "From the Soul," in a radio interview. "I feel like we do everything from our heart and soul. Why don't we call ourselves From the Soul?" However, Trugoy refined it. "Why don't we say De La Soul?" Posdnuos attributes Trugoy's suggestion to his ability to coin terms, but also to his upbringing as a Haitian American. In an interview in 2016, Trugoy told drum impresario Questlove, "My family are Haitian. A little bit of that lingo, a little bit of French in there, a little broken French, had me thinking of an option, or an alternative, of 'of the soul.'" Ironically, De La Soul's name also caused some confusion, as the members recount how they surprised a mostly Latinx audience. "People thought we were Spanish," Posdnuos recalls. "Our in-store [performance] was in the Bronx and nothing but Dominicans and Puerto Ricans showed up," Maseo chimed in.

Mason, Mercer, and Jolicoeur also needed to choose their individual names. "Posdnuos" is one of rap's weirdest and unique names. Mercer explained the origins of his name to Questlove. "One of the names I wanted to call Easy Street was Sopsounds. Dave was like, 'Nah . . .' So let me use it: DJ Sopsounds. So, when I turned 'sop' backwards, it became 'Pos'; 'sound' became 'dnuos.'" Jolicoeur also chose a weird name—"Trugoy the Dove." Trugoy is "yogurt" spelled backward and was a testament to his love for the dairy product. Mason seemed to choose the most "normal" hip-hop moniker—"P. A. Pasemaster Mase." By choosing his name, Maseo paid homage to DJ sound system culture. Additionally, the trio would be among the first to establish aliases—Posdnuos also soon became known as "Plug 1"; Trugoy was "Plug 2"; Maseo was "Plug 3." Their "plug" names stemmed from their rap routine that became the song "Plug Tunin'," referencing stereo inputs.

Stage names in any performing arts culture are important. They provide a way to exercise more agency, especially for marginalized youth, and to express more self-definition and self-determination. The group's name, "De La Soul," evokes spiritual and Black cultural traditions going back to the enslavement of African peoples in the Western hemisphere. Black people have relied upon their relationship with a spirit world for shelter and strength since enslavement. This human struggle against violent oppression helped shape Black culture and much of Black politics over the last four hundred years. Thus, it is no surprise that Black intellectuals, singers, dancers, and comedians generally theorized about, performed, and embodied the concept of "soul." Black sociologist and historian W. E. B. Du Bois famously named his 1903 book *The Souls of Black Folk*, and used it to ruminate on the meanings of "soul" in Black thought, politics, and culture, including music. Black poet, activist, and scholar Amiri Baraka (known then as LeRoi Jones) also argued that spirituality is central to Black music. "Indeed, to go back in any historical (or emotional) line of ascent in Black music leads us inevitably to religion, i.e., spirit worship. This phenomenon is always at the root in Black art, the worship of spirit—or at least the summoning of or by such force." However, one of the important features of Black experiences in enslavement and emancipation was a devotion to forward-looking, forward-thinking, and forward-living. Black Americans have engaged in the centuries-long struggle to survive, fight, and endure oppression, all in an attempt to pave a future for their children and their children's children. In doing so, they've often had to articulate their visions for the future to inspire themselves and others.

Consequently, it is not a coincidence that Posdnuos, Trugoy, and Maseo called themselves "De La Soul" and "soul brothers and sisters" and "soul children" rather than hippies. Their simple, yet weird, name reached back to an ancestral past while they devoted themselves to the ethic of constantly looking forward—to being futurists in their artistic direction. But this futuristic drive ties De La Soul back to a history of Black music that includes not only the enslaved who sang spirituals but also blues singers like Bessie Smith and vocalist Nina Simone, jazz performers like John Coltrane and Ornette Coleman, and funkateers like George Clinton.

De La Soul came together at a time when more progressive Black artists used their work to comment on social issues and challenge racism in US popular culture. Long Islanders Carlton "Chuck D" Ridenhour and William "Flavor Flav" Drayton formed Public Enemy the same year, 1985, creating one of rap music's most dynamic groups. Living Colour guitarist Vernon Reid and music critic, intellectual, and artist Greg Tate formed the Black Rock Coalition in 1985 to challenge racist stereotypes in rock and popular music. Then, Prince, who had already challenged gender norms within Black music and sexual norms in broader society, released his brooding and conscious *Sign O' the Times* in 1987. Other progressive Black artists, like Tracy Chapman and Lenny Kravitz, soon followed.

Plug Tunin'

By 1986, Trugoy, Posdnuos, and Maseo were already performing locally. The nascent group had not produced much music outside of their live routine and a few songs that would comprise their demo tape. The showcase consisted of three tracks—"Freedom of Speak," "De La Game" (which would become "D.A.I.S.Y. Age"), and "Plug Tunin'." The last track, "Plug Tunin'," comprised the group's live concert set. Constructed from a pause tape—a crude, yet intricate form of production where artists sequenced segments of beats from other songs—"Plug Tunin'" took the opening horn riffs from The Invitation's "Written on the Wall" and laid it over a drum beat. The demo, which the group later released with their 35th Anniversary edition of *3 Feet High and Rising*, reflects the do-it-yourself feel of pause tape production as the individual samples are pronounced while Trugoy's and Posdnuos's vocals remain muffled. However, the work still illustrates how De La Soul distinguished themselves from their peers, many of whom were producing rock-infused or James Brown–sampled tracks. In fact, the The Invitation sample on the demo version almost sounds as if it were "chopped and screwed" in the style that Houston's DJ Screw would become known for innovating.

While De La Soul worked on producing a compelling demo tape, none of them had reached the status of DJ Prince Paul. Since he joined Stetsasonic, the group had released several singles that became local hits, including the infamous "Go Stetsa." Based on a pulsating drum loop, "Go Stetsa" turned into a robbery anthem as the break signaled to stick-up kids that it was time to demand unsuspecting clubgoers' belongings. Trugoy reflected, "We were just the average high schoolers clowning around and being goofballs and trying to be part of the 'in-crowd.' Seeing Paul made us think making music was possible."

Maseo connected with Prince Paul first. Maseo had served as DJ for another rapper, Gangsta B, who'd signed to a small record label that had grown frustrated with their artist's inability to produce. After the label hired Prince Paul to construct a beat for Gangsta B, Paul and Maseo came together and agreed that the rapper's skills failed to reach their standard. Maseo suggested that Paul should check out a group he had been working with—De La Soul. Maseo, Posdnuos, and Trugoy met Paul at his house with a rough copy of "Plug Tunin'." Impressed with the song, Paul began working to improve it. The nucleus was in place.

"Three Black Guys from Way Out in Long Island"

Stetsasonic's founder, Daddy-O, introduced De La Soul's music to Tommy Boy Records executive Monica Lynch. Tom Silverman, Tommy Boy's CEO, owned and ran the record label, which built its reputation by signing DJ legend Afrika Bambaataa and the group Soul Sonic Force and managing a diverse roster that included artists Stetsasonic and Force M.D.'s. De La Soul's offbeat appearance and demo left Lynch and Silverman intrigued. For Silverman, taking on De La Soul would be a worthy risk. "When I heard De La Soul the first time, I remember saying, 'This is going to do nothing, or it's going to be really big.' Because when you listen to it, it was so bizarre compared to anything out. And whether it did something, or didn't do something, we loved it and we thought it was important that it came out." De La Soul signed with Tommy Boy Records in 1987.

The consensus at Tommy Boy Records was that De La Soul was "different." Posdnuos's, Trugoy's, and Maseo's stage names and their eclectic appearance struck Lynch. "And they had, you know, these unusual haircuts and their style was completely antithetical to the prevailing aesthetic of hip-hop at the time, which is much more driven by black leather and gold chains and such. They were definitely like these introverted, nerdy guys that were very cool," Lynch said in the 2016 documentary *De La Soul Is Not Dead*. Dante Ross, Tommy Boy's A&R who oversaw De La Soul on the recording of their first album, wrote in his memoir, "When I first met them, I was confused. They were three Black guys from way out in Long Island. . . . But they dressed way out, even by my downtown standards. . . . They were progressive cats, and we clicked right away."

LIVING IN A D.A.I.S.Y. AGE

De La Soul differentiated themselves from other rap soloists and groups coming out of New York in the mid-1980s. Run-D.M.C., the first rap group to sell more than a million records, had revolutionized rap's sound, pioneered the culture's street fashion, and remained at the height of their powers. Def Jam Records' young upstart, LL Cool J, demonstrated an aggressive style over hard, Rick Rubin–produced, rock-tinged beats. The Beastie Boys, comprised of three Jewish kids from New York City, burst onto the scene as rap's newest phenomenon. Their debut album, *Licensed to Ill*, also produced by Rubin, extended rap's reach to young white Americans, many of whom identified with the group's masculine sound and punk and frat sensibilities.

However, De La Soul constructed their own aesthetic elsewhere. Between their formation and *3 Feet High and Rising*'s release in 1989, the group found inspiration in old-school hip-hop artists and groups. One can hear the influence of early 1980s rap groups like Crash Crew, a Sugar Hill Records group that pioneered rapping *and singing* on tracks like "Breaking Bells (Take Me to the Mardis Gras)" and "On the Radio." While De La Soul did not sing on songs, tracks like "Plug Tunin'" and "Buddy" reflected their ability to translate the fluidity of a live routine onto a limited recording. Beatboxer and rapper Doug E. Fresh, his Get Fresh Crew, and British rapper Slick Rick also influenced De La Soul's sounds. Tracks such as "The Show" and "La Di Da Di" were standout rap storytelling songs featuring Doug E. Fresh's beatboxing and both artists bragging about their lyrical prowess while spinning tales about their excursions in New York City, partying, and interactions with women. These tracks surely helped influence De La Soul's approach on *3 Feet High and Rising*. Doug E. Fresh and the Get Fresh Crew hit the market in 1985, the same year members of De La Soul began collaborating.

The group also credits the Ultramagnetic MC's as one of their main inspirations. Led by lyricist Kool Keith and backed by Ced Gee, TR Love, and DJ Moe Love, the group dropped their left-of-center debut, *Critical Beatdown*, in 1988. To listen to *Critical Beatdown* is to hear somewhat of a *3 Feet High and Rising* prototype, as the group pioneered new sampling techniques. Most importantly, Kool Keith and Ced Gee delivered abstract verses using rhyme schemes and terminology no rappers had used before. Instead of straightforward lyricism and songs declaring one's superiority like LL Cool J's "I'm Bad" or Run-D.M.C.'s "Sucker MCs," Kool Keith and Ced Gee dove into unorthodox ways to demonstrate their lyrical prowess on songs like "Ego Trippin'." "Of the average formulation, apply mechanically, maintainable display expressed by alternate microwave frequencies, directly inorganic, operating logically," Kool Keith rapped on the song. Maseo later said in his Red Bull Music Academy lecture in 2012, "It was really Ultramagnetic that was the catalyst to want to be different and to speak your own language. . . . But Kool Keith was on something else. And that was the inspiration. We gon' be different. We gon' come up with our own language. We gon' make you believe what we believe."

De La Soul also wanted to look different. They stayed away from the track suits, Adidas shoes, fat gold chains, and the Dapper Dan–inspired outfits. Instead, they donned colorful button-up shirts, medallions with peace and flower signs, and weird haircuts. Posdnuos and Maseo credit Trugoy for influencing the group's colorful and offbeat style. And just like they appropriated records from their parents' music collections, they also liberated threads from their dads' wardrobes. According to Posdnuos, "Dave would be like, 'Let's take our fathers' old pants that were bell bottoms but straight-leg them. Then they'll look how Lees look, but the patterns will be different." They also helped pioneer the Afrocentric look, alongside the Jungle Brothers, A Tribe Called Quest, and Queen Latifah, as they often wore African-inspired dashikis. As the visual artist of the group, Trugoy fashioned their notable fade hairstyle that looked like he forgot to cut the top of one side of his hair. De La Soul made fashion cool for the kids who could not or did not want to be like Run-D.M.C. or LL Cool J. They unknowingly inspired later artists like Questlove and Common.

But being different and coming from left field was risky, especially in a genre as young as rap with rigid standards of Black masculinity. They did not look like "typical" Black male rappers. They did not rap like proven stars LL Cool J, Kool Moe Dee, or Chuck D. Their music did not sound like Eric B. and Rakim or Boogie Down Productions. Tommy Boy's executives understood this when they released "Plug Tunin'" as a 12-inch single in June 1988. The song might thrive because De La Soul did not sound like any rappers out at that moment. Consequently, according to Trugoy, Tommy Boy wanted to release the song right away. For Lynch, "Plug Tunin'" would represent the group's introduction to the wider rap world in New York. Tommy Boy A&R representative Dante Ross spirited the record to DJ Red Alert at Kiss FM, and the song caught the ears of many. The single's success opened up other important doors. Tommy Boy decided they wanted to release another single, and it also caught Red Alert's attention. He then connected his nephew, Mike Gee from the Jungle Brothers, with Trugoy, Maseo, and Posdnuos, laying the foundation for the creation of the Native Tongues.

"Transmitting Live from Mars"

De La Soul recorded *3 Feet High and Rising* in two months. They and Prince Paul came to the studio prepared with ideas and sketches of songs. With Prince Paul producing and mentoring Maseo, Trugoy, and Posdnuos, the group developed a collaborative approach to recording. However, not one person in the group was the "sole producer" of the album. Trugoy told journalist Brian Coleman, "Whatever idea was brought to the table, we'd all just expound on it. . . . It didn't matter who brought it. It could have been us four, it could have been my sister. It was all about enjoying music and creating more music." The ecstatic tone of *3 Feet High and Rising* reflected the group's excitement during the recording. Posdnuos later told the *New York Times*, "It was just a process of all our separate lives and the music within them just being dumped into sessions of fun."

The group's sampling technique distinguished their first record from many others in the late 1980s. Rather than relying on known samples from people like James Brown and popular drum breaks circulating on compilations, De La Soul dug deep into the archives to gather scores of samples. As Prince Paul explained in the 1989 short documentary *De La Speaks*, "If you have a creative mind, you can basically use anything. . . ."

De La Soul's approach to sampling was almost ecumenical in its breadth. It is hard not to dream in technicolor after a listening session with *3 Feet High and Rising*. They pulled from contemporaries Public Enemy and Beastie Boys, but also television shows like *Schoolhouse Rock*, and sampled tracks from the 1960s, 1970s, and 1980s, carving out sections from doo-wop, rock, psychedelic pop, funk, R&B, and soul. They seamlessly layered and stitched together these samples over drum loops, giving the record its sonic buoyancy. Today, the record would cost millions of dollars to produce with all the samples, making such a feat virtually impossible. But according to Tom Silverman, the record cost less than $30,000 to make in its day.

The short skit "Transmitting Live from Mars" exemplifies the album's psychedelic sound. De La Soul adapted the first few seconds of The Turtles' 1968 recording "You Showed Me," slowed it down, and looped it throughout the rest of the song. The group overlays a French language lesson on top of the newly constructed beat, illustrating Prince Paul's point that one could take *anything* and use it.

3 Feet High and Rising was introduced to the world on March 3, 1989. Their debut album dropped amid a string of astonishing rap releases in the late 1980s—Eric B. and Rakim's *Follow the Leader*, Boogie Down Productions' *By All Means Necessary*, Slick Rick's *The Great Adventures of Slick Rick*, N.W.A's *Straight Outta Compton*, and Public Enemy's *It Takes a Nation of Millions to Hold Us Back*. De La Soul somehow matched Public Enemy's sample-based style.

Yet, while Public Enemy were scientists of sound, De La Soul were human synthesizers, seamlessly juxtaposing various genres to produce more infectious melodic tracks. Like Greg Tate declared in his review of *3 Feet*, "If PE advanced the art of sampling-and-stitching to the level of microsurgery on *It Takes a Nation of Millions to Hold Us Back*, De La Soul take that knowledge to the bridge and drop it off in Toontown." Of course, De La Soul's collage style of rap production eventually got them into legal trouble with The Turtles. However, the group demonstrated how rappers could extend their sampling reach far beyond classics of R&B and hip-hop, to also Johnny Cash, Parliament Funkadelic, and Daryl Hall & John Oates.

Maseo, Prince Paul, Posdnuos, and Trugoy also preempted another group that used a collage of samples to produce a hip-hop gem. Seeking to distance themselves from the frat-boy aesthetic found on their debut album, the Beastie Boys' Ad-Rock, MCA, and Mike D fled to Los Angeles, where they connected with the production duo The Dust Brothers (Mike Simpson and John King) to construct *Paul's Boutique*. Together they expanded the group's sonic palette as they also pulled from various genres to produce a lo-fi and dense record. Although the album still contained the brash, obnoxious, and playful lyrics that their fans loved on songs like "Hey Ladies," the album was seen by many as too much of a departure at the time. Yet *Paul's Boutique* would become totemic in its influence on the genre.

Like *Paul's Boutique* and other albums such as Run-D.M.C.'s self-titled debut album, *Paid in Full*, and *It Takes a Nation of Millions to Hold Us Back*, De La Soul's *3 Feet High and Rising* elevated rap in the album format. From the music to their Day-Glo cover art and comic strip explaining the group's mythical origins in their liner notes, this was a complete work of art. De La Soul illustrated how artists wove silly songs, serious tracks, verbal manifestos, dance music, and comedic skits (or as Prince Paul called them, "bug out pieces") together cohesively. The album used the music, their image, and creative marketing to articulate an ethos of creative individualism De La Soul would adhere to for the rest of their career. It scrambled critics' and their peers' understandings of what it meant to be rappers in the late 1980s with its expansive, yet whimsical and surreal demonstration of free imagination. The group not only built their own world but also hinted at constructing their own universe. They created their own language. They told stories that had not been told before in rap. They revealed an identity that complicated Black masculinity by being vulnerable, silly, ironic, and serious. The group also took inspiration from cultural futurist George Clinton, leader of Parliament Funkadelic. As one reads in a comic book–style fictionalized origin story about De La Soul in *3 Feet High and Rising*'s insert, Prince Paul summons the group from Mars for an "ultimate mission" to record *3 Feet High and Rising*.

These characteristics are why *Los Angeles Times* critic Robert Hilburn surmised that the album "may well be the 'Sgt. Pepper' of rap." With *3 Feet High and Rising*, De La Soul accomplished what The Beatles, The Beach Boys, Marvin Gaye, and Sly & the Family Stone did for pop music album construction in the late 1960s and early 1970s. *Sgt. Pepper's Lonely Hearts Club Band*, *Pet Sounds*, *What's Going On*, and *There's a Riot Goin' On* innovated the pop album into artistic pieces that created their self-contained worlds. De La Soul's Black sci-fi comic announcing the group's arrival recalls Funkadelic's futuristic imagery and messaging on covers of albums like the group's 1975 record *Let's Take It to the Stage*.

Critics heralded *3 Feet High and Rising* at the time of its release. Robert Christgau called De La Soul's debut "an inevitable development in the class history of rap, they're new wave to Public Enemy's punk" in his A-review. Michael Azerrad wrote that *3 Feet High and Rising* was "one of the most original rap records to ever come down the pike" in his three-star *Rolling Stone* review. Most importantly, other rappers and musicians raved about the album and group at De La Soul's release party. "The music they're doing is not like anything out right now. . . . Not even my album is compared to this madness," exclaimed Boogie Down Productions frontman KRS-One. Living Colour guitarist and Black Rock Coalition founder Vernon Reid said earnestly, "I think De La Soul is some of the freshest music I've heard in a long time. And it's going to change the world as we know it."

A "Change in Speak"

While fans, critics, and scholars often credit Rakim with pioneering complex rhyme schemes in rap, De La Soul stretched the genre's use of the English language. With songs like "Change in Speak," "Potholes in My Lawn," "Plug Tunin'," and "Buddy," De La Soul asserted a new form of language, or what they themselves called "speak." Like fantasy author J. R. R. Tolkien, Posdnuos, Maseo, and Trugoy built a world and spoke in a manner outsiders could not understand without context. Listening to their debut album might leave one wondering, "What's a Derwin?" "What do they mean by 'Delacratic'?" "Who is Dan Stuckie"? They infused new meanings into terms like "buddy" and coined others like "Delacratic" and "schwingalokate." (The latter means "to change.") Posdnuos, Trugoy, and Maseo also famously referred to the oft-misinterpreted "D.A.I.S.Y.," reflecting the group's desire to make music from the soul. They distinguished themselves from other top rappers like Rakim, KRS-One, Big Daddy Kane, and MC Lyte by calling themselves "speakers." And speakers, in De La Soul's world, signified a higher level of lyricism.

"Change in Speak" announced the group's new style of lyricism and language. Trugoy told Brian Coleman, "That was the album version of 'Freedom of Speak.' . . . It was definitely a declaration about us, like, 'We've landed, we're here.' But it wasn't boasting. . . . It was more about letting people know that there's room for a change and this is what we're about." Over a beat based on The Mad Lads' "No Strings Attached," Pos and Trugoy match their first verses by ending every line with the same word, or a word containing the same sound.

Pos's lines end with a version of, or a word rhyming with, "soul." In contrast, Trugoy concludes every line with "step," spelling out the group's creative ethos. Trugoy rapped that De La Soul were "true to the soul" and they'll never "half step." In other words, they would never compromise their style nor stay in a single place creatively.

While De La Soul announced their new rap style on "Change in Speak," the track preceding it introduces the listener to De La Soul's complex language, laid-back rap style, and the group's identity. No song on the album captures De La Soul's idealism and innocence like "The Magic Number." Anyone who watched *Schoolhouse Rock* cartoons recognized the beat. Over Robert Dorough's "Three Is the Magic Number," Posdnuos, Trugoy, and Maseo deliver a mission statement on the record to be different, to stay true to themselves or their soul, and to express a lyrical style that could not be duplicated. "'Cause seein' and doin' are actions for monkeys," Posdnuos raps. De La Soul's take on the childhood jingle captured the wonder reflected in 1980s popular movies like Stephen Spielberg's *E.T.* While "The Magic Number" is an upbeat articulation of the group's ethos, the group demonstrates their uncanny use of juxtaposition. As the song concludes, listeners hear Johnny Cash's voice echoing the line inspiring the album's title, "Three feet high and rising." Cash's "Five Feet High and Rising" is also childlike, but it is more of a tale of lost innocence as the singer tells how he and his family escaped the 1937 Mississippi River flood.

In "Potholes in My Lawn," De La Soul deployed a quirky suburban metaphor to weigh in on the rap game of the late 1980s. Trugoy critiquing rappers for stealing his lines tipped me off to the fact that De La Soul was commenting about the rap game when I listened to the song for the first time. Yet, I never thought about what their references to "potholes" meant. Dante Ross states, "De La Soul took their abstract song crafting up a notch, creating a secret metaphor-filled rap language with their cryptic rhymes. A lot of people still don't know that the lawn in the song is their lyrical style and that potholes were a metaphor for what's left behind when you bite. The tune was a message to their biters. I thought it was brilliant." Journalist and cultural critic Jeff Chang refers to the song as "a battle rhyme refracted through the brutal status consciousness of the 'burbs," in his *Pitchfork* review of the group's debut. Chang explained, "De La played the family on the block coming into success, only to be met with the envious rage of the Joneses next door."

I would never claim to be a country music fan, but I fell in love with "Potholes." It appeared on many of my own mixtapes in my teenage years. I found De La Soul's sampling of the mouth harp in Parliament's "Little Ole Country Boy" incredibly catchy. While the track reflects De La Soul's suburban upbringing, "Potholes in My Lawn" is a multilayered example of De La Soul reaching back to the past to create something that rappers had not up until that point. "Potholes in My Lawn" is not just a suburban battle rap song but one that collapses multiple overlapping Black spatial experiences—suburban, urban, and rural—into a track.

In his review of *3 Feet High and Rising*, Chang reminds us, "The musical chorus of 'Potholes in My Lawn' pointed not only to Parliament's 1970 debut *Osmium*, but to the African American roots of country and western music." While Black folk are often associated with the urban in modern US politics and culture, many of us have country or rural roots. Black people moved from rural southern spaces to northern industrialized cities after emancipation and during the Great Migrations of the late nineteenth and twentieth centuries. Thus, like all groups who migrated to new geographical and regional settings, Black people brought aspects of their culture with them, from the people who played banjos and mouth harps to those who continued their farming practices in cities. This conclusion should not come as a surprise considering Parliament recorded the album and the song sampled, "Good Ole Country Boy," in Detroit, a city with a history of rural farming.

De La Soul's dense lyricism on *3 Feet High and Rising* exemplifies what historian William L. Van Deburg calls "soulful talk," or Black Americans' capacity to engage in "in-group dialogue," which might be indecipherable to some outsiders. De La Soul, like many Black artists, drew from various traditions particular to Black culture—so-called "African American Vernacular English," or "Ebonics"; the "trickster" tradition found in comedy and blues music; and toasting. Like many working-class Black youth, De La Soul recorded an album under the cover of what anthropologist James C. Scott called a "hidden transcript," which refers to "a dissident political culture that manifests itself in daily conversations, folklore, jokes, songs, and other cultural practices."

"Jenifa Taught Me"

De La Soul's form of speak and their D.A.I.S.Y. aesthetic complicated prevailing expressions of Black masculinity in rap. De La Soul did not present themselves in a harder cast like Run-D.M.C. and LL Cool J, or with the cool street intelligence of Rakim or KRS-One or the gangsta chic of Schoolly D, Ice-T, or N.W.A. Instead, the group offered, to paraphrase The Roots drummer Questlove, an "alternative" Black masculinity. Rather than a brand of Black hardness, the group leaned into their nerdiness, whimsicality, and playfulness. De La Soul was political but not as militant nor preachy as Chuck D. (I mean "preachy" in a good way.) Posdnuos, Maseo, and Trugoy displayed a combination of innocence, vulnerability, and, frankly, horniness rarely seen in rap up until that point. As many artists, critics, and fans testified later, De La Soul allowed Black youth to be their complicated selves.

De La Soul was not the only rap group positioned at the vanguard of this new individuality in hip-hop culture. They formed one pillar of the Native Tongues collective, initially comprising the Jungle Brothers, A Tribe Called Quest, Monie Love, and Queen

Latifah. The Jungle Brothers released their debut album, *Straight Out the Jungle*, in 1988. The group, with members Michael Small (Mike Gee), Nathaniel Hall (Afrika Baby Bam), and Sammy Burwell (DJ Sammy B), exemplified African Americans' embrace of Afrocentricity amid the global anti-apartheid movement and racist violence of the 1980s in a less oppositional manner than Public Enemy. "The Jungle Brothers' album *Straight Out the Jungle* was a blueprint," Monie Love declared in the documentary *Hip-Hop Evolution*. They featured Q-Tip on an album track, "Black Is Black," which helped introduce the world to A Tribe Called Quest. Q-Tip, Phife Dawg, Ali Shaheed Muhammad, and Jarobi White formed their group the same year Posdnuos, Maseo, and Trugoy established De La Soul.

The Native Tongues emerged as hip-hop's most dynamic collective since the Juice Crew formed by major East Coast rappers a few years prior. In addition to sharing an ethos of positivity, playful spirit, and pro-Blackness, the group stood at the cutting edge of Black masculinity and femininity in rap. On her debut album, *All Hail the Queen*, Queen Latifah wore a militaristic yet regal suit, looking like she would fit in with Public Enemy as well as she did with the Native Tongues. Queen Latifah presented herself as a tough yet tender Black feminist willing to advocate for anti-apartheid activists abroad, represent Black women historical leaders, and make listeners want to dance. The men in the collective did not present themselves as slick-talking rappers like Slick Rick and Big Daddy Kane. They were not rock stars sporting big gold chains like Run-D.M.C. and LL Cool J. Nor did they claim to be masculine "teachas" like KRS-One. They were not hard, nor did they devote their songs to outright bragging about how nice they were on the mic. They sought the third space of masculine Afrocentricity, vulnerability, and mischievousness.

Maseo, Posdnuos, and Trugoy show their complicated masculinity on songs like "Jenifa Taught Me (Derwin's Revenge)," "Eye Know," and the Native Tongues posse track "Buddy." Skits like "De La Orgee," which sonically simulates the group participating in group sex, were among the genre's most wacky NSFW moments. "Jenifa Taught Me (Derwin's Revenge)" captures the teenage wonder that accompanies young sexual desire and the pursuit of one's first sexual experience. As an answer record to the Jungle Brothers' song "Jimmy," Trugoy and Posdnuos present themselves as kids who stumble into sexual adventures. The artists reverse what we might think are the roles in young sexual exploration—it's Jenifa who is taking the lead in all the moves on the curious boys. "Grabbed my jeans, Jimmy screamed. Jenifa, oh Jenny," Pos rapped.

If "Jenifa" takes listeners back to their first encounters, then "Eye Know" sets a standard for hip-hop love songs. It's playful, sunny, and naïve. The group juxtaposed the whistling from Otis Redding's "(Sittin' On) the Dock of the Bay" and a sample from Steely Dan's "Peg" to perfection to create a beautifully poetic love song. The video is extremely colorful, and Posdnuos and Trugoy almost appear bashful as they awkwardly start rapping at the beginning of their verses. Of course, as part of the group's adherence to D.A.I.S.Y., Maseo, Posdnuos, and Trugoy perform alongside flowers, peace signs, and other psychedelic designs. It is not hard to see the influence of this song and video on like-minded rappers like A Tribe Called Quest and Common. In fact, Common holding signs in his *Electric Circus*-era love song, "Come Close," recalls Posdnuos and Trugoy holding signs displaying lyrics on "Eye Know."

Of De La Soul's flirtatious songs of desire, the posse tracks "Buddy" and "Buddy (Native Tongue Decision)" illustrate De La Soul's creative use of language, playful approach to sexuality, and rap homosociality the best. At the time of its release, it seemed few understood what the term "buddy" meant. Cultural critic Greg Tate wrote in his review of *3 Feet High and Rising*, "'Buddy' is either a euphemism for womens or the P word." I always took a literal approach to the term—that "buddy" was a friend, or even an affectionate term for "friends with benefits." However, Prince Paul explains at the beginning of the "Buddy (Native Tongue Decision)" music video. "'Buddy' doesn't mean girl, or sex, for that matter," Paul says. "'Buddy' simply means body—bodies of all kinds."

This makes sense. "Buddy" is a horny song with Posdnuos, Trugoy, Mike Gee, and Baby Bam all rapping playfully about the gravitational pull that other bodies have on them. *Village Voice* columnist Tate wrote about the original song, "What the song really gets deep into is how tight De La Soul are with their dicks. More specifically about how tight De La Soul, the Jungle Brothers, and Q-Tip are with every man's favorite flop-along toy." This was especially the case with Q-Tip, who raps about sticking out his "jimmy." He also plays with the multiple meanings behind "buddy," including using it to refer to a friend.

"Buddy" reflects male bonding over heterosexual activity in a homophobic world. Naturally, the male lyricists in the song are always clear that, while they all recite euphemisms about being led by and using their penises, they are pursuing women's bodies. Even if "Buddy" can take on multiple meanings in that song, they are clearly chasing "Jennys." This heterosexual clarity in hip-hop culture, especially among men, has long reflected the culture's homophobia, especially during the 1980s and 1990s.

While the original "Buddy" celebrated male bonding over sexual activity, De La Soul recorded a remix in the spirit of gender inclusivity. This version features British rapper Monie Love (it also features A Tribe Called Quest's Phife Dawg), who also shined on Queen Latifah's "Ladies First." In a short verse preceding Q-Tip's and Queen Latifah's sung bridge, Monie Love expresses her attraction for bodies while also rapping about her own sexual pursuits. She's serious about her hunt for the "B," she quips. While Love's verse did not entirely undermine the song's bent toward masculinity, it was a gesture toward some gender inclusion.

De La Soul songs like "Eye Know" and "Buddy" are very much in a similar vein to LL Cool J's "I Need Love" and their Native Tongues brethren A Tribe Called Quest's "Bonita Applebaum."

They are earnest rap love songs. "Eye Know" and "I Need Love" demonstrate a sentimentality often downplayed in rap. "Buddy" and "Bonita Applebaum" are important examples of the Native Tongues' flirtatious approach to sex and love. All these songs are masculine, but they don't sound aggressive. These love songs are inviting, playful, and sincere expressions of affection, similar to what we hear from artists like Common, Talib Kweli, Mos Def, The Roots, and Pharrell. These records demonstrated how young Black men could articulate or show romantic interest while being discerning, not objectifying too much, and not being too awkward.

"Take It Off"

De La Soul's creative ethos particularly shines on the album's skits. "Take It Off" is probably the most explicit critique of following dominant trends in hip-hop as, over a sparse beat, Prince Paul urges listeners to shed articles of the typical hip-hop uniform. The listener can figure out the tropes, or even the popular artists, De La Soul refers to when instructing listeners to discard the shell-toe Adidas shoes, fat laces, do-rags, Kangol hats, and the Jheri curl. As many hip-hop fans know, Ice Cube was one of the most prominent rappers to sport a Jheri curl. While Ice Cube says he did not direct "Jackin' for Beats" at anyone, it is hard to see that "Jackin' for Beats" is not in conversation with "Take It Off," especially his references to artists with weird haircuts. De La Soul were not necessarily known for dancing like other rappers in the new jack swing era, but Trugoy sported a funny haircut, the half-fade, half-grown-out cut.

"Take It Off," for members of the group, however, represented a clear statement about individuality in rap. Trugoy later told *Rolling Stone*'s Evan Serpick,

> That was another one of those moments where there were 25 people in the studio. There was a song out there at the

time called "Kick the Ball" and it used the same Headhunters beat, so we basically mimicked the sound of their single and, instead of saying "kick the ball," we said, "take it off," and thought about all the cliché hip-hop stuff that people should just change and find some individualism or some of their own personality, as opposed to falling in line with what hip-hop was supposed to be. It was something we felt strongly about. We felt like there shouldn't have been guidelines for hip-hop.

As students in my hip-hop history class pointed out, "Take It Off" is Kendrick Lamar's "N95" predecessor as Kendrick urged his listeners to "take off" many of the trends of the 2020s, from clothes to what he believed were false appeals to social consciousness ("take off the fake woke") amid the racial justice protests in the summer of 2020. Lamar commands everyone to discard the "weird-ass jewelry" and other evidence of materialism and conspicuous consumption. Like De La Soul, Lamar name drops brands like Chanel. However, Lamar's tone on "N95" was not as playful as De La Soul's on "Take It Off." "N95" is frenetic and cynical. This makes sense, however, as "N95" matches the frantic times of the 2020s dominated by crises such as the COVID-19 pandemic and the economic crash that accompanied the global shutdown. Most of us felt we all had descended into hell.

"Say No Go"

Although *3 Feet High and Rising* is famous for the group's whimsicality and playfulness, De La Soul also responded to the tumultuous politics of the Reagan era. The decade in which hip-hop culture matured was characterized by racial violence, the federal government's abandonment of social policies, police brutality, and the Reagan administration's failure to address crises like the HIV/AIDS epidemic. The Reagan era also became synonymous with the War on Drugs.

As one of the drug war's signature laws, the Comprehensive Crime Control Act of 1984 required a five-year mandatory minimum sentence for anyone convicted of using a gun in a violent crime and a sentence of fifteen years to life for a third strike. The Anti-Drug Abuse Act of 1986 doubled funding for crime and drug control programs from the administration's first term. And drug warriors existed across party lines. Many Democrats, including New York's Charles Rangel, supported the 1986 law, which established mandatory minimum sentences for heroin, cocaine, and crack cocaine possession. The federal government ramped up its rhetoric against drug dealers and users. In 1982, Delaware senator Joe Biden declared dramatically, "Crime is a national-defense problem. . . . You're in as much jeopardy in the streets as you are from a Soviet missile."

The federal government and law enforcement also waged the war using soft power. The Reagan administration launched the "Just Say No" campaign to persuade young Americans to refuse drugs. First Lady Nancy Reagan served as the leading spokesperson for the campaign, appearing on popular TV shows like *Diff'rent Strokes* and in commercials alongside director and actor Clint Eastwood. The Los Angeles Police Department (LAPD) coupled its militaristic approach to anti-drug enforcement with more soft tactics when LAPD Chief Daryl Gates created the Drug Abuse Resistance Education (DARE) program in 1983. Ultimately, the federal government, local law enforcement, and local news media aimed to scare the public in an attempt to keep them from participating in the drug trade, whether through relying upon irrelevant metaphors like likening addicts' brains to a fried egg; transmitting images of police arresting suspected drug dealers and addicts who were mostly Black and Brown; or, as historian Max Felker-Kantor argues in his study of the DARE program, encouraging students to "snitch" on those they suspect of drug use.

De La Soul engaged the national conversation about crack cocaine addiction in their fifth single, "Say No Go." While songs like Grandmaster Flash & the Furious Five's "The Message" and Public

Enemy's "Night of the Living Baseheads" address urban decline and drug use with a sense of sonic urgency, De La Soul famously sampled Daryl Hall & John Oates's "I Can't Go for That," a very catchy pop song, to create what Havelock Nelson and Michael Gonzales describe as the "most-danceable anti-drug song." As on the album's other conscious record, "Ghetto Thang," the group narrates the ravaging effects of crack cocaine on Black people in a manner similar to Melle Mel's rap on "The Message." In the last verse of "The Message," Melle Mel mournfully states, "A child is born with no state of mind, blind to the ways of mankind." Posdnuos starts "Say No Go" with "A baby is born into a world of pits. And if it could've talked that soon in the delivery room, it would've asked the nurse for a hit." However, Posdnuos's words feel more bleak as he narrates the birth of a child already addicted to crack cocaine because of their mother's drug habit. Later in the song, Posdnuos nods to some truth in Nancy Reagan's "Just Say No" campaign without endorsing the Reagan administration's politics.

Posdnuos later confirmed that the group took inspiration from "The Message" for "Say No Go." Pos told *Rolling Stone*, "By the time we were with Tommy Boy we were able to give it a better beat, give it a better keyboard, and it wound up becoming a song that talked about things that happen in the ghettos of America. We said, 'Let's make sure we have something like "The Message" from Grandmaster Flash, like, wow, that's a whole other level of looking at things.' I think it was important for us, already being known from our singles as being funny and witty, to have something like that added as well."

Posdnuos and Trugoy chastised dope pushers and drug users over the catchy disco and pop track. The group holds both the mother of the crack baby and the drug dealers equally responsible for the scourge in Black communities. They call them "jerks" and "zombies." (Public Enemy also portrayed drug addicts as zombies in the music video for their anti-crack song "Night of the Living Baseheads.") While De La Soul's critique of crack addiction is noble, it's a behavioral explanation that lacks a discussion of the structural forces contributing to chronic drug use in America's cities in the 1970s and 1980s. However, as journalist Donovan X. Ramsey illustrates in his oral history of the drug war, *When Crack Was King: A People's History of a Misunderstood Era*, De La Soul articulated a view common among those Black Americans who lived amid the crack cocaine crisis. Songs like "Say No Go" contributed to a general cultural milieu that ridiculed hard drug use (as well as risky sexual behavior for fear of contracting HIV/AIDS). We not only watched crack's deleterious effects on people in movies like *New Jack City* and television shows like *Chappelle's Show* but also made crack users laughingstocks and the butts of jokes. None of us were perfect in this regard, as I recall my friends and myself using terms like "crackheads" to describe all sorts of "weird" behavior, thus reinforcing the stigmatization of crack addiction.

Decades later, according to Ramsey, many health officials and Americans reversed their view of the crack epidemic. He cites neonatologist Hallam Hurt's 2015 study of the effects of prenatal cocaine exposure, which found that the panic over "crack babies" was overblown as many children born to addicted women lived lives unaffected by their mother's drug use. In the era of opioid addictions and sudden fentanyl overdoses, many Americans learned some of the right lessons from the crack wars—that drug addiction and deaths are a *health emergency*, not merely a problem of criminalized behavior. Yet, our current crisis is still haunted by the racist, classist, and sexist response to the crack cocaine epidemic. It is difficult to imagine the FBI, DEA, and the LAPD bringing the full weight of their resources down on white Americans living in the suburbs over the use of crack cocaine. Our collective turnabout on drugs does little to undo the stigmatization, incarceration, and deaths of African Americans, casualties of an epic policy failure and our addiction to racist, sexist, and classist punishment.

The song "Tread Water" might not qualify as social criticism for some listeners, but it is one of De La Soul's most imaginative efforts at addressing the precarity of Black life during the Reagan years. Spinning a surreal tale, the members tell stories of themselves talking with animals, working through fears of death, receiving survival tips, and reifying their commitment to their ethics. Anticipating rap songs featuring lyricists interacting with nonhuman characters such as Dan the Automator and Kool Keith's "Cartoon Capers," Trugoy and Posdnuos talk with crocodiles, squirrels, and fish. However, in conversing with animals, Trugoy and Posdnuos learn of the specter of harm haunting their lives. The crocodile warns Trugoy of the "villains" who would try to drown him and wonders whether the rustling in the ferns was an animal that would harm him.

Journalist Harry Allen asserts that De La Soul's "Tread Water" is connected to a deeper African spiritual and storytelling tradition in which people communicate with animals. According to Allen, "There's a very deep tradition in many African cultures of people consulting spirits through animals, being advised by animals, animals being guides of various kinds. . . . And I remember Dave saying that as a Haitian, in a lot of Haitian culture, there was folklore of animals being guides, advisors, counsel of that kind."

The title of the song could also serve as a slogan for the Reagan era as many Black Americans found themselves outside the workforce, cut from welfare rolls, enduring police surveillance and violence, and seeking to avoid drug addiction, gang culture, and violence. And while it may not appear so on the surface, "Tread Water" offers an ingenious rejoinder to rapper Melle Mel on "The Message" when he raps about struggling to "keep from goin' under." De La Soul's answer is to listen to *3 Feet High and Rising*. Their music will keep us from drowning. And while they tell listeners to follow their path, Posdnuos reiterates the group's commitment to their D.A.I.S.Y. ethos, or following their inner sound. Posdnuos later explains how the song served as a mantra. " 'Cause it's just about keeping your head and trudging on, above all the negativity. And this song is just a lighthearted but really powerful record in terms of cleverly using animals," he told *GQ*.

De La Soul distinguished themselves from socially conscious rap artists and projects of their era. Unlike the straightforwardly political music of KRS-One's and Nelson George's Stop the Violence Movement's "Self-Destruction," Public Enemy's "Fight the Power," and X Clan's album *To the East, Blackwards*, De La Soul's "Tread Water," "Say No Go," and "Ghetto Thang" demonstrate music producer Ian Brennan's point that the "most political music is the least obviously so." De La Soul vacillated between silliness, whimsicality, and political consciousness. Music scholar and funk expert Rickey Vincent contends that much of Black culture is animated by a silly-serious dichotomy, or Black people's willingness to confront existential threats with silliness. Hence, De La Soul recorded the most "danceable" drug song and tales of survival, told by talking animals.

"We Hate This Song"

Commercially, "Me Myself and I" is the crown jewel of De La Soul's *3 Feet High and Rising*. However, while the track demonstrates the group's creative individuality, it was also born out of great tension with their D.A.I.S.Y. or "hippie" image. The song and video also captured the group's willingness to engage in irony and articulate iconoclastic critiques of rap.

As the story about the recording of "Me Myself and I" goes, Posdnuos and Trugoy responded to Tommy Boy's requests for a radio-friendly single with reservation. According to Prince Paul, they thought recording a commercial single to move records was "selling out." Yet, Maseo took Tommy Boy's request as an opportunity to use a desired record, Funkadelic's "(Not Just) Knee Deep." As the centerpiece of the 1979 album *Uncle Jam Wants You*, Parliament recorded the song "intending to try to identify and isolate the essence of p-funk," George Clinton explains in his memoir. "(Not Just) Knee Deep" seemed to be crafted with hip-hoppers in mind more than disco dancers. The song runs long, like the first hip-hop singles, at more than fifteen minutes. According to Clinton, while Warner Bros. failed to push the song, the track hit in cities like Detroit, Richmond, and Los Angeles. Naturally, hip-hop DJs picked it up. According to Maseo, he and Trugoy heard a DJ at a Zulu Nation party drop the record, and "the crowd went bananas." Prince Paul, another fan of George Clinton and Parliament Funkadelic, agreed to base "Me Myself and I" on it.

After repurposing Parliament's beat for a rap track, Posdnuos and Trugoy articulated their message of self-expression in the most deadpan fashion. Adopting the Jungle Brothers' flow from their song "Black Is Black," the group calmly explained the meanings of their lyricism and aesthetics. Trugoy and Posdnuos confront those who believe the group is just trafficking a gimmick and those who might try to bully them over it. In maintaining the group's commitment to childlike naivete and their surrealism, Trugoy famously adopts lines spoken by *Snow White*'s Evil Queen to open the song, "Mirror, mirror on the wall. Tell me, mirror, what is wrong?" Trugoy and Posdnuos then spend much of the song challenging the notion that the group's image was purely a marketing ploy.

While George Clinton sings about the "freak of the week" on his version of the track, De La Soul present themselves as "social freaks" in the video. Surrounded by classmates in hip-hop's classroom sporting jumpsuits, Kangol hats, and fat gold chains, and carrying large boomboxes, Pos, Trugoy, and Maseo sport funky haircuts, bright-colored shirts, and African medallions. Referring to his eyeglasses in his verse, Posdnuos points to the unfair and untrue notion that people, especially young Black men, who wear glasses are nerds and social outcasts. The group members are teased, bullied, and treated like class clowns and dunces by their classmates for their appearance, dark skin tone, and general disposition. Classmates threw rolled-up paper at them, even put Posdnuos in the corner and placed a Kangol hat with "dunce" written on it on his head. In a surrealist moment in the video, doppelgängers wearing pink shirts appear before the group's members to give them each detention passes. While teachers and school administrators gave kids detention as punishment, De La Soul, probably like many others, saw it as an opportunity. In the video, detention allows them to go somewhere where they can be more creative. The video's ending recalls how all the members found themselves creatively while attending summer school.

"Me Myself and I" drips with irony. Trugoy and Posdnous were not enthusiastic about recording what became their biggest hit. In effect, "Me Myself and I" was a means to an end, and Posdnous and Trugoy acted accordingly. They tucked the song near the end of the album out of annoyance. Later, the lyricists seemed to perform the song as though it were a chore. Maseo said in *Hip-Hop Evolution* that Posdnuos and Trugoy sandbagged its performance. "They tried to take that song and make it the worst record possible because in their mind, the more stupid it is, the less it's going to be accepted." "We took a piss on that song," Posdnous smirked. However, as the whole group admits, the song blew up despite Trugoy and Pos's attempts to sabotage it. "They put it out, the record just blows up," Prince Paul says. "We were like, 'How did that happen?'" Maseo attributes the significance of the song to the group's silliness: "Nobody in hip-hop was silly. Nobody else was being class clowns. Everybody else had a bravado."

De La Soul's hit song and video gave kids like me, teenagers, and young adults hope that we could be ourselves without interference. I was a little too young and shy to consider wearing bright-colored shirts and a wacky haircut. But "Me Myself and I" showed me that I could be different, and there was nothing wrong with looking a little nerdy. However, this remained a difficult lesson to internalize, especially at such a young age. I still had to learn how to negotiate and navigate everything that made me feel different. My family and I seemed to move every few years, which always made me feel like the new kid. I was shy, and I wore glasses with large frames and hand-me-down clothes. And, of course, who retains all the lessons they learn when they are eight or nine years old?

"Me Myself and I" was both a gift and a curse. It shot the group to the vanguard of rap music, but it also symbolized their efforts to resist the identity they had created for themselves. Naturally, the problem with creating a hit song one does not like is that most artists are condemned to perform it for the rest of their careers. This explains how they came to ridicule the song while performing it on stage, as they sometimes shouted "We hate this song" as the chorus. As the track thrust De La Soul into rap stardom, they had to contend with the "hippie" image and the industry expectation to create more hit songs.

"Straight Up Soul Brothers and Sisters"

While critics and listeners fell in love with De La Soul's playfulness, positivity, and countercultural aesthetic, the group openly bristled at suggestions that they were hippies and pacifists. Posdnuos, Trugoy, and Maseo thought journalists, critics, listeners, and other artists misinterpreted D.A.I.S.Y. Everyone seemed to focus on the imagery rather than the meaning of the acronym. In their 1989 press video, when they explained the meaning of the term "D.A.I.S.Y.," Posdnuos said that the flowers were a visual representation of their production. He explained, "We consider our production 'Da Inner Sound, Y'all.'" Posdnuos, Trugoy, and Maseo admitted they valued peace, explaining why they might wear signs in their hair, medallions, or clothes. However, they still denied being hippies. "It really had nothing to do with being hippies in the sixties. . . . We can have a psychedelic sound in some of our cuts, but we are not hippies," Posdnuos declared.

De La Soul's resistance to the "hippie" label appeared to be a reaction to its gendered and racial implications. The "hippie" label put too much distance between Maseo, Posdnuos, and Trugoy and their Black masculinity. While some critics mistook the group for being unserious, other people they encountered, especially while on tour, thought the group was "soft" because of the D.A.I.S.Y. imagery and their nerdy appearance. As a result, group members found themselves engaging in fisticuffs with strangers who tried to test them. "Random people would come up to me and [be] like, 'Yo, you know your boys on the road, I heard they beat up such and such.' I'm like, 'What?!' . . . I would hear all of these different stories that people would come up [with] because . . . obviously, I worked with them," Paul said excitedly on *De La Soul Is Not Dead*. However, Paul stated that the group admitted the stories were true when asked. They had to protect themselves. Tales of their altercations formed the emotional basis for the group's second album, *De La Soul Is Dead*.

Also, the emphasis on the D.A.I.S.Y. persona threatened to leave Posdnuos, Maseo, and Trugoy boxed in as nonthreatening flower-power rappers. Tom Silverman expressed disappointment in De La Soul's reaction to its "hippie" image. The stakes were high regarding the group's ability to build careers, not to mention retain their artistic autonomy. De La Soul, like many artists, could be one-hit pop wonders, or their peers could label them as "soft," either of which would short-circuit their careers. P.M. Dawn were never thought of in the same way after KRS-One and members of Boogie Down Productions rushed Prince Be during their performance and threw him offstage in 1992.

There are questions about how the group's image became synonymous with hippiedom. Of course, the group created the D.A.I.S.Y. acronym to describe their musical style and ethos. Even so, Posdnuos, Maseo, and Trugoy maintain that Tommy Boy ran away with the concept in its brilliant marketing campaign. The "o" in De La Soul was replaced with a peace sign in Tommy Boy ephemera. The company engaged in guerrilla marketing as they paid to produce thousands of De La Soul stickers, encouraging its promoters and, most importantly, the group's fans to stick them everywhere. Even Questlove admits that he almost got into trouble for sticking them on school property when he was younger. Then, according to Trugoy, daisies were ubiquitous at photo shoots. This frustrated Trugoy and the other members of the group. "I mean, every damn photo shoot, you can bet there was a florist hanging around with flowers. . . . It was just like, 'C'mon, man. Flowers?'

That's not really what it's about. . . . I can understand the connection, but we're beyond that." The group's music videos also featured flowers, brightly colored imagery, and Day Glo designs.

The marketing emphasized De La Soul as a group with crossover appeal, which underplayed the group's Black masculinity. They got (presumably middle-aged) people to pose in ads holding a vinyl copy of *3 Feet High and Rising* with the admission, "I came in for Patti Labelle, and came out with De La Soul." At the bottom of another of these flyers read a paraphrase of Hilburn's review of the group, "The Sergeant Pepper's of the eighties." Yet, Tommy Boy's street game seemed to be working. On the "I came in for . . ." flyers, the record label declared De La Soul was "making hip-hop history" with nearly 1 million records sold, and *3 Feet High and Rising* reaching the Top 40, especially due to the popularity of "Me Myself and I." But what would it mean for this trio of Black teenagers to appeal to white listeners and those of middle age rather than Black youths?

While De La Soul attempted to protect their artistic autonomy, seeing them as descendants of flower children was not entirely unreasonable. Much of their aesthetics and ethos overlapped with those who called themselves hippies in the 1960s. In his book analyzing the American counterculture, historian Damon Bach explains the meanings of "hippie" and "counterculture": "Hippies distinguished themselves by donning eclectic—and from the perspective of outsiders—bizarre clothing that was frequently bright and colorful. Flowers became entities that symbolized love, harmony, and beauty." De La Soul did not wear flowers in their hair, but they often looked the part in some interviews and music videos. And, if we think about Bach's characterization of hippies, some of De La Soul's principles overlap with those shared by the 1960s and 1970s counterculture, like "cooperation, truthfulness, love, empathy, and egalitarianism."

Anyways, Native Tongues mentor and DJ, Red Alert, disagreed. He evoked George Clinton while challenging the characterization of the group as hippies at their *3 Feet High and Rising* release party: "People consider them as the hippies of hip-hop. They [are] not the hippies of hip-hop. They are considered the new funk. The new Parliament. The new Funkadelic."

Ironically, George Clinton called himself a "hippie" in his autobiography. He admitted that Jimi Hendrix and The Beatles inspired his groups, Parliament and Funkadelic. Yet, Clinton also acknowledged his hippiedom was not limited to popular portraits of flower children. Clinton sought to go musically where none had gone before. De La Soul shared this artistic instinct on *3 Feet High and Rising* and later records such as the *Art Official Intelligence* series. Like De La Soul later, Clinton remarked how his groups' aesthetics elicited racial confusion. However, he saw this confusion as part of Parliament Funkadelic's plan. Clinton explained, "We were too white for black folks and too black for white folks. We were a source of confusion. And that's exactly how we wanted it."

Yet, as De La Soul often asserted, the fact that their first album reflects a countercultural aesthetic misses the point. De La Soul operated in a different social and cultural context. While Clinton embraced the "hippie" label, it still carried racialized and gendered implications. According to Bach, few Black folks considered themselves hippies in the 1960s and 1970s. De La Soul addressed the racialized aspects of the term on the song "Ain't Hip to Be Labeled a Hippie." At the end of the song, Posdnuos and Paul engage in a dialogue clarifying that De La Soul were not in fact hippies. Posdnuos instead refers to the group, by extension of their parents, who came of age during the civil rights era, as "soul brothers and sisters." Posdnuos, using this reference, acknowledges they were more descendants of the Black Power movement than the hippies.

Ultimately, Posdnuos's, Maseo's, and Trugoy's resistance to misinterpretations of D.A.I.S.Y. reflected their longing for autonomy and a desire to exercise agency as young Black men. They were learning the lesson of being Black male artists in the United

States. They lived in a country where people tried to use Black masculine stereotypes to trap them artistically and to provoke them into physical altercations. Of course, agency, creative control, and freedom are among the first principles of any artist, let alone Black working-class rappers living in the United States with narrow options and even narrower margins for success in a volatile music industry. The group hinged much of their debut album and subsequent records on expressing themselves fully as authentic artists. Doing so entailed controlling their image and output as much as possible while also maintaining the right to change course in the rap game. "Shwingalokate" is a weird and funny-sounding word when one tries to pronounce it, but it carries real meaning for the group. Change turned out to be De La Soul's North Star in an industry that transformed rapidly, often leaving artists who dropped classic first singles and debut albums behind. Maseo, Posdnuos, and Trugoy believed their best chance at rap longevity was to be able to change with the times and not be boxed in by critics, Tommy Boy, or fans who sought to keep them trapped in a creative and aesthetic amber.

The music industry also sought to challenge De La Soul's creative freedom. The years 1988 through 1990 were the zenith for the type of collage sampling that made the record famous. De La Soul released *3 Feet High and Rising* amid other similar albums like Public Enemy's 1988 release *It Takes a Nation of Millions to Hold Us Back*, the Beastie Boys' 1989 album *Paul's Boutique*, (which was underappreciated at the time) and PE's 1990 album *Fear of a Black Planet*.

While De La Soul helped revolutionize rap production, along with the Bomb Squad, the Beastie Boys, and the Dust Brothers, their collage style of music-making provoked legal backlash. Much has been written about the Turtles suing De La Soul for using the band's "You Showed Me" for a one-minute-and-eleven-second skit in "Transmitting Live from Mars." Black artists and critics have covered the ironies of the long history of white artists sampling, if not stealing, and profiting from Black artists. Jeff Chang explains this irony perfectly in his retrospective *Pitchfork* review of *3 Feet High and Rising*:

> It is true that many of the Black artists sampled by hip-hop producers have also been denied the profits of their work. It is also true that works by so-called minorities—whether the sampled or the sampling—suffer disproportionately from the land-grabbing, barbed-wire-fence-erecting, tons-of-guns-defending mentality that drives the growing corpus of intellectual property law. What is currently called copyright protection is also the wholesale locking away of people's labor, legacy, and inheritance. The current structure of sampling law functions like—because it is—a process of cultural erasure, a glaring and expanding cultural injustice.

Members of De La Soul obviously pushed back against restraints to their creativity after *3 Feet High and Rising*'s release, hence their desire to disregard any of the rules in hip-hop and Trugoy's wish not to have any "guidelines for hip-hop." I would love to see hip-hop without guidelines besides an adherence to one's truth and creativity. Nevertheless, the lesson of De La Soul, as well as Public Enemy, the Beastie Boys, and graffiti artists, is that when young people, especially young Black folks, find new ways of expressing themselves, the legal system will try to regulate them. De La Soul, Public Enemy, the Beastie Boys, and Biz Markie opened a moment of sonic and creative anarchy that paved new avenues for hip-hop production into the 1990s. However, these acts also galvanized other artists skeptical of hip-hop and lawyers who wasted little time taking action that set limits on rap production. Producers in the next wave, like DJ Premier and Pete Rock, did not stop sampling, but they found more creative ways to get away with it. The legal clampdown on collage rap production also fueled other producers willing to toil in obscure music and to get weirder, like DJ Shadow, Dan the Automator, The Alchemist, and Madlib.

As we know, records containing scores, if not hundreds, of samples eventually became obsolete as other artists, lawyers, and record companies began the clampdown on uncleared samples, engaging in restrictive lawsuits and/or charging exorbitant prices for each sample. Yet, Prince Paul and De La Soul, along with Public Enemy's Bomb Squad, the Beastie Boys, the Dust Brothers, and even Q-Tip and A Tribe Called Quest unlocked the door to another realm in the sonic imagination in rap that shaped the genre in the years to come. Numerous producers walked through this door—DJ Premier, Pete Rock, Large Professor, DJ Shadow, DJ Muggs, DOOM, Madlib, Kanye, El-P, J Dilla, 9th Wonder, The Alchemist, and many others.

Black Freedom Dreaming

De La Soul shouldn't be confused for radical political activists; however, their debut album illustrates the power of the Black radical imagination. The artists engage in what historian Robin D. G. Kelley calls "Black freedom dreaming." *3 Feet High and Rising* is one of the few rap albums imagined and produced at the height of creative freedom. It is a utopia set to music. De La Soul drew from every musical genre and any sound without restriction to musical or rap norms before the artists, lawyers, and record labels came to extract their cut from the artists' proceeds. De La Soul developed their own language and aesthetic; they imagined telling different types of stories in rap, from conversing with animals to women pursuing them to finding love. De La Soul, at the end of the Reagan era, imagined themselves free.

De La Soul used their imaginations to construct a world just outside Earth. Even though they addressed the drug war and urban devastation wrought by capital and federal divestment, Maseo, Posdnuos, and Trugoy created a musical world just beyond the crises of the 1980s. After George Clinton and jazz musician and arranger Sun

Ra, De La Soul were among hip-hop's first afrofuturists. The trio were hip-hop's first aliens as they traveled from Mars to Earth to elevate rap to a higher art form. Like Clinton, they constantly challenged themselves to embrace the future and adapt to change artistically.

De La Soul produced a revolutionary rap album for a revolutionary moment. While other artists like Michael Jackson and Neil Young commented on world events, De La Soul's aesthetic—using Day Glo imagery and wearing peace signs—also captured the democratic zeitgeist of the end of the Cold War. De La Soul's D.A.I.S.Y. and peace symbols make sense when thought of in the context of rebellions against authoritarianism in South Africa, China, East Germany, and the rest of Eastern Europe. As Kelley asserts in *Freedom Dreams: The Black Radical Imagination*, "The most radical art is not protest art, but works that take us to another place, envision a different way of seeing, perhaps a different way of feeling."

3 Feet High and Rising is utopian in its sonic anarchy and lyricism. Trugoy, Posdnuos, Maseo, and Prince Paul took disparate sounds and songs across genres and produced a cohesive record filled with idealism, whimsy, sarcasm, and surrealism, clear in its intention to be different and grounded in their truth.

CHAPTER 2

De La Soul Is Dead

"They were young Black men and they had to deal with all the things that come with being young Black men. They were being marketed in a way that, for them, was emasculating, in a sense. And led them to be stereotyped in a way that would potentially question their 'Blackness.'"

—Dante Ross, A&R representative for De La Soul's first album, *3 Feet High and Rising*

De La Soul proclaimed the beginning of the "D.A.I.S.Y. Age" at the end of *3 Feet High and Rising*. Then, they responded to the success of their revolutionary album by kicking over the flowerpot, killing the D.A.I.S.Y. Maseo, Trugoy, and Posdnuos believed the D.A.I.S.Y. had given them more trouble than it was worth and made this drastic move for their art, careers, and sanity. "There wasn't really room to go back into the studio and make more music. And what was going on with D.A.I.S.Y. age, what we'd intended to be a movement felt more like a trend, a misinterpreted trend. Trends come and go—we wanted to kill that trend before it killed us," Maseo explained.

De La Soul Is Dead is an ultimate "departure album": records that negate a previous work, especially when artists understand that a classic work could not be topped. The Roots drummer and music historian Questlove defines the "departure" record in an Instagram post praising Lil Yachty's *Let's Start Here*: "Departure albums are when musicians pull a COMPLETE creative left turn—most times as a career sabotage of feeling doomed to not be able to live up to a standard they set."

While De La Soul changed its tone and aesthetic on *De La Soul Is Dead*, the record follows a similar formula in its production. Prince Paul and the group relied upon a bevy of samples and dabbled in various musical genres—rap, R&B, rock, and house music. Also, like *3 Feet High and Rising*, *De La Soul Is Dead* followed a theme that went meta—three young Black men who discover the album in the trash and proceed to listen to it and give it commentary. We follow this storyline in the liner notes and the album's thirteen skits.

On *De La Soul Is Dead*, Posdnuos, Maseo, and Trugoy boldly confronted those who tested them physically while they were on the road, those who tried to keep the group in the D.A.I.S.Y. Age and hippie box, and the critics who would surely complain about the album's tonal change by embarking on their greatest act of creative freedom—killing off the D.A.I.S.Y. image. *De La Soul Is Dead* was punk. It negated *3 Feet High and Rising* by presenting a counternarrative to the D.A.I.S.Y.—knocking over the flowerpot. And they displayed it on the cover for the world to see.

The group remained as thoughtful, imaginative, political, and fun as they were on their first record. Importantly, though they demonstrated that their identity and authenticity was constantly under construction. De La Soul presented a more nuanced form of masculinity in their evolution. They channeled a simmering anger fitting for a group that the market and the streets tried to label as nonviolent hippies. On *De La Soul Is Dead*, they allowed listeners a deeper glimpse into their psyches. And Trugoy, Posdnuos, Maseo, and Prince Paul became more personal, slightly more serious, and unyielding in their follow-up.

The New World Order

De La Soul Is Dead arrived in music stores as geopolitical and cultural tectonic plates shifted in the United States and abroad. The Reagan era seemed to be over, with President George H. W. Bush entering his second year in office. The idea that the world was heading in a different direction after the fall of the Berlin Wall and the revolutions in 1989 could not have been clearer as I watched President Bush announce that the US military had launched attacks on Iraqi targets in Kuwait in January 1992. "We are at war," Mom said with a sigh.

Two weeks later, Bush delivered his infamous "New World Order" speech to Congress, setting off alarm bells among the anti-government and conspiracy minded. I remember the ubiquity of yellow ribbons displayed on cars and houses. One time, as we took a class picture, my fourth-grade teacher admonished those of us who flashed peace signs because "the world wasn't peaceful." Yet, by the end of the year, the world had changed. That year, the last nail in the Cold War's coffin arrived as General Secretary Mikhail Gorbachev resigned as head of the Soviet state in December, following an August coup attempt. The Soviet Union, wrote journalist Serge Schmemann in the *New York Times* the day after Christmas, "died . . . after a long and painful decline. It was 74 years old." The West was jubilant again.

Racial identity in the United States remained in flux as geopolitics shifted. De La Soul articulated their new Black masculinity at a time when more African Americans raised questions about the meanings of Blackness. The anti-apartheid movement reinvigorated Afrocentrism. Soon, Afrocentricity circulated among academics, artists, and even rappers. Reverend Jesse Jackson encouraged Black Americans to adopt the term "African American" to highlight perceived ties to the African diaspora. Lena Williams wrote about this "search for identity" in the November 30, 1991, edition of the *New York Times*. "The ever-changing black experience in America is being assessed with a new intensity. Skin color, how you talk, more specifically what you say and how you live your life are examples of the tests being used to determine what it means to be black in the 1990s," Williams declared.

Of course, debates around racial identity among Black folks go back to the early days of the republic. These discussions often intersected with party politics, gender, and class. As African Americans grew more distant from the Civil Rights and Black Power movements, more moved to the suburbs, went into middle-class professions, were elected to political office, and sent their kids to colleges and universities. The class divide among Black Americans became more apparent than ever. More Black people in the United States were living stereotypically middle-class lives. Television shows and movies like *The Cosby Show*, *A Different World*, and *School Daze* interrogated the meanings of personal identity and one's relationship to community, colorism, racism, gender, culture, education, and socioeconomic mobility in what cultural critic Nelson George called "post-soul" America.

Then came a rude awakening on March 3, 1991.

I was ten years old when I watched the video footage of four Los Angeles police officers kicking and pummeling Rodney King. In my mother's living room in our apartment in Pensacola, I viewed the grainy video footage on what seemed to be an endless loop. I could not believe what I was seeing. I knew I was watching something terrible—multiple police officers beating a Black man—but it still seemed unfathomable. Mother watched and expressed anger and dismay at the horrific display. It also served as another moment for Mom to remind me, "Young Black men are an endangered species. You have to be careful, especially around the police." Mom's articulation of a gendered characterization of Blackness informed me that my life would be defined, at least in part, by avoiding racist state violence.

The Rodney King beating in Los Angeles, a city that had become infamous for its racist police force and gang culture, highlighted the development of the "gangster" Black masculinity arising from these conditions. Several months after LAPD officers beat King, in September 1991, *The Source* magazine published an issue with "Endangered

Species" emblazoned on the cover along with a photo of Ice Cube, who by then had left the group N.W.A. In the issue, Ras Baraka and dream hampton interviewed Ice Cube and movie director John Singleton about their movie, *Boyz N the Hood*. The movie follows a group of young Black men living in Los Angeles who try to navigate personal and family relationships, gang rivalries, and a racist legal system. *Boyz N the Hood* features typical storylines underscoring Black struggles and tragedies that led to promising Black youths' fall from grace. They get trapped in gang life and crime, unwanted pregnancy, or they have their dreams extinguished in a violent death. For working-class and poor Black folks living in segregated and economically depressed inner-city neighborhoods, the conditions in which they live define their Blackness, especially for those policymakers who claim they live in "cultures of poverty."

The Rodney King moment, Mom's warnings, and gangster rap shaped my outlook when De La Soul railed against "hard" rap. I was attracted to gangsta rap's in-your-face, anti-authoritarian ethos. My friends and I started listening more often to Ice Cube's *Death Certificate* and *The Predator* as both albums demonstrated strong responses to racism. These albums represented one example of Black masculinity we idolized as teenagers.

Stretched Identities

Thurgood Marshall's retirement from the Supreme Court as its first Black justice and George H. W. Bush's nomination of Clarence Thomas were additional flashpoints in conversations about the meanings of racial identity for Black Americans in the early 1990s. Bush's nomination and the Republican Party's support of Thomas demonstrated a vapid and superficial expression of identity politics. Thomas grew up racially conscious and even dabbled in a little bit of Black nationalist politics before he turned into an anti-anti-racist or colorblind Black conservative who seemed to oppose affirmative action as much out of self-loathing as a matter of principle. However, Thomas and his white conservative allies cynically mobilized his racial identity to bolster his claim to Marshall's former seat. They summoned histories of racism to excoriate those who supported lawyer Anita Hill and her testimony detailing instances of sexual harassment she faced while working for him at the Department of Education and the Equal Employment Opportunity Commission (EEOC). Democratic senator Joe Biden failed to confront his male Republican colleagues for their attempts to publicly humiliate Hill in front of a nationally televised audience.

The confirmation hearings simultaneously reached their political zenith and rhetorical low when Thomas sneered that he suffered from a "high-tech lynching." Thomas's comments were another example of how the Republican Party had warped racial politics after the Civil Rights and Black Power movements. Black folks could only articulate a racial consciousness when they supported the Republican Party. Otherwise, we had to act as if we were colorblind.

In response to Thomas's testimony and the Judiciary Committee's mistreatment of Hill, Black women rallied to her defense while some African Americans, especially Black men, defended Thomas. Black scholars Barbara Ransby, Debra King, and Elsa Barkley Brown organized a group of Black women in solidarity with Hill called African American Women in Defense of Ourselves. In November 1991, the organization bought space in various newspapers, including the *New York Times*, to publish their statement against Clarence's confirmation and sexist treatment of Hill in the public conversation around the hearings.

The statement carried forward the tradition of Black women advancing an intersectional analysis of power and demanding an end to sexism, racism, classism, and all forms of exploitation and oppression. Public debates around Thomas and Hill propelled conversations about race and gender in Black and US public discourse during the 1990s that would culminate with the debates around Louis Farrakhan's Million Man March.

"What Is Alternative Hip-Hop?"

The music world also entered a transition in 1991. While rap music had grown in popularity during the 1980s, it seemed that record companies and music store owners failed to pay attention or were in denial. Rock and pop music typically dominated the *Billboard* charts, while rap and country were seen as marginal, if not faddish. But, on May 25, 1991, *Billboard* made an announcement that altered the course of popular music—rap music had "arrived." Eleven days after De La Soul released *De La Soul Is Dead* and three days before N.W.A dropped their second album, *Efil4zaggin* (*Niggaz4Life* spelled backward), *Billboard* started using barcodes to track sales. SoundScan's tracking system displaced record store owners who would "count" records they sold. Of course, these human counters were biased, tending to favor pop and rock while discounting country and rap. To the surprise of critics, record store owners, radio programmers, and consumers, N.W.A's polarizing second album overtook R.E.M.'s *Out of Time* to become the number one album on *Billboard*'s Top 200 chart. Proclaiming themselves on the album as the "world's most dangerous group," N.W.A confirmed what many already knew—rap music and hip-hop culture were growing commercial forces, not just among Black fans but also among white consumers. Rap might have been in transition, but it was here to stay.

Artists in popular culture unfailingly express concern or anxiety around success and "selling out." But some in the rock and rap world seemed to express more discomfort, if not consternation, about the trappings of success and authenticity. Even though performers toiled in rock's underground during the 1980s, grunge finally hit its stride later in the decade and in the early 1990s. Seattle's Nirvana released *Nevermind* in September 1991. Grunge, like punk rock, arose in response to the excesses of rock music. Grunge was a negation of the big-hair rock music of the 1980s. Groups like Nirvana with frontman Kurt Cobain arrived on the scene questioning the authenticity of other artists and performed lyrics demonstrating their discomfort with sudden success. Culture critic Chuck Klosterman cites how Nirvana's lead singer disdained groups like Pearl Jam and Alice in Chains. "They're obviously just corporate puppets that are trying to jump on the alternative bandwagon," Cobain explained in an interview.

Ironically, De La Soul and alternative hip-hop remained in its nascent stages while grunge reached its zenith, leading the press to question whether the post–punk rock form remained underground. Similar to punk bands and early hip-hop groups like The Clash and Grandmaster Flash & the Furious Five, grunge and hip-hop groups like Nirvana and De La Soul shared an affinity, even if they were not directly conversing with each other. Members of both groups chafed at fame and success. And starting with *De La Soul Is Dead*, Posdnuos, Trugoy, Maseo, and Prince Paul became more vocal about De La Soul's oppositional stance to commercialism in rap over the next few years.

Black Nerd Status

Pivotal events took place in my life in the early 1990s. Mom received her military discharge papers in February 1990, and we left the air force base in Altus, Oklahoma and returned to Pensacola. Mom and Dad's relationship grew untenable, and they split up. Dad traveled back to Mansfield, and we stayed in Pensacola. Our stay in Florida was short-lived, unfortunately. Sometime in the summer of 1991, I was talking with my best friend Charles on the phone. We planned a sleepover so we could stay up and play Nintendo. His mother said it was okay for me to stay. Unfortunately, my mother dashed my hopes. She said abruptly, "You can't go to his house. We're moving. I need you to get off the phone and pack."

"Wait. What do you mean?" I said.

I told Charles, sadly, that I could not come over. "We are actually moving," I said. It was one of the saddest conversations I had with anyone.

I hung up the phone. Mom told my sister and me that we were allowed to pack whatever we wanted to take with us into our bookbags. I grabbed my new Nintendo console and games and stuffed them in the bag.

"What about the rest of our stuff?" I asked sadly.

"We'll come back and get it," Mom replied.

Of course, we never returned to Pensacola to get our stuff, but Mom knew what she needed to say to get me moving. Later that night, we went to a Greyhound stop, boarded a bus, and traveled to her hometown, Mansfield, Ohio. We left everything behind—toys, trophies, books, and memories. Mom even abandoned her record collection, which still haunts me as a music lover and grieving son. I did not know the reason why we left so abruptly. Looking back, I can only speculate that Mom thought it was best for us to live near family.

I officially entered nerdom upon arriving in Mansfield. After I'd spent weeks squinting at everything—the TV, the chalkboard in the classroom, my books—my mother took me to an eye doctor. I failed the eye tests, and the doctor delivered the news that I did not know I dreaded: I would need to wear glasses.

"Ugh," I thought sadly.

Not only was I the new kid in my fifth-grade class, but I would also have to wear these large-framed glasses that made me look like a nerd. I resisted wearing them for a few weeks. I left them at home or brought them with me but never put them on. Then, my fifth-grade teacher, Ms. Mahoney, inquired about my performance. She and my parents encouraged me to wear them. I put them on and have hardly abandoned them since. I was excited to be able to see the board and to participate in class again. But my participation drew the ire of a classmate (I won't reveal his name) who never failed to point out my contributions in a passive-aggressive and ridiculing way. It was not the first time I had been bullied, but it was the first time someone else, a peer, had tried to use my intelligence against me. As a result, I withdrew, participated less, and downplayed my intelligence. I continued to do so until my junior and senior years of high school, when I took my studies and hip-hop fandom more seriously.

"This Is a Very Mean Record" / "Yo, We Need a Single"

De La Soul Is Dead is a great act of negation. Drawing on cultural studies scholar Lawrence Grossberg's argument about the reliance on "excorporation" to establish legitimacy in culture, philosopher Jeffrey T. Nealon argues that authenticity "depends on saying 'no' to some very specific things," or rejecting popular artists like "Justin Bieber or Taylor Swift." Ironically, De La Soul said "no" to a past version of themselves, at least the version that recorded "Me Myself and I," who posed with flowers in photo shoots and utilized Day Glo flower designs on the *3 Feet High and Rising* cover and in music videos like "Eye Know."

Nealon argues that this negation highlights the ascension of "every-man-for-himself neoliberalism and the parallel commodification of everything, even . . . authentic oppositional or subcultural identity." Maybe this is the case for De La Soul, considering their commitment to a creative individualism. But, also, the group's act of negation was pragmatic. *Posdnuos, Trugoy, and Maseo* understandably aimed to free themselves from the unwanted identity projected onto them by record labels, fans, and critics. For them, D.A.I.S.Y. had become more of an obstacle. The flowers and hippie image gave license to others to challenge the group's authenticity and to test their masculinity. Prince Paul told rapper and podcaster Open Mike Eagle about the group's consternation around the term and image, "We're in hip-hop, and there's a certain amount of bravado and masculinity that kinda comes along in that era in hip-hop. And you come across, 'Hey, we're daisies. Peace and happy.' And that brought a lot of people testing them."

The album title was a joke about their labor. According to Posdnuos, Trugoy wrote "De La Soul Is Dead" on the tour calendar because of their grueling schedule. While the joke stuck, it also contained a philosophical and existential meaning. Posdnuos told journalist Sway Calloway in 2023 that their "death" marked a transition—"Death is a way to transitioning to something else." The negation was natural. So, instead of continuing to try to answer questions about whether they were hippies, they displayed a knocked-over flowerpot with dying daisies on the cover and killed their image. Posdnuos is right: Death and change are the natural course of events. The second album suggested that embracing both was necessary to build a lasting career in rap.

De La Soul also used the second album to say "no" to popular rap, mocking artists like Vanilla Ice. The illustrated panels in the *De La Soul Is Dead* album insert display a group of women gushing over Vanilla Ice. In the context of the album, it is difficult to read praise like "He's better than any rapper I have seen!" as anything but sarcastic. Nevertheless, in the early 1990s, performers like Vanilla Ice and MC Hammer were that popular. Both artists blasted themselves into pop culture stardom using conspicuous sampling as rocket fuel. Songs like "U Can't Touch This" and "Ice Ice Baby," which sampled Rick James's "Super Freak" and Queen and David Bowie's "Under Pressure," were ubiquitous on MTV, and the lyrics were on the tips of the tongues of many. Vanilla Ice's *To the Extreme* sold six million records in the first few months of its release, while MC Hammer's *Please Hammer Don't Hurt 'Em* more than doubled *To the Extreme*'s sales a year later by selling nearly 15 million records in the United States.

While some hip-hoppers frowned at the parachute pants–wearing MC Hammer, Vanilla Ice stirred the most consternation and anxiety. Vanilla Ice was an interloper in hip-hop culture, and everyone knew it. This white rapper seemed to have taken MC Hammer's style and run with it. He danced. His single, "Ice Ice Baby," utilized a conspicuous sample, and, most infamously and offensively, the white rapper claimed that he grew up in Miami in an appeal to authenticity. Late night talk-show host Arsenio Hall, who had also introduced De La Soul as "the hippies of hip-hop," confronted Robert Van Winkle about his upbringing. As it turned out, Van Winkle grew up middle class in South Dallas, not Miami. Of course, there was nothing wrong with white lyricists—the Beastie Boys conquered the mainstream in 1986. There was nothing wrong with being from the suburbs—De La Soul was from the 'burbs. There was something wrong with producing wack music and then lying about where one was from to gain some clout. Van Winkle tried to partake in and profit from Blackness. Hence, A Tribe Called Quest's Phife Dawg called Van Winkle, and the music industry, "ridiculous" on the "Scenario (Remix)."

Prince Paul recalls the recording of *De La Soul Is Dead*. "As we were recording the album, I remember telling the guys, 'This is a *very* mean record.'" This is evident in the overarching counternarrative De La Soul spins on the record. On the introduction to *De La Soul Is Dead*, we encounter a group of kids who find a De La Soul tape in the trash. A group of bullies, played by members of De La Soul, run into the kids, beat them up, and take the tape. Instead of a game show host, the bullies are the ones who guide listeners through the album. De La Soul, or the bullies, also provide us with feedback. In doing so, as Prince Paul acknowledged, the group would beat all the potential critics to the punch by dissing themselves! No bad review could be worse than them dissing themselves. This is how they would take back control of the narrative.

Posdnuos, Trugoy, Maseo, and Prince Paul drew on their personal experiences to produce a genre-bending, reality-based, yet at times fantastical album. Prince Paul and the group relied on their *3 Feet High and Rising* production formula—using samples from various sources to craft songs and skits. However, they offered a more sophisticated sonic backdrop. *De La Soul Is Dead* incorporated punk, hard rock, house music, and disco. And, as with *3 Feet High and Rising*, De La Soul sampled from their creative predecessor, Parliament Funkadelic. The dozen "bug out pieces" are some of the group's best skits, using quiet storm to slow down the album's tempo and other genres to turn it up to a frenetic pace.

De La Soul's counter to the D.A.I.S.Y. age relied on taking control of their narrative by reframing their identity and reconciling that with their newfound fame, articulating a meta anti-corporate and anti-rap industry critique and engaging in tough, more personal conversations about social issues. The group's abandonment of their innocence on *3 Feet High and Rising* also included more direct verbal confrontations with women on songs like "Bitties in the BK Lounge" and a more straightforward expression of their sexual desires.

The group addressed the rap industry's and their challengers' attempts to lock them in a D.A.I.S.Y.-inspired pacifist box on songs like "Oodles of O's," "Pease Porridge," and "Afro Connections at a Hi 5 (In the Eyes of the Hoodlum)." While it sounds like De La Soul is rapping about cereal or SpaghettiOs on "Oodles of O's," the group uses their inside language, describing their experiences with fame by ending all of their lines with an "O"—all of the shocked faces when they encounter fans, the (possible) respect they garner from others due to their fame and money, and the fistfights they got into along the way. As the beat tumbled over me, I was struck by Posdnuos's use of onomatopoeia while threatening to beat up challengers on this song and sporting peace signs on his clothes.

The threats and fictionalized depictions of violence negates the group's emphasis on peace signs, flowers, and bright colors featured on *3 Feet High and Rising*'s album cover and in its music videos. "Pease Porridge" is another track where Trugoy and Posdnuos employ a different rhyme style over a familiar, if unorthodox, sample of an eighteenth-century English nursery rhyme, "Pease Porridge Hot." Of course, in this song, "pease" is a play on "peace," and the group contrasts the nursery rhyme with their tales of beating down those who approached them. Moreover, De La Soul highlighted not a contradiction but the misinterpretation of their previous D.A.I.S.Y. identity with their fistfighting tales. Critics mistook them for carefree pacificist hippies, while challengers took the group for easy opponents. De La Soul instead used this and other songs on the album to illustrate an actual reality for many Black men, especially those marked for bullying.

Presenting as willing to defend oneself from physical threats might appear counterintuitive for those who prefer to move through life nonviolently. However, the failure to look intimidating can elicit unwanted interactions that could escalate into a physical confrontation. Of course, wearing my big glasses and being quiet as a kid never helped me out, either. I still encounter moments when I think some perceive me to be an easy target. I have lost count of the times when I have had to sternly address a stranger or even, in a few cases, step to someone to get them to leave me alone. I experience these types of interactions with many men from various racial backgrounds to this day, and I believe it is in part because I am far from an intimidating-looking person (which is also probably why some of these men act surprised at my reactions to them).

Trugoy's, Posdnuos's, and Maseo's displays of physicality on *De La Soul Is Dead* is for all of us Black folks who deal with the times when people test our patience. In 1989, De La Soul demonstrated that Black people could present a weird and nerdy side. Two years later, they also showed that young Black men who looked like them were more than capable of defending themselves. Thus, to paraphrase a later Posdnuos lyric, they added a bit of a hard edge to their music. This hardness, then and now, is a survival tactic in a racist and patriarchal society that often fuses physical prowess with masculinity and Blackness. In this type of society, questioning one's ability to scare off other people might provoke existential questions about one's racial identity. Consequently, De La Soul's responses to physical threats were not just about some people thinking they were "soft," the group's fights were about protecting their freedom, their ability to move through the world and express oneself freely.

The fictional beatdowns on *De La Soul Is Dead* were not the group's only appeals to authenticity through an expression of a harder Black masculinity. Posdnuos, Trugoy, and Maseo address sex and women more directly, if not with more ire, on "Let, Let Me In." Unlike the playful "Jenifa Taught Me," where Jenifa initiated sexual encounters with Posdnuos, Trugoy, and Maseo, De La Soul turn the tables and demonstrate their sexual prowess over a sample of Lowell Fulson's "Tramp" on "Let, Let Me In."

Yet, sometimes women turn the tables on De La Soul and ridicule the group and hold them accountable. A lover calls out Posdnuos's sleeping around on the cute skit "Talkin' Bout Hey Love." And on the panoramic "Bitties in the BK Lounge," group members engage in an acerbic game of dozens with "bitties" Almond Joy, Jenette, Monique, Naima, and Tonya. The three-part, airy and fantastical track features Trugoy, who enters Burger King and encounters a woman working at the register who ignores him. He captures her attention after taking off his cap because, upon seeing his dreadlocks, she thinks he's Tracy Chapman. She asks for an autograph, and he plays along, claiming to have sung the now-iconic song "Fast Car."

Posdnuos, on the other hand, plays a BK worker who is serving a group of women (Shushawna, Rosita, and another woman) unhappy with the service. After they recognize each other, Shushawna harangues Posdnuos for failing to respond to her and informs him that she has a "real job." Posdnuos then criticizes Shushawna's appearance. They go back and forth, with Shushawna bragging about the cost of her clothes, her partner, and her higher economic standing, at least compared to Posdnuos's, and Pos replying with more cuts about her hair, her appearance, and her guy, whom Pos claims he could beat up. On "Talkin' Bout Hey Love," "Let, Let Me In," and "Bitties in the BK Lounge," Pos abandons the carefree, flirty, and poetic approach to love and women heard on "Eye Know," "Jenifa," and even "Buddy." Instead, he locates Black masculinity in his ability to engage in sexual conquest, control, and ridicule. Yet, ironically, neither he nor the rest of the group escapes accountability.

"Bitties in the BK Lounge" echoes Otis Redding's and Carla Thomas's battle of the sexes on "Tramp." Soon after the recording of Fulson's "Tramp," Otis Redding and Carla Thomas recorded a version where they dissed each other. With Booker T. & the MG's playing what became an oft-sampled funky beat, Carla Thomas calls Redding a "tramp" and tells him "you probably haven't even got twenty-five cents." Redding, unlike Posdnuos, replies by bragging about how he owns more than two dozen vehicles. Thomas also attacks him for being "country," while Redding replies, "That's good." Like the women confronting Posdnuos, Thomas controls the verbal sparring match.

"Bitties in the BK Lounge" also captures a common experience of working-class youth—laboring in fast food and service. (In fact, working in food service is so common that Vice President Kamala Harris not uncontroversially touted her work at McDonald's in her 2024 campaign for president.) His own experience, according to Trugoy, partly inspired the song. Trugoy later explained to *GQ*, "Bitties in the BK Lounge" was

> . . . like reading De La's journal, something that really happened—an actual situation that took place in life and we put it to song. Our experiences working as employees of Burger King definitely adds to it. We worked in Burger King at some point together or at the establishment. And there were so many memories there and those memories spilled onto the record.

While Burger King never employed me, I worked in a couple of pizza places as a teenager and remember engaging in the same type of resistance, directed either at my employer or customers. I snuck food for myself and friends because we couldn't afford to eat at the places we worked. I talked back to customers who exhibited way too much impatience when we were busy. While working at another pizza place, I egged on a man who threatened to "leap over the table and wipe the smile off my face" because he was unhappy that his pizza order would not be enough to feed his family. The company ran a special that led him to believe he would receive more pizza if he ordered it. But, of course, the pizza special was a scam. We cut two pizzas in half and stuck them in the narrow, three-foot-long box corporate gave us. I sympathized with the man because the pizza corporation fooled him. But my empathy ran dry after he threatened to leap over the counter and beat me up. I laughed at him because he wasn't going to win that fight.

As Robin Kelley contends in his book *Race Rebels: Culture, Politics, and the Black Working Class*, De La Soul and their collaborators acting out scenarios of working more slowly and playing the dozens, as well as my experiences working in food service, are examples of everyday resistance at work. Kelley advances this point upon reflecting on his own experiences working at McDonald's in the late 1970s.

> And while all of this was going on, folks were signifying on one another, talking loudly about each other's mommas, daddys, boyfriends, girlfriends, automobiles (or lack thereof), breath, skin color, uniforms; on occasion describing in hilarious detail the peculiarities of customers standing on the other side of the counter. Such chatter often drew in the customers, who found themselves entertained or offended—or both—by our verbal circus and collective dialogues.

De La Soul and their collaborators, like many of America's fast-food workers, documented instances of what anthropologist James Scott calls the "hidden transcripts" of "infra politics," or the everyday acts of resistance that fall outside the parameters of established politics (e.g., voting, canvassing, lobbying, etc.).

Even De La Soul's playful singles are related to work. I fell in love with "A Roller Skating Jam Named 'Saturdays'" and "Ring Ring Ring (Ha Ha Hey)" instantly when I first listened to *De La Soul Is Dead* as a junior in high school. Both songs underscore labor themes, albeit in different ways. Both are fun, and at the time of my first listening, they evoked nostalgia for a moment I had never really experienced. I attended a couple of roller-skating parties, but I doubt either was as fun as is depicted in the "Saturday" song and video. And while my mom listened to R&B music that sounded like "Ring Ring Ring," I was never old enough to experience hearing the song in a party context. Yet, these tracks also negate previous singles like "Me Myself and I." Why? Because they were meta. De La Soul recorded these songs to appease Tommy Boy's desire for another hit. The record label wanted radio-friendly songs, so why not give them a song with an extremely on-the-nose title like "A Roller Skating Jam Named 'Saturdays'" or rap annoyingly on "Ring Ring Ring" about wannabe musicians chasing them down like zombies to give the group their demos?

The group did not intend to record "Saturdays" for the album until, Posdnuos told *Rolling Stone*, "Tommy Boy was bothering us about, 'Yo, we need a single.'" The beat was originally for a Native Tongues spinoff group, The Fabulous Fleas, which, in an incredible hip-hop "what if," consisted of A Tribe Called Quest's Q-Tip, the Jungle Brothers' Afrika Baby Bam, the Beatnuts' Juju, and Posdnuos. "'What I'ma come up with,'" for the beat, Posdnuos remembered in a 2023 *Rolling Stone* interview. De La Soul plotted a disco-inspired song that one might hear in a roller rink. "Saturdays," like other songs on the album including the three-part "Bitties in the BK Lounge," featured more sophisticated production. Featuring multiple samples from the Mighty Ryders, Chic, Chicago, and Frankie Valli's "Grease," the song included a blood-pumping beat change (which I am a sucker for) where Trugoy triumphantly enters, "Oh Mr. Sprinkler, Mr. Sprinkler."

The rapper breaks up a crowd of women in the video by spraying them with a sprinkler. And the "disco diva singer," otherwise known as Vinia Monica, sings the chorus. De La Soul was not hiding what feelings they were trying to instill in its listeners on the song.

"Saturdays" represents one of De La Soul's lighter moments on *De La Soul Is Dead*. The light tone of the song is illustrative of Saturday as a day for rest and partying for those fortunate enough not to have to work on the weekends. After a disco-inspired WRMS radio introduction, Q-Tip delivers a flirty and carefree verse about a boy pursuing a girl only to be stood up on Saturday. Monica and Posdnuos address one of the few motivations of engaging in capitalist labor besides avoiding starvation—working to reach the weekend. Monica sings, "Five days you work, one whole day to play." Posdnuos urges listeners to "toss the briefcase" and "unfasten that noose around your neck," or one's necktie, to free oneself from the doldrums of oppressive capitalist labor. There's a reason why we hate Mondays. As scholars like Robin Kelley and Tera Hunter show us in their histories of the Black working class, exploited workers using their bodies for pleasure instead of labor can also represent resistance. On "Saturdays," De La Soul is freeing themselves, albeit momentarily, in two ways: first, by submitting an ironically named single to satisfy the Tommy Boy dictates, and second, by giving their listeners a soundtrack to dance to on their days off from capitalist work.

Of course, "Ring Ring Ring" is another example of the group's belief that rap authenticity arises from one's direct experience. What is funny about the infectious song is it arose out of a joke the members used to play with each other. In their encounters with aspiring artists looking for record deals, Prince Paul, Posdnuos, Trugoy, and Maseo would give out the other members' phone numbers rather than their own. Prince Paul said, "Random people will come up to us . . . and they would go, 'Prince Paul, I got this demo. I want you to check it out.' Aw, man. I don't have that much time, but if you contact Trugoy, he'll listen to your demo. Here's his number." Hip-hop culture is full of stories about aspiring artists looking for their big break—just one shot, whether it was through an impromptu freestyle or a rapper getting a demo tape into the hands of an artist, producer, or A&R. Back in 1989, EPMD made a song urging people to listen to their demos. Responding to their experience, De La Soul recorded a song expressing their annoyance at others for seeing them as an onramp into the rap industry. In the song, each of the members, sans Paul, performs lyrical evasive maneuvers where they would give would-be artists fake numbers and pass them off to the other members.

But before "Ring Ring Ring" is a zany horror skit with another long title, "Not Over Till the Fat Lady Plays the Demo." On this "bug out piece," Trugoy narrates a story about running from a woman pursuing him with a demo tape. The skit contains a callback to "Bitties in the BK Lounge," as Trugoy scampers there for a burger after being denied a ride by a cabdriver. Who is it taking his order this time, he wonders. It's the woman. "Oh Chrissie!" Trugoy screams. The skit ends with a familiar horror scene as she stalks Trugoy while he is showering. "What did she want from me?" Trugoy keeps yelling, and it's for him to take her demo.

De La Soul's lyrics express annoyance, which might strike a listener as pretentious if it were not set to an R&B-inspired dance track, and the group's lyrics were not so catchy. The song was tailor-made for me. It was one of the first songs from the album I could memorize. I still love every verse. Its beat evokes memories of Mom and me listening to Janet Jackson in the car as she drove around running errands. The song features a beat change where Maseo tells the fictional driver that Posdnous was the group's main producer. The video feels like a Soul II Soul spoof, showing slow-motion dancing and the group looking bohemian.

Remember when De La Soul tried to sandbag their performance on "Me Myself and I" and despite that, the song became a big hit? Well, "Ring Ring Ring" obviously was not as big, but De La Soul created their infectious pop song to negate popular trends in R&B

during the 1990s. "Ring Ring Ring" was one of rap's first ringtones, or answering machine song messages, as the group apologized for the caller not being able to reach them on the chorus. And like "Me Myself and I," the group tucks the song toward the album's end (Track 21). Posdnuos and Trugoy also seem to rap with a similar reserved tone in "Ring Ring Ring" and "Me Myself and I."

While De La Soul addressed social issues on *3 Feet High and Rising* in songs like "Ghetto Thang" and "Say No Go," their second album delivered more dark meditations on social ills from a more personal perspective. "My Brother's a Basehead" and "Millie Pulled a Pistol on Santa" both form the social consciousness of *De La Soul Is Dead*. Posdnuos drove the creative direction for both songs. "My Brother's a Basehead" negates "Say No Go" sonically and lyrically. Rather than the familiar pop sample guiding "Say No Go," Posdnuos raps about his older brother's drug addiction over a track inspired by 1960s British pop group The Mindbenders. While this does not make the song less danceable, the sample's unfamiliarity and the beat's slower tempo focus ears on Posdnuos's story of his brother. Saying no to drugs was no longer a dancing matter as it was on "Say No Go." Of all the disses and spoofs on *De La Soul Is Dead*, Posdnuos's narrative of his brother is probably the most scathing. He addresses him as a "basehead," or a crack addict, throughout the track.

De La Soul continues their journey into bleaker aspects of life on "Millie Pulled a Pistol on Santa." While the title might evoke a sense of comedy, "Millie" might be De La Soul's darkest and most affecting song. On this masterful storytelling track, Posdnuos and Trugoy narrate the story of Millie, a girl who was sexually and physically abused by her social worker father. Posdnuos and Trugoy capture the levels of primary and secondary trauma in this unfurling and disturbing narrative over a slightly sped-up sample of Funkadelic's "I'll Stay" (which sounds ominous itself). Posdnuos narrates the story from the point of view of an admiring peer. Meanwhile, Trugoy plays the role of the peer who dismisses Millie after she confides in him about the abuse at the hands of her father. There was no way her father, Dillon, could have inflicted that type of harm because Dillon has a favorable reputation as "cool" among Millie's friends. Without support from her peers, Millie seeks another way out of her hell—by calling Trugoy and asking if he could get her a gun. Trugoy rebuffs her request and again questions how Dillon could assault her. Yet, like many Americans seeking firearms, Millie succeeds. She "floats" into Macy's "like a zombie" and murders her father while he's playing Santa for the kids. Posdnuos's narration ends as suddenly as the gunshot to Santa Claus's head.

While I did not listen to "Millie Pulled a Pistol on Santa" until my junior year of high school, I found De La Soul's narrative similar to Aerosmith's in the "Janie's Got a Gun" music video. Aerosmith's 1989 song tracks a similar story about Janie, who also sought revenge for abuse. I remember being horrified at the video and the song's content, yet vaguely understanding the song's meaning. While Steven Tyler was inspired by news reports about gun deaths, Posdnuos claims the group developed the story about Millie from the experience of someone they knew. After deriving inspiration from seeing a houseless man wearing a "really dirty Santa Claus outfit" while riding the subway, Posdnuos wrote, "Millie pulls a . . ." "So later on," Posdnuos told *GQ*, "someone close to me went through a situation with their father. I then applied that situation to the title. 'So, it could be about this. The girl being molested shoots her father at the end who plays Santa Claus.'"

Both songs capture the complexities of the unspeakable shame, depression, entrapment, trauma, and pain that many assault victims must feel. Both stories reflect the harsh reality that most victims know their attacker. According to the Rape, Abuse & Incest National Network, 8 out of 10 assault victims know their perpetrator. In each case, Millie and Janie not only relive their trauma when they encounter their fathers, they also must contend with their abusers seemingly being respectable in the public eye. Neither Janie nor Millie can find any support, and their fathers' public persona contributes more to their trauma and their desperation. Both songs also critique men. De La Soul and Aerosmith remind us that any seemingly "good" man could perpetrate such acts. In fact, these acts often go unaddressed because perpetrators become effective in utilizing both fear with victims and charm with others in their community to create the buffer needed to continue to perpetrate such gruesome acts. Then women and other vulnerable people like Millie are subjected to further trauma as those who know the perpetrators deny such gruesome acts, and the experiences of people like Millie, because the perpetrator constructs a public image as an upstanding citizen. "Millie Pulled a Pistol on Santa" also offers another lesson when it comes to dealing with sexual and physical abuse and trauma—it takes a community to deal with, if not protect each other from, violence.

"A Short Film by De La Soul." The "Hippies of Hip-Hop." "Head Full of Dreads, but Knowledge Inside."

While not heralded as a revolutionary album like *3 Feet High and Rising*, *De La Soul Is Dead* was critically acclaimed. *The Source* magazine, which eventually served as hip-hop's bible during the 1990s, awarded the group's second album its highest rating—five mics. Critic and scholar Scott Poulson-Bryant raved about the album in his four-star review for *Rolling Stone*. "The record revels in hip-hop's eternal commitment to the 'street' and finds a warranted and sensitive rap authenticity," he wrote. Although Poulson-Bryant praised De La Soul's turn toward realism and negation, other reviewers gave *De La Soul Is Dead* less favorable reviews than *3 Feet High and Rising*. Famed rock critic Robert Christgau gave De La Soul's second effort three stars after awarding *3 Feet High and Rising* an A-. David Browne in *Entertainment Weekly* asserted that De La Soul's zany, yet realist, album was "closer to the sophomoric high jinks of Cheech and Chong." He also stated that the group "comes off as smug and self-righteous."

Despite the few bad reviews and some of the disappointment with De La Soul's abandonment of their whimsy and innocence on *De La Soul Is Dead*, the group's sophomore album might be as influential as its predecessor. Prince Paul's and De La Soul's willingness to produce an album that mashes up many genres set a standard for rap producers like Kanye West and Pharrell. Besides N.W.A's *Efil4zaggin*, in which Dr. Dre was undoubtedly influenced by *3 Feet High and Rising*, few rap albums at the time used the album form to tell a full story. *De La Soul Is Dead* paved the way for other cinematic albums like Gravediggaz's (which included Prince Paul) *6 Feet Deep* (1994), Raekwon's *Only Built 4 Cuban Linx* (1995), Jay-Z's *Reasonable Doubt* (1996), and Biggie's *Life After Death* (1997).

For Prince Paul, one can draw a line from *De La Soul Is Dead* to *6 Feet Deep* and his first two solo albums, *Psychoanalysis (What Is It?)* (1996) and *A Prince Among Thieves* (1999). "Who Do U Worship," from *De La Soul Is Dead*, is a prequel to Prince Paul's "Beautiful Night," the first song on *Psychoanalysis*. While Prince Paul juxtaposed the main character's optimism with metal riffs on "Who Do U Worship," the producer reverses the equation on "Beautiful Night" and features its main character calmly recounting a night of violence and murder over a chill, jazzy beat. Prince Paul became rap's prince of darkness as he helped bring together other artists who were once on Tommy Boy and were now at a down point in their careers (except for the RZA)—Frukwan, Poetic, and the RZA. *6 Feet Deep*, which appears as the more bizarro *3 Feet High and Rising*, ushered in the brief horrorcore moment in hip-hop culture as the group produced songs about taking psychedelics, drinking blood, and murdering people. Songs on *6 Feet Deep* carried the same darkness as De La Soul tracks like "Millie Pulled a Pistol on Santa" and the same horror as "Not Over Till the Fat Lady Plays the Demo."

We can also draw a line from *De La Soul Is Dead* to rap musicals, even those like *Hamilton*. And if De La Soul pioneered cinematic recording in rap, albeit chaotically, then Prince Paul built on *De La Soul Is Dead* in his rap musical, *A Prince Among Thieves*. The album features main characters Tariq, played by rapper Breezly Brewin', and True, played by rapper Big Sha. The listeners follow the two as the former seeks to raise enough money to record a demo for Wu-Tang Records. Of course, Tariq turns to drug dealing in pursuit of his dream. Throughout the story, he visits Crazy Lou, a weapons dealer played by Kool Keith, engaged in selling drugs to addicts (De La Soul); he's arrested by the police (played by Everlast) and is imprisoned with Sadat X and Xzibit. Afterward, Tariq confronts his former partner in a decisive and fatal battle, and he loses the urban duel. While Lin Manuel Miranda frames his musical around a fantastical biography of Alexander Hamilton, it is hard not to think of the parallels of both pieces culminating with a duel. But *De La Soul Is Dead* is not just a predecessor of *A Prince Among Thieves* and *Hamilton*. It is hard to imagine the existence of Kendrick Lamar's album *good kid, m.A.A.d city*, which also carried the subtitle "A Short Film by Kendrick Lamar," without the influence of *De La Soul Is Dead*.

De La Soul Is Dead had a profound impact on my tastes and my identity. Before *De La Soul Is Dead*, I enjoyed listening to all the popular rappers in the mid-1990s. I listened to gangster rappers like Ice Cube, Scarface, Tupac, and The Notorious B.I.G. Still, I could not identify with any of these artists in the way that I could with De La Soul on their second album. The record matched my cerebral disposition. (I was, and am, a nerd.) This album helped me become what I thought was a "real" hip-hop head.

I loved this album because it was left, but not so far left that it could be misread or not entirely understood. I often felt misunderstood by most people, except for my closest friends. *De La Soul Is Dead* was hard, but it was hard for thinking persons. I saw myself in Posdnuos—a Black, nerdy-looking kid who wore glasses and did not quite possess the confidence that many of my male peers seemed to have. But, after listening to Posdnuos express confidence in his lyrical and fighting abilities and his interactions with women, I found a model of Black masculinity I could identify with. I could understand the need to flex to ward off anyone who would want to challenge me while remaining somewhat in touch with my feelings.

After listening to *De La Soul Is Dead*, I recognized it was neither wack nor soft to care about the culture and the people in it, including my friends. *De La Soul Is Dead*, along with the group's 1996 album, *Stakes Is High*, helped me identify with Common's lamentations about rap music's decline on his 1994 song "I Used to Love H.E.R." I better understood Common's introspective songs on his second and third albums, *Resurrection* and *One Day It'll All Make Sense*. It also guided me into the burgeoning underground scene where artists and groups like Company Flow dropped dense rhymes over dense beats and Mos Def and Talib Kweli critiqued mainstream rap.

Next to "My Brother's a Basehead" and "Millie Pulled a Pistol on Santa," *De La Soul Is Dead*'s nineteenth track, "Pass the Plugs," might be the album's most personal song, where the artists address their struggles for creative control and with fame most directly. Over a simple beat sampling funk ensemble group the JB's that evokes nostalgia and melancholy, Posdnuos gets meditative about his growth, describing it in a way similar to how I would have liked to have seen myself, "smart and mature." Posdnuos called out Arsenio Hall for dubbing the group the "hippies of hip-hop," and *Soul Train* host Don Cornelius for not liking rap.

Initially, Posdnuos's verse was my favorite, but over time, Trugoy's verse became just as meaningful as he signaled where De La Soul was heading after their second album. Trugoy remarked how De La Soul always contained multitudes. Trugoy, Posdnuos, and Maseo always were hard; they claim the expectations stemming from *3 Feet High and Rising*'s success cast them in a "new" light. With his "head full of dreads, but knowledge inside," he addresses Tommy Boy's and the industry's expectations for De La Soul to continue cranking out catchy hits. Trugoy remarked mockingly, "Watch the Daisy, watching it die, see. Tommy Boy wants another 'Say No,' huh." Trugoy then goes on to remark about how the rap industry necessitates a loss of autonomy for artists as record labels and others in the industry seek to "pimp" and "work" them for profit. At the end of Trugoy's first verse, he articulates his need to live without the rules that prevented groups like his from producing music without creative limits. Making a bid for his freedom, Trugoy threatens, "watch me steppin', now I'm dancing, then disappear with a hocus pocus."

CHAPTER 3

We Might Blow Up: The Theory of *Buhloone Mindstate*

"I am tired of these popcorn radio records that the label is looking for us to do when we have so much more that we can create and that we're about. . . . It almost felt like a slave record."

—Trugoy

When I first listened to *Buhloone Mindstate*, I did not understand much. The album's title, cover, and song names confused me. I did not get the balloon ("buhloone") metaphor. I did not know what "stickabush" meant. It was probably because I had not matured enough to understand the album's mesage. I still listened to and derived meaning from Ice Cube's *Death Certificate* and *The Predator* and mixtapes with songs from Eazy-E, Dr. Dre, Scarface, and Tupac Shakur.

Nevertheless, two aspects of the album stuck out to me, even at my rather young age—Posdnuos's claim, "Fuck being hard. Posdnuos is complicated," and his vulnerability on "I Am, I Be." I could not recall more affecting lyrics.

While I found *Buhloone Mindstate* to be a mystery wrapped in a riddle, over time I recognized the title as their theory of rap artistry. The "buhloone" is the album's central metaphor, and the mantra that we hear after the sound of someone blowing up a balloon until it pops is "We might blow up, but we won't go pop." Posdnuos told *Vibe* magazine writer Scott Poulson-Bryant, "We could blow up, but not go pop as in Top 40, or we could have a hit in the Top 40 and still not go pop, meaning explode or have a backlash." Trugoy added, "A lot of people don't see hip-hop as an art. They just out there doin' it. . . . It's not just something done to make money. It's a business, but that's aside from the creative part." Settling into a buhloone mindstate in rap meant pushing artistic boundaries without compromising a sense of themselves and their art. Now, in a way, this theory is not novel for artists. One could throw a rock into a crowd of musicians and artists of all sorts and hit twenty who will claim to care at least as much, if not more, about their art as they do the fame and money. Also, the 1990s concerns of "selling out" or "compromising art" reflected a general unease with corporate culture after the "greed is good" 1980s. So De La Soul, like some other rap artists such as EPMD, A Tribe Called Quest, 3rd Bass, and more, voiced their discomfort with crossing over.

On *Buhloone Mindstate*, the group advanced two theses about confinement—one about the rap industry and another about Black masculinity. On about half of *Buhloone Mindstate*, De La Soul confronts certain truths about rap fandom and the limitations of "crossing over," rap fame, and ego. For Maseo, Trugoy, and Posdnuos, these elements trapped Black artists, especially, within an industry mostly controlled by white Americans. De La Soul did not want Tommy Boy, nor any entity, whether BET, MTV, or *Billboard*, dictating how they should create their art. And on their third album, De La Soul used jazz as a canvas for their presentation of complicated Black masculinity. They joined rap soloists and groups like A Tribe Called Quest, Digable Planets, The Pharcyde, and Guru from Gang Starr at the vanguard of what critics called "jazz rap." De La Soul's articulation of this subgenre reflected jazz's historical inclination toward artistic freedom and innovation.

This is where De La Soul's second thesis—"I'm not hard, I'm

complicated"—is relevant: De La Soul also criticized those in rap who allowed ego and the pursuit of fame and wealth to define their identity. At the center of this ego, for the group, was a specific expression of Black masculinity that focused on being "hard" and "gangsta." De La Soul had rebelled against the "D.A.I.S.Y." image on the previous album by presenting a harder edge. With their jazz rap, De La Soul aimed to break out of the creative limitations the rap industry, the market, and critics placed on them. Now, they presented a different vision of racial and rap authenticity that suggested it was okay for Black men and Black youth, generally, to be "complicated."

"The Nineties Will Be the Decade of a Jazz Thing."

Mom introduced me to jazz and jazz-inspired rap when she bought Quincy Jones's 1989 album, *Back on the Block*. At eight years old, I did not know who Quincy Jones was. I was too young to know he was a legendary jazz composer and producer of some of my parents' favorite albums, such as Michael Jackson's *Off the Wall* and *Thriller*. Yet, I can recall the Afrocentric design on the *Back on the Block* cassette J-card. Mom loved songs like "Wee B. Dooinit," which incorporates beatboxing and R&B. Watching and listening to Mom sing along to "Tomorrow (A Better You, Better Me)," sung by a very young Tevin Campbell, comforted me.

The rappers' contributions on *Back on the Block* caught my ears. Ice-T, Melle Mel, Kool Moe Dee, and Big Daddy Kane verbally stomped through the percussive title track. One could argue, though, that "Jazz Corner of the World" and the updated rendition of "Birdland" served as the album's jazz centerpieces. To start the former, "Jazz Corner of the World" incorporated the sampling element of rap music as Jones and other arrangers interspersed portions of Charlie Parker talking with Jones about Miles Davis playing at the Booker T. Washington Hotel. Big Daddy Kane and Kool Moe Dee follow the spoken introduction with rapid-fire verses giving a lesson in jazz and demonstrating rap's natural fit within the form of (Black) America's "classical music." They lyrically cue artists like legendary singers Ella Fitzgerald and Sarah Vaughan and saxophonist James Moody. Then as Kane and Kool Moe Dee finish their verses, the rhythm of "Birdland" kicks in.

I loved "Birdland" when I first heard it. I remember it sounding very lush and smooth. My parents' factory-installed speakers in their two-door burgundy Pontiac Grand Am must have sounded great because I felt like the production surrounded me. I did not know Joe Zawinul wrote the song in the 1970s, and Weather Report first recorded it in tribute to the club dedicated to Charlie "Bird" Parker. It was very catchy, and I did not care that the song featured little vocals other than those by Ella Fitzgerald and Sarah Vaughan. And, of course, I had no clue that this song, as well as the others they performed on, including "Jazz Corner of the World," were among Fitzgerald's and Vaughan's last official recordings. Who would have thought that they went out with rap?

From the late 1980s into the 1990s, jazz and rap often swung together. Gang Starr's collaboration with saxophonist Branford Marsalis on "Jazz Thing" for Spike Lee's 1990 film *Mo' Better Blues* represented the joining of the two genres. Similar to Big Daddy Kane's and Kool Moe Dee's raps on "Jazz Corner of the World," Guru adapted Lolis Eric Elie's poem telling the history of how jazz musicians such as Louis Armstrong, John Coltrane, and Ornette Coleman helped build and innovate the genre despite attempts of some white Americans to claim it as their own, which is the underlying thesis of the development of much popular music in the United States. Guru then punctuated the song with a declaration, "The nineties will be the decade of a jazz thing."

Over the next couple of years, it seemed that Guru's declaration would turn prophetic. A Tribe Called Quest splashed hip-hop with its stellar, if not its most critically acclaimed, piece of jazz rap, *The Low End Theory*. In addition to featuring bassist Ron Carter, *The Low*

WE MIGHT BLOW UP

End Theory drew from notable jazz artists like Gary Bartz, Weather Report, Art Blakey and the Jazz Messengers, Lonnie Liston Smith, Grant Green, Cannonball Adderley, and Eric Dolphy in their recordings of songs like "Excursions," "Butter," and "Buggin' Out." A Tribe Called Quest caught rap's zeitgeist on *The Low End Theory*, which earned the coveted five-mic rating from *The Source*. Q-Tip called *The Low End Theory* "one of the most on-time records we ever did."

Jazz rap was not limited to the east coast, as groups like The Pharcyde and Freestyle Fellowship dropped jazz-sampled or jazz-infused albums in 1992 and 1993. The Pharcyde's 1992 debut album, *Bizarre Ride II The Pharcyde*, based its production firmly on live instrumentation and jazz, sampling artists like Lou Donaldson, Louis Armstrong, Herbie Mann, Donald Byrd, Ramsey Lewis, Thelonious Monk, John Coltrane, and Roy Ayers. De La Soul's Trugoy reported that *Bizarre Ride II The Pharcyde* inspired him on *Buhloone Mindstate*. He told music critic Miles Marshall Lewis in *Rolling Stone* about the recording of "Eye Patch": "The time was really experimental for us. I remember being influenced by The Pharcyde's release [*Bizarre Ride II The Pharcyde*]. It felt like those guys are just rhyming, having fun. And once again just feeling like, 'Let's go past our norm. Let's try something different.'"

Rappers adopted jazz to express another version of authentic Black masculinity, or even Black cool, in the early 1990s. It is no coincidence that artists like Guru, A Tribe Called Quest, Freestyle Fellowship, and De La Soul articulated their visions of authentic Black musicality on jazz-infused songs. According to music scholar Justin A. Williams, "The process that established jazz rap as a formative rap subgenre saw the construction of an 'alternative' to other rap subgenres such as 'gangsta' and 'pop rap,' creating, ideologically speaking, a unique type of high art within the rap music world." A Tribe Called Quest's Q-Tip and Phife Dawg articulated this distinction more explicitly on two of their album's singles, "Check the Rhime" and "Jazz (We've Got)," dissing MC Hammer and new jack swing artists like Wreckx-N-Effect.

De La Soul criticized "hard" rap and distinguished themselves from the west coast on *Buhloone Mindstate*.

While jazz rap might have been seen as a more elevated form of rap, at least in comparison to the more popular forms of the genre, some artists viewed their adoption of jazz in class terms. Q-Tip offered a class-based reasoning for getting bassist Ron Carter to play on *The Low End Theory*. "When it came to hip-hop and jazz, the work we were doing was a unique opportunity to combine both of them, like the way we used Ron Carter on 'Verses from the Abstract.' Both musics come from the black underclass, and both are very expressive." Guru told Danyel Smith in *Vibe* in 1994: "The whole so-called jazz hip-hop movement is about bringing jazz back to the streets. It got taken away, made into some elite, sophisticated music. It's bringing jazz back where it belongs. Rap got messed up by labels: gangsta rap, jazz rap. It's not about that. It's about phat beats, skills, original voices, original flows." Even on *Buhloone Mindstate*, De La Soul reflected on how some Black artists remained working class compared to many popular white artists. Record labels were more likely to exploit and discard Black artists. And, to De La Soul's consternation, record executives were not afraid of dictating the type of music they want Black artists to record, all to profit. They believed profit-hungry record executives did not mind encouraging rappers' gassed-up egos, especially if that meant more for the label's bottom line. Thus, on *Buhloone Mindstate*, De La Soul deepened their critiques of Tommy Boy Records and the industry that appeared on *3 Feet High and Rising* and *De La Soul Is Dead*.

As Trugoy told journalist Greg Watkins, *Buhloone Mindstate* was "on the jazz tip." De La Soul did not just rely on sampling jazz artists like Milt Jackson and looping it up, they "infused" jazz into the project. Prince Paul and Posdnuos devised a plan to enlist instrumentalists into this project. Prince Paul told *Variety*: "Pos and me were both listening to [legendary James Brown and p-funk saxophonist] Maceo Parker's album at the time and he was like, 'We should get

WE MIGHT BLOW UP

Maceo on the record.' His record was a contemporary record at the time; it wasn't an old JB's record. So we were listening to what was going on in the pulse at the time and that was partly an influence." Thus, the group secured the participation of James Brown's old horn section—Maceo Parker, Fred Wesley, and Pee Wee Ellis.

Parker, Wesley, and Ellis were living embodiments of the history of modern Black music. All three men were born in the South and took to music early in their lives. As a child, Wesley played the piano and trumpet before switching to the trombone. Maceo Parker also learned the piano when he was young after watching others play and learning their finger movements. Ellis started his musical career in jazz, studying the saxophone under Sonny Rollins in the 1950s. The trio joined James Brown's band as its horn section and, along with drummer Clyde Stubblefield, helped create funk music. Wesley served as Brown's band and musical director, and Ellis co-wrote the pro-Black anthem "Say It Loud (I'm Black and I'm Proud)." The trio left James Brown in the mid-1970s to play with George Clinton's Parliament Funkadelic. From there, they collaborated with other artists such as Van Morrison and Prince, pursued solo work, and recorded as a trio—The J.B. Horns.

The album Prince Paul and Posdnuos might have been listening to at the time of recording was probably Maceo Parker's *Life on Planet Groove*. On this recording of a live show in Cologne, Germany, in 1992, Maceo led a band consisting of Ellis, Wesley, and others in renditions of "Soul Power" (titled "Soul Power '92"), "Georgia on My Mind," and "Shake Everything You've Got." Parker cites "Pass the Peas" as "the big hit on the record" and "a song that would eventually become something of a calling card for me" in his autobiography, *98% Funky Stuff*. Of course, De La Soul sampled the studio recording of "Pass the Peas" on one of my favorites from *De La Soul Is Dead*, "Pass the Plugs."

While De La Soul and many other rap and R&B artists grew in popularity due to their use of samples, Parker raised ethical questions about how sampling became a cottage industry as rap grew in popularity. "Fred [Wesley] and I were hired to go to the studio and told to 'just play.' No specific key, no real melody in mind—just play. A few months later, we saw the CD marketed as horn samples to be used in hip-hop tracks. We were furious, because packaging our music like this was never discussed during the session," Parker explains in his memoir, *98% Funky Stuff*. Indeed, artists like George Clinton recorded jam sessions for the purpose of providing samples for music producers; that way Clinton could control what sounds could be used. However, the request that legendary Black musicians like Parker and Wesley create decontextualized sounds for another producer to use seems exceptionally alienating.

Yet, Parker praised De La Soul, who helped pioneer sampling scores of songs on an album, for hiring the J.B. Horns for *Buhloone Mindstate*. "I really respect De La Soul who, rather than sample a bunch of funk records, actually brought my band (which included Fred and Pee Wee) into the studio to record a few tracks on their album *Buhloone Mindstate*," Parker wrote. While it is not entirely accurate to suggest that De La Soul did not rely on samples for their third album, Parker is right to say that the group's inclusion of the J.B. Horns helped achieve a more sonic cohesiveness, one where the samples sounded more in-sync than on their previous albums.

Jazz's move back to the center of Black culture in the early 1990s also probably played a role in influencing rappers. Spike Lee followed *Do the Right Thing* with *Mo' Betta Blues*, a film starring Denzel Washington playing a fledging jazz musician caught between his work and two romantic partners. Two years later, Toni Morrison published *Jazz*, which centered on a love triangle among characters Violet, Joe, and Dorcas, set in 1920s Harlem. The shape of the narrative reflected the genre's form. "I wanted the work to be a manifestation of the music's intellect, sensuality, anarchy; its history, its range, its modernity," Morrison wrote. Even the Recording Academy seemed to somewhat accept jazz rap's surge in popular culture. Digable Planets won the

1994 Grammy for Best Rap Performance by a Duo or Group for their jazzy track "Rebirth of Slick (Cool Like Dat)," beating out Snoop Dogg, of all people. Jazz was in the air.

Jazz aesthetics also influenced Black scholarship. Philosopher Cornel West used jazz references in his 1993 book, *Race Matters*, to analyze race relations in the United States. "I use the term 'jazz' here not so much as a term for a musical art form, as for a mode of being in the world, an improvisational mode of protean, fluid, and flexible dispositions towards reality suspicious of 'either/or' viewpoints, dogmatic pronouncements, or supremacist ideologies," West wrote. He continued, "The interplay of individuality and unity is not one of uniformity and unanimity imposed from above but rather of conflict among diverse groupings that reach a dynamic consensus subject to questioning and criticism."

While West spent much ink criticizing gangsta rap and Black youth "nihilism" in *Race Matters*, he neglected to mention how he shared similar concerns with rap artists A Tribe Called Quest, De La Soul, Digable Planets, and Guru, and others drawing from jazz. These rap artists infused this way of being into their art. Groups like A Tribe Called Quest and De La Soul might have utilized jazz to express their authentic selves in the early 1990s. Furthermore, jazz rap provided these groups with a critical lens that they applied to hip-hop and the music industry. While record executives and some artists sought to take control over the mainstream, De La Soul, Guru, A Tribe Called Quest, and the Freestyle Fellowship pushed to keep rap creatively and intellectually honest. Like "underground" and "backpack" rappers later in the 1990s, they also took it upon themselves to embody hip-hop's diverse spirit. The "dynamic consensus," in West's words, could be interpreted as balance, or an equilibrium that would not always hold, but if it did, then the whole culture would benefit. But if this balance, equilibrium, or consensus among the various subgenres could not settle among each other, then a conflict among rappers could follow.

LIVING IN A D.A.I.S.Y. AGE

"We Might Blow Up, but We Won't Go Pop."
The De La Soul fan who picked up *Buhloone Mindstate* on September 21, 1993, the day of its release, probably found the whole project—the album cover, some of the beats, and the lyrics—surreal. While consumers were greeted by a tipped-over flowerpot on the cover of *De La Soul Is Dead*, on the group's third album, I encountered a dreamlike cover with Trugoy, Maseo, Posdnuos, and Prince Paul looking into a body of water. I could only see Maseo's face clearly while ripples in the water obscured the others. Then I noticed what could be construed as a lily pad, or even a deflated balloon, floating in the water, and on it was printed the name of the album, *Buhloone Mindstate*.

Then I opened my CD case, and the first things I saw were drawn caricatures of Trugoy's, Maseo's, and Posdnuos's faces with their mouths tied shut. Honestly, I did not think much about the photo then, but the images suggested that someone or something was muzzling them. Was it Tommy Boy? Was it the music industry, generally? Was it the rap game?

The front cover provokes questions, too—What are Posdnuos, Maseo, Trugoy, and Paul looking at? Are they looking for themselves in the mainstream? Maybe I am just overthinking it.

Buhloone Mindstate's cover represents an apt reflection (no pun) of De La Soul's willingness to engage in obfuscation on their third record: They triple downed on the metaphors, secret language, and allusions. They deployed satire and irony. They wallowed in malaise and melancholy. The cover demonstrates the album's tendency toward the illusory. We see reflections of Posdnuos, Trugoy, Maseo, and Prince Paul. And, we see them in the water from their vantage point. In essence, they are letting us into their minds.

Buhloone Mindstate also featured a new voice in the Native Tongues. Terressa Thompson, the Boston-born, yet Philadelphia-based MC known as Shortie No Mas(s), appeared on songs like "En Focus,"

"Ego Trippin' (Part 2)," and "In the Woods." Thompson moved to Philadelphia in 1985, when she was eleven, in the same year that the city's first Black mayor, Wilson Goode, oversaw the Philadelphia Police Department's bombing of a stretch of row houses on Osage Avenue, where Black radicals from MOVE lived. While in Philadelphia, Thompson befriended artists such as producer Mel "Chaos" Lewis and started recording songs. A few years later, two aspiring hip-hop artists, drummer Ahmir Thompson and Tariq Trotter, formed a band called The Square Roots, later The Roots. Thompson encountered the group's bassist, Leonard Hubbard, and entered a talent show organized by Rich Nichols, The Roots's manager. Shortie No Mas(s)'s success in Philly's hip-hop scene earned her a place in The Roots' budding collective, and we first hear her voice on the group's debut album, *Organix*, released in the same year as *Buhloone Mindstate*.

Shorty No Mas(s) also caught the attention of De La Soul's Posdnuos, who wanted to feature her on the group's third album. Shorty No Mas(s) later told John Morrison, "Posdnuos said, 'You're gonna be on an album,' but he wasn't really descriptive on what that entailed," Thompson recalls. "So I would just hang out [in the studio]. I just was always there." In addition to contributing verses on songs, she provided ad-libs, as rappers like Jeezy and Quavo would on songs in the 2000s and 2010s. While it is likely that De La Soul fans did not anticipate Shortie No Mas(s)'s participation on the album, her presence did not seem as jarring as Consequence's on A Tribe Called Quest's *Beats, Rhymes and Life*. In fact, her voice complemented Posdnuos's and Trugoy's superbly.

While *Buhloone Mindstate* included some new voices, Prince Paul told writer, rapper, and podcaster Open Mike Eagle that he took more of a step back from the recording. Paul seemed on his way to accomplishing one of his initial objectives with the group—making sure they were self-sufficient artists. Consequently, according to Prince Paul, Posdnuos "really took the lead on a lot of this [*Buhloone Mindstate*]."

LIVING IN A D.A.I.S.Y. AGE

The group undertook a more efficient route in producing their third album. Prince Paul told *Variety* in a 2023 interview, "And we strayed away from making fifty songs on an album and streamlined it. It was definitely a different vibe." It's true. *Buhloone Mindstate* was the group's most focused record to date. Critic John Bernard called De La Soul's third effort "economical" in his A+ review in *Entertainment Weekly*. The album boasts eleven strong, jazz-infused tracks addressing expanding minds and exploding egos. Rather than multiple "bug out pieces" on a twenty-plus track album, *Buhloone Mindstate* only featured four standalone skits.

In the first batch of songs on the album, "Eye Patch," "En Focus," "Patti Dooke," "I Be Blowin'," "Long Island Wildin'," and "Ego Trippin', Part Two," De La Soul articulate their critiques of the music industry. "En Focus" is an interesting track. It is not one that I took to when I first heard *Buhloone Mindstate*. Yet, "En Focus," featuring Shortie No Mas(s) and Black Sheep's Dres, addresses the hypervisibility that accompanies success and the invisibility of the fall-off. The rappers reference "the light" in the song, which refers to popularity, attention, and sales. Of course, De La Soul experienced much of this "light" upon the release of "Me Myself and I" and *3 Feet High and Rising*. The newfound attention and fame encouraged much focus (no pun) on, and misinterpretation of, the group's D.A.I.S.Y. aesthetic. For De La Soul, the light caused some consternation, leading others to test them. Consequently, it is possible they dimmed their own shine with *De La Soul Is Dead*. This is a weird assertion considering that De La Soul's second effort was a better lyrical and, for lack of a better term, theatrical performance. *The Source* even awarded it a perfect five-mic rating! Yet, some of the critics of their sophomore album did not see De La Soul similarly.

If it was De La Soul's turn to deal with the invisibility of the fall-off, then who among their Native Tongues colleagues held the light? A Tribe Called Quest and Queen Latifah are sure answers, but the rapper who appeared to be "next" rapped alongside De La Soul and Shortie No Mas(s) on that song—Dres. Black Sheep dropped their debut album, *A Wolf in Sheep's Clothing*, in 1991. The album marked another classic for the Native Tongues crew. Yet, Dres would become known for his show-stealing performance on the group's smash hit, "The Choice Is Yours (Revisited)." Now, with rap fans waiting for Black Sheep's next move, De La Soul acknowledged that their own group might have taken a step back and that Dres was in the spotlight on "En Focus." Posdnuos referenced De La Soul's fading commercial popularity while describing Black Sheep's and Dres's rise, suggesting that being "flavor of the month" meant being trapped in a music industry that was really a zero-sum game, even for those in the Native Tongues. We cannot forget that De La Soul released *De La Soul Is Dead* the same year that Black Sheep released their first album. While *De La Soul Is Dead* garnered more critical acclaim than *A Wolf in Sheep's Clothing*, the group perceived Dres and Black Sheep as the ones occupying the spotlight. In a rap world governed by a theory of the buhloone mindstate, however, there would be room for both groups in the spotlight. No one would confuse Posdnuos with Positive K.

Many rappers and the rap industry have embraced this zero-sum thinking around hip-hop success. This competitive impulse drove the whole battle for coastal supremacy in the mid-1990s, which helped create the atmosphere for the murders of Tupac Shakur and The Notorious B.I.G. And up until recently, the rap industry, or better yet, the larger music industry, seemed to only have room for one or a few top women emcees. This manufactured and industry-created scarcity in the rap market rendered many Black women rappers invisible. If a male rap artist's shelf life was five years, then maybe a woman artist's was three years, if they were lucky. This manufactured, tight work market for women also encouraged unnecessary rap beef; only a few, like Lauryn Hill and Missy Elliott, could transcend this trend in the 1990s and 2000s.

Of course, many Black folks are also confined in the space between visibility and invisibility in everyday life and in death. I've experienced this pressure plenty of times in my adult life—a white professor publicly acknowledging my race as if I could represent all Black people to my classmates, assuming I share the same cultural cues and values as my Black peers. Some white Americans had a way of hitting me with the one-two punch of racist visibility and colorblind ignorance.

Even more seriously, racist and misogynist tropes such as the matriarch, welfare mother, and Jezebel render Black women's experiences invisible, especially if they are working class and/or poor. We often fail to consider the negative impact of the lack of access to reproductive health care and of state violence on Black women. Usually, white women and Black men might get that type of shine in political discourses around abortion and police killings. For this reason, my mother focused more on keeping me out of trouble than my younger sister. Over the course of the twentieth century, American policymakers have spent much ink trying to address joblessness among Black men while chastising Black women for raising families alone. In this context, Black women become hypervisible in relation to sexuality or public policy deemed deplorable by conservatives. While De La Soul made fun of themselves in their illustrations of being caught between visibility and invisibility, or neglect, "En Focus" hits a theme embedded in many Black Americans' experiences.

"Patti Dooke"

The confidently Black "Patti Dooke" takes aim at cultural appropriation in rap music. The song's name refers to Anna Marie "Patty" Duke, a teenage actor who became the youngest Academy Award winner at age sixteen in 1963, winning for portraying Helen Keller in *The Miracle Worker*. Yet, like many child and teenage actors, Duke experienced the negative effects of sudden and early success. She suffered from depression, lived with bipolar disorder, and later became a mental health advocate. Duke's story recalls those of other child celebrities who could not escape success unscathed, such as Michael Jackson and Macaulay Culkin.

The name "Patty Duke" is a double entendre as it has roots in hip-hop culture. Dancers in the 1970s popularized a move called the "patty duke." The move grew so popular that disco band Cloud One produced an instrumental track called "Patty Duke," which formed the sonic backdrop for Spoonie Gee's "Spoonin' Rap." So, De La Soul's "Patti Dooke" is a callback and an homage to an earlier time in hip-hop's history when some might have considered the production of the music more "authentic," or at least less encumbered, by the dictates of a record label and music market.

To establish "Patti Dooke" as a comment on cultural appropriation and racism within the music industry, De La Soul samples a scene from the 1991 film *The Five Heartbeats*. In the clip, the Black members of The Temptations–like group express their frustrations about the cost of crossing over—they would have to deny their Blackness by not displaying themselves on the cover of their album in order to appeal to a white audience—a problem as old as the history of modern popular culture in the United States. In using this sample and redefining "Patti Dooke," De La Soul asked, What was the cost of success? This is especially true for a group that inadvertently experienced much crossover success due to their own ingenuity but also due to the massively popular song they grew to hate after a while, "Me Myself and I." For De La Soul, as well as many other hip-hop artists, the notion that certain Black artists should present themselves as nonthreatening or make their music palatable to white audiences was part of the problem with the rap industry. According to this view, the crossover forced artists to abandon their artistic principles, and those artists who willingly pursued the crossover were "less" hip-hop than their peers.

"Patti Dooke" is assertive in its Blackness. From the confident opening "Woohah," to Guru's recitation of the song's hook, to Posdnuos's declaration, if not reminder, of De La Soul's Blackness and commitment to making music "from the soul," it seemed that De La Soul and their collaborators were at the height of their creative powers. Posdnuos and Trugoy use the song to confront emerging trends like gangsta rap and remind listeners that Blackness and masculinity contain multitudes.

Posdnuos's last verse is an excellent illustration of this masculine expression. Continuing to deploy metaphors related to light and the third eye, Posdnuos affirms his connection to Black social consciousness. He then proceeds to distinguish himself and the group presumably from west coast gangsta rappers as he admits to not being from Compton or owning a gun. Posdnuos says he respects gangsta rappers, but not all authentic rappers need to be gangsta. He then proceeds to remind listeners of his connections to 1980s rap and his lyrical prowess as he and Millie from "Millie Pulled a Pistol on Santa" are pursuing "Patti Dooke," or the rappers trying to run through the rap game seeking commercial gain.

Many Americans, including some Black scholars like Cornel West, began to closely identify Black youth masculinity with a gangsta persona due to the popularity of artists like Dr. Dre, Scarface, and Tupac Shakur and movies like *New Jack City*, *Boyz N the Hood*, and *Menace II Society*. Rather, De La Soul proved that hip-hop artists could succeed on their own terms; they did not have to be "gangsta," "hard," or "down" to be confident Black men or to be Black, generally. And, by presenting non-gangsta confidence, if not a hardness grounded in intelligence, De La Soul also refused to cater to misguided beliefs held by whites about Black masculinity. Instead, non-Black listeners had to recognize and adjust to the group's Blackness.

In an album full of artistic statements, "Patti Dooke" represents a primary example of De La Soul's buhloone mindstate as a theory of rap, if not Black, culture. For De La Soul and many Black rap artists, those who practiced the culture had to respect it. Of course, rappers, producers, DJs, and others associated with rap music could get paid. But De La Soul drew a line between those who engaged with the culture with some degree of respect for it and those they believed sought to exploit it. "Patti Dooke," initially, seemed to be aimed at white interlopers like Vanilla Ice. As *The Source*'s Jennifer Perry explained, "'Patty Duke' calls out those who purposefully infiltrate hip-hop for cash, specifically artists who don't know shit about our culture."

Presidential candidate Bill Clinton's efforts to use jazz to appeal to Black folks and attacks on hip-hop and Black youth to appeal to whites might be the most conspicuous example of a Patti Dooke in politics and culture. During the 1992 campaign, Clinton famously tried to adopt a version of "Black cool" while playing the saxophone on *The Arsenio Hall Show*. Ten days later, while giving a speech at Reverend Jesse Jackson's Rainbow Coalition meeting, Clinton aired out hip-hop artist and Public Enemy affiliate Lisa "Sister Souljah" Williamson for her comments to David Mills in the aftermath of the 1992 uprising in Los Angeles. "So if you're a gang member and you would normally be killing somebody, why not kill a white person?" Williamson asked rhetorically. Clinton took her comments literally because few white Americans are willing to entertain a Black person suggesting committing political violence against them. Also, chastising Williamson was politically expedient—it was a way for Clinton to publicly distance himself from Jackson, one of the most prominent Black figures in the Democratic Party. Clinton's comments also demonstrated to white Americans that he was willing to discipline Black people on the political stage. Still, what is often missing from the "Sister Souljah moment" is Williamson's critique of white America—that many white Americans didn't value Black lives. So, within two weeks in June 1992, Bill Clinton pulled a Patti Dooke. He utilized racialized doublespeak. He donned sunglasses.

He played the saxophone on *The Arsenio Hall Show* to appeal to a sense of Black masculine cool, and then he attacked a Black woman hip-hop artist on Reverend Jackson's home turf to show he was willing to stand up to Black political leadership. The Sister Souljah moment could just as well be referred to as the Patti Dooke. And let's not forget Clinton signed the 1994 crime bill, too. (I will come back to that in the next chapter.)

"Ego Trippin' (Part Two)"

In addition to the appropriators, De La Soul also took aim at the outsized egos in rap. "Ego Trippin' (Part Two)" is one of De La Soul's most brilliant songs. Instead of relying on musical samples, Posdnuos and Trugoy adapt others' lyrics to poke fun at braggadocio rap satirically. Listening to them rap, one can detect traces of Melle Mel, Big Daddy Kane, KRS-One, Pete Rock & C.L. Smooth, Digable Planets, Jungle Brothers, and Salt-n-Pepa littered throughout their lyrics. It's like an audio version of cutting out printed words and then rearranging them onto another page. The song is a bit of clever doublespeak. They walk a thin line between parodying braggadocio rap and engaging it without parodying themselves. Again, there's nothing wrong with having an ego.

While poking fun at the rappers, they use other lyricists' words to demonstrate their prowess. Posdnuos and Trugoy are no longer the self-deprecating emcees they were on "Me Myself and I." They possess the supreme confidence of rappers who believe they should be considered among the elite. They could take your rhymes and run lyrical circles around you while laughing in your face.

The song's title, "Ego Trippin' (Part Two)," like "Patti Dooke," is also a double entendre. In the immediate context, De La Soul continues to pay tribute to the Ultramagnetic MC's classic track, "Ego Trippin'." Therefore, the group saw their track as a sequel to their predecessors'. Yet, "Ego Trippin' (Part Two)" also taps into the

Black radical tradition. Two decades before *Buhloone Mindstate*, poet Nikki Giovanni wrote "Ego Tripping (there may be a reason why)" where she also drew from Black cultural traditions of boasting and toasting and articulates a swaggering poem depicting herself as an omnipresent and omnipotent queen who can conceive of pyramids, drink with God, and give birth to royalty. Giovanni was a goddess in her own mind and rhyme. On "Ego Tripping," Giovanni kept up with the best boastful lyricists like Muhammad Ali, who is sometimes credited as a progenitor of modern rap.

Yet, De La Soul's "Ego Trippin' (Part Two)," the song and video, warn of the perils of ego in rap. The video itself is about the buhloone going pop. The group spoofs the conspicuous consumption and wealth that was starting to emerge in the genre and would remain staples as rap grew more in popularity, the artists grew richer, and the genre blew up. They took shots at many rap video tropes—the use of the ground-up shots, the faux stomping on the video camera, and rappers' displays of conspicuous wealth. In the first couple of scenes, Trugoy is driving in a Mercedes Benz convertible, but to make sure we understand, we see a caption that says, "It's a rental." Then we eventually see the group performing in, around, and on top of a mansion. At times, Posdnuos is rapping while sitting at a table near the backyard pool. Another caption informs us that Trugoy and the group don't really live there. Then, of course, there are the images of jewelry-wearing and shirtless rappers who dance with each other, in a very conspicuous depiction of the homosocial behavior of "hard" Black men. Another image that caught people's attention featured a short-haired, slender, yet muscular rapper wearing sunglasses and chains and sitting in bed with a woman.

Rapper Tupac Shakur took issue with De La Soul's parody of contemporary rap videos. It is true that the video for "Ego Trippin' (Part Two)" resembles Shakur's "I Get Around." "I Get Around" stands in between the late 1980s' playful Digital Underground images and the early 1990s gangsta rap party videos featuring Black male rappers using Black women's bodies as props and accessories. In a way, "I Get Around" symbolized rap's early transition to g-funk. The pairing of gangsta rap lyrics with funk samples of groups such as Parliament-Funkadelic captured the essence of this budding subgenre. After "I Get Around," Tupac and his brash masculinity and sex appeal overtook the conscious yet playful style of Digital Underground and other like-minded rap acts on the west coast.

Tupac Shakur was born in 1971, during the Black liberation movement in the United States. His mother, Afeni Shakur, born Alice Faye Williams, served as one of the leaders of the Harlem Black Panther chapter along with her then-husband, Lumumba Shakur. She was arrested with twenty other Black Panthers in New York in 1969 and accused of conspiring to bomb police stations. While freed on bail in 1970, and with her marriage to Lumumba in dire straits, Shakur befriended a Panther from Jersey City, Billy Garland. Soon after consummating their relationship, Shakur was pregnant. She and the rest of the "Panther 21" were acquitted in 1971 after a lengthy trial. As the Harlem chapter disintegrated, Afeni decided that it was time to leave the Black Panthers and New York and move to Baltimore to raise her son.

Tupac Shakur's emergence as a lyrically piercing gangsta rapper seemed somewhat unlikely at the beginning of his career. Shakur got his start in the rap industry rolling with De La Soul's western counterparts, Digital Underground, as a roadie and dancer. Shakur eventually debuted his rap skills on the Digital Underground single "Same Song." Reflecting the resurgence of Afrocentricity in rap, politics, and academia, Shakur made a grand entrance in the video dressed as African royalty. Shakur's first solo album, *2Pacalypse Now*, displays Shakur's social and political consciousness, his lyrics railing against structural racism and state violence on songs like "Soulja's Story" and "Violent." He also developed a talent for speaking to Black women's plight on his lamentation about race, unwanted pregnancy, and failing social services, "Brenda's Got a Baby."

WE MIGHT BLOW UP

By the time De La Soul released *Buhloone Mindstate*, Shakur had evolved into a budding rap and movie star. He played the menacing and homicidal Bishop in the 1992 movie *Juice*. Shakur dropped his second album, *Strictly 4 My N.I.G.G.A.Z. . .* , in 1993, which hued closer to the Death Row and Dr. Dre model of a gangsta rap album. Shakur's second album still featured hard-hitting social critique, like the anti-police brutality track "Holler if Ya Hear Me" and another ode to Black womanhood, "Keep Ya Head Up." Shakur even dedicated the video for the latter to Latasha Harlins, the fifteen-year-old Black girl shot by Korean shop owner Soon Ja Du in Los Angeles in 1991. Yet, *Strictly 4 My N.I.G.G.A.Z. . .* also featured songs and videos depicting rap culture's increasing focus on party life and pursuing women. The song and video for "I Get Around" fit neatly within this formula. The video includes multiple scenes of Tupac and other men partying with women and drinking champagne. Women caress a shirtless Tupac, and the lyricist often raps as if he's engaging in playful banter with women. After "I Get Around," it seemed Tupac and his style of brash masculinity and sex appeal might overtake the conscious, yet playful, style of groups like Digital Underground on the west coast.

De La Soul would not be the only group to piss off notable rappers with video spoofs of commercial and gangsta rap. Three years after De La Soul released *Buhloone Mindstate*, The Roots produced an almost identical video for "What They Do," with the band hosting a party at a mansion; Black Thought sitting at a table in front of a pool; the group poking fun at the stomping, rapping on top of buildings, and other popular imagery. Yet, instead of Tupac getting angry at the group, The Notorious B.I.G. became flummoxed and angered by The Roots' satirical depiction of commercial rap videos. Questlove recounts the Brooklyn rapper's displeasure in his autobiography: " 'I had mad love for those guys. I'm the one who put them on to Brooklyn. My feelings were really hurt, man, because they were one of my favorite groups. I love Thought. He's one of my favorite MCs. Why'd he go and shit on me?'" The Roots, like De La Soul, contended that they never had any particular artist in mind when shooting the video. They just wanted to make a statement about commercial rap's materialism, worship of wealth, and false imagery. And while Questlove claims the group felt confused by Biggie's response, they did not want to backtrack. "We didn't want to act like a bitch and say we didn't mean it," Questlove admitted. "What we were critiquing was obvious, and the satire was clear." In response to Biggie's comments, Questlove said that he and Rich Nichols, the group's manager, planned a response— "a manifesto where we tried to clearly articulate what was happening in hip-hop . . . It was long. It was righteous, maybe self-righteous in parts." Unfortunately for us rap fans and scholars, the planned manifesto never saw the light of day. Biggie was murdered before the group could release the manifesto.

"I Am I Be"

"Fuck being hard, Posdnuos is complicated," or refusing limitation in their masculinity, is *Buhloone Mindstate*'s second thesis. With this lyric, uttered on "In the Woods," Posdnuos drew another line in the sand. One did not have to fit into a stereotypical image of rappers claiming to be gangsta or appealing to a sense of hardness to be an authentic participant in the culture. Instead, it was okay for rappers and Black youth, whom policymakers and Black intellectuals often saw as nihilists, to express a wide range of feelings and to contain nuance. Songs like "I Am I Be," "Breakadawn," and "In the Woods" illustrate the lyricists' willingness to show vulnerability and doubt, address the complications of their masculinity, and experience melancholia, which serves as the flipside to the group's consternation with the rap industry.

"I Am I Be" is *Buhloone Mindstate*'s emotional centerpiece. If one does not know that De La Soul uses an earlier track on the album, the jazz song "I Be Blowin'," which shares the same Lou Rawls sample that appears on "I Am I Be," to prepare us for what is coming, track eleven arrives as kind of a surprise. Shorty No Mas(s)'s voice is the first one we hear when the song comes on: "I am Shorty. I be four-eleven." We hear the voices of several people stating their names and then describing themselves. Then Posdnuos proceeds to perform one of his greatest verses. After naming himself, an important aspect of rap that underscored Black youths' abilities to redefine themselves in the face of structural racism, Posdnuos declares himself a "new" slave, decades before Kanye West would come out with a song by that title.

The vocalists' declarations on "I Am I Be" (not just Posdnuos's and Trugoy's, but those of the chorus of voices appearing at the beginning of the song) echo a hip-hop version of philosopher René Decartes's declaration, *"Cogito, ergo sum,"* or "I think, therefore I am." It also illustrates the importance of naming in hip-hop culture. From graffiti artists, to dancers, to DJs and emcees, giving oneself a new name underscored Black, Brown, and even white youth's ability to redefine themselves in the face of structural racism and economic exploitation and inequality since the 1970s. Posdnuos references the intersection of racism and economic exploitation at the beginning of his verse when he states that he's unable to pay rent on time because his employer did not pay him adequately for his labor as a rapper.

Meanwhile, Posdnuos's verse is like opening his diary and reading a long entry documenting his feelings about laboring in the music industry as a Black artist; coming of age as a father; dealing with fraying relationships, fame, and loss; and trying to make ends meet financially. There is no insider language or jokes from Posdnuos. He's just telling us what's on his mind at the time. Then there's Posdnuos's declaration that some in the Native Tongues had stopped speaking. His admission of strife within the Native Tongues disappointed me, and it caught the attention of plenty of listeners.

Was the group already done? How could this be? Q-Tip is part of the role call in the song! What was up with the Native Tongues? Posdnuos's statement was straightforward, yet rather opaque, leaving us having to put together clues.

Some of the details of the internal strife appear in interviews after the fact. Posdnuos told music critic Miles Marshall Lewis, "At the moment in time, me and Q-Tip actually had an issue with each other—that's what I was gonna talk about." Tension also brewed between A Tribe Called Quest and Jungle Brothers in the early 1990s. DJ Red Alert managed both groups initially. Eventually, A Tribe Called Quest left Red Alert for Russell Simmons's Rush Management. Soon, Chris Lighty started handling Tribe. While this was probably a sound business move for the group, Tribe's decision strained the collective. Q-Tip admitted to *Vibe* in 2007, "Jungle didn't fuck with us. Everybody was hurt." Combine this development with the fact that the Jungle Brothers' excellent second album, *Done By the Forces of Nature*, sold poorly, and they struggled with their label, Warner Bros., to release their third album, and the group's growing resentment comes into better focus. Not to mention, the Jungle Brothers basically organized the Native Tongues collective, and now De La Soul and A Tribe Called Quest, as well as Queen Latifah, had all gone on to experience more success. (Jungle Brothers' unreleased album, *Crazy Wisdom Masters*, was set to be more experimental than any of the Native Tongues records.) Few things can spark discord among creative people like fame.

Maybe I'm reading too much into some of this. But this is what we rap fans did in the 1990s when we only had CDs, tapes, monthly subscription hip-hop magazines, and the occasional report on MTV and BET. We parsed interviews and songs for clues and asked each other questions, hoping to learn more about our favorite groups.

Also—and this is a more obvious point, but one that is related to the theme of *Buhloone Mindstate*—all talented artists in collectives must navigate egos, especially when they are competing in a marketplace. There is typically friction within groups, whether artistic in nature, personal, political, or all of the above. One can always find the source of conflict among two or more individuals within any rap group, whether it involves Q-Tip's and Phife Dawg's creative and personal differences in A Tribe Called Quest, Ice Cube's conflicts with the rest of N.W.A stemming from the former's refusal to sign an unfavorable contract, or, famously, Busta Rhymes and Charlie Brown of Leaders of the New School arguing during an episode of *Yo! MTV Raps*. And rap is competitive, so naturally there was artistic competition. Singer Vinia Mojica, who appeared on De La Soul's "A Roller Skating Jam Named 'Saturdays'" and A Tribe Called Quest's "Verses from the Abstract," explained in 2012, "The boys had a lot of love-hate rivalries. . . . They always wanted to one up each other." When one thinks of a confederation of various rap acts, many of whom are famous on their own, hearing one member announcing to the world that someone within the group is going back on their word, or not being faithful to the group, can negatively affect internal dynamics, especially when someone from a group expresses their feelings publicly, and especially on a song.

Posdnuos later expressed regret for divulging too much about the relations among the Native Tongues on "I Am I Be." He told Lewis, "I lean more towards talking about what's going on in my life. Even unfortunately, in this record. I treated it like a journal." After mentioning his problem with Q-Tip, Posdnuos continued, "But now, honestly, I wish I wouldn't have did that. That was something we got over. It was hard for us to get over because the world was going to listen to it for the rest of their lives." Q-Tip confirms feeling hurt by Posdnuos's words on the song:

> Pos hurt me when he did that. It's like airing it out to a whole bunch of people. And now everybody's gonna get this perception that we've been reinstated when to me, we never

left. For him to make that statement was really bugged out, and maybe a little anal. More than anything, what we really are, is family. We just happened to be doing the music thing. But when the music stops, I'm still gonna be going over to Pos' crib, I'm still gonna call up Mase. We still gonna see each other. . . .

Although Posdnuos declared the "Native shit" dead on "In the Woods," the principal artists continued to collaborate. Trugoy performed the chorus for A Tribe Called Quest's "Award Tour." De La Soul and Q-Tip also appeared on a Jungle Brothers song, "How Ya Want It We Got It (Native Tongues Remix)," featured on their 1997 album, *Raw Deluxe*. I missed "How Ya Want It" at the time, but when you listen to it, you notice what you tend to hear from old friends who reunite—a song where all the lyricists picked up where they last left off. Unfortunately, though, the strained relations between Jungle Brothers and A Tribe Called Quest remained. Sammy B told *The Source* in 1997, "The only ones I feel from the Native Tongues is De La. I ain't feeling nobody else except De La." Baby Bam then credited De La Soul with getting them all back together: "Shout out to De La for initiating the reunion."

On "I Am I Be," Posdnuos also took aim at rap clichés and narrowing conceptions of masculinity and identity in the genre. He articulates some aspects of respectability politics. He brags about staying away from selling drugs, which was consistent with his stance on drug use. And he informs listeners of the type of working-class ethic that he applies to rap. He boasts that he would rather be the best "rug cleaner" than drug dealer. Here it is hard not to think of Dr. Martin Luther King, Jr., telling audiences that "all labor has dignity" as he supported Black sanitation workers striking in Memphis in the late 1960s. Posdnuos, Maseo, and Trugoy took this kind of pride in their work as hip-hop artists.

In addition to maintaining his antipathy toward the drug trade,

Posdnuos addresses the shifting context of hip-hop. The notion that a career in rap served as an alternative to participating in the drug trade had been a common refrain for some. On one hand, for some rappers that was probably true, at least in the cases of lyricists like The Notorious B.I.G., Jay-Z, Raekwon, and Ghostface Killah, who all expressed some version of this idea. Yet, on the other, the concept of "realness" is equated with living the street life. Instead, Posdnuos explains that he always lived according to a different set of expectations, which was evidenced by the fact that he, Maseo, and Trugoy were on their way to pursuing more legitimate paths before they blew up.

The group's anticipated career journeys also illustrate the complexity of other rappers making such declarations. Rappers like The Notorious B.I.G., Raekwon, Ghostface Killah, and Method Man also arose from working-class environments, but in New York City, where the drug game dominated and the economy might have presented few illicit options. Ultimately, however, Posdnuos's critique of this line of thought reminded his listeners, namely Black and Brown working-class youth, that one should remain open-minded regarding their ideas of what personal success looks like.

"I Am I Be" was the song I can recall that helped me understand rap music's power to convey confession, romanticism, and self-declaration. Of course, many other rappers like Queen Latifah, Ghostface Killah, Chuck D, Drake, and Eminem, have expressed more serious emotions in their lyrics. Tupac Shakur is often cited as one of the most affecting rappers. He demonstrated a capacity to express sorrow and empathy for Black women like the fictional Brenda, as well as love for his mother, Afeni. Also, Shakur is often known for his verses full of derision and anger—at racism, at women, and at his foes.

But while Tupac harnessed his anger, we, or I, needed more from rap than anger. We got plenty of it over time. And it's not like I never got angry. Of course I did. But I understood, or at least vaguely knew, that I felt more than anger. The problem with me, like with a lot of young men, is that I did not possess the emotional intelligence and the vocabulary to express melancholy or sadness. Consequently, I retreated into myself. (I'm not claiming that I was more emotionally intelligent as a teenager. That came much, much later.)

In "I Am I Be," Posdnuos provided me a blueprint for expressing the more nuanced feelings floating in my brain. At times, I felt a sense of malaise and melancholy, and listening to that song allowed me to focus on those emotions. Posdnuos and Trugoy demonstrated that one could be contemplative about their life without obsessing over their potential demise, like Biggie; and that thinking about where one stood in relation to their friends, family, partners, and society was natural and more relatable than trying to emulate someone like Tupac, who believed death haunted and stalked him. So when I finally got to "I Am I Be," I kept hitting the Back button on my CD player after listening to it. I was enraptured by the song. Also, the longer I played it, the more I wanted to sit in my feelings. The song, like any good track, can be hypnotic.

"I Am I Be" is one of the most mature rap songs ever recorded, and it anticipated what's become known as "grown rap" in the last decade and a half. The song also foresees De La Soul's future as they reexamine these issues in their music for the rest of their careers.

Can't Help It 'til the "Breakadawn"

Hearing the Michael Jackson "I Can't Help It" sample on "Breakadawn" for the first time unleashed all kinds of serotonin and dopamine in my brain. All I felt was a hazy euphoria after listening. Of course, the song took me back to my childhood, when Mom swayed and sang to Jackson's *Off the Wall* album.

Naturally, Tommy Boy demanded a "radio record" for *Buhloone Mindstate*. De La Soul, as we know from the singles off their first two albums, hates the request for a *palatable* single; they resent having to record the songs, perform them, and even shoot videos for them. This is when their music production changed from creating art for art's sake into working a job for a corporation. "For me, 'Breakadawn' almost felt like, 'Okay, do that. That's your job right there. You go do that,'" Trugoy would tell *GQ*. Yet, as Posdnuos later told radio host Ebro in a 2018 interview, he'd been listening to "I Can't Help It" on the turntable while watching the Motown 25 anniversary concert. Posdnuos had something after combining "I Can't Help It" with Smokey Robinson's "Quiet Storm."

For a group that typically resists making commercial singles, De La Soul is among the best rap outfits at producing earworms. Just about every album features one—"Me Myself and I," "Ring Ring Ring (Ha Ha Hey)," "Breakadawn," and later, "Oooh" and "Baby Phat." And that's not to mention the harder anthemic singles like "Stakes Is High" and "Much More." De La Soul is probably so good at constructing radio singles because of the creative tension their label produced when they reminded the group that albums (at that time) needed radio singles. The group refused to cave to industry pressures. One of the reasons why "Me Myself and I" and "Ring Ring Ring" worked was not just the catchy beats, but because the group spit clever verses filled with a degree of self-deprecation and disdain for the idea of the commercial rap single itself. Even if De La Soul adhered to a pop music formula, as Sean "Puff Daddy" Combs pushed his artists to do in the mid-1990s, they tried to undermine that formula with their deadpan and/or sarcastic tone of rapping.

"Breakadawn" took two recognizable R&B samples from the disco era and produced a dreamy and surreal song that seemed to capture the group's melancholy that was also exhibited on "I Am I Be." The beat seems to float in the air. The setting of the music video is more of a hazy sunshine. "Breakadawn" continues with key themes and aesthetics contained in the album—the use of insider language, hip-hop and pop culture references, and an implicit critique of the rap industry. The verses are filled with references to *Star Trek*, R.E.M., Sugarhill Gang, Genesis, and Phil Collins, as well as to the Native Tongues. And, as if we needed any one of them to confirm this, it is not a coincidence that the song served as the first single for *Buhloone Mindstate* because it departs from the jazz-infused sound contained in much of the record.

"Breakadawn" also felt like a coming-of-age song for the group as they rapped about their journey, social mobility, their artistic legitimacy, and the ability to beat up anyone who tested them. Posdnuos kicks off the song acknowledging his place of origin (the Bronx), which is credited as hip-hop's birthplace. Trugoy reflects on growing up with his parents in Amityville. Trugoy also raps about the struggle, again bringing up working-class themes: "Freak the WIC call and get a tap on my shoulder 'cause the days of the breaks be just about over." Much of "Breakadawn" is about authenticity, or at least De La Soul uses the single to display their realness through the struggle of navigating a fickle music industry. Posdnuos again uses inside language to remind listeners and others in the rap game that the group was not to be played with. They could still hold their own lyrically and physically.

Most importantly, Posdnuos and Trugoy use the single to stake their claim among rap's royalty. They were approaching a decade in the industry and had made deep marks on the culture. Building on the performance of songs like "Patti Dooke," Posdnuos and Trugoy remind everyone that De La Soul is better at making songs appealing to the mainstream than many mainstream artists. They could take catchy samples like "Knee Deep" and "I Can't Help It" and make them into clever rap songs without compromising their values years before Puff Daddy got famous for sampling pop hits for profit.

While the video for "Breakadawn" is not as colorful as those for "Me Myself and I" or "Eye Know," it is certainly surreal. The director and the group are playing with camera images; members of the group disappear offscreen and reappear. One could argue that the artists' reflections in certain scenes resemble their reflections on the album cover. The video, generally, is also subdued as it seemingly captures the group's wistful nature. Yet, the video is also somber, resembling the black-and-white visuals of "Say No Go" and "Ring Ring Ring (Ha Ha Hey)."

When I think of surreal rap videos, I usually go to Ice Cube's "It Was a Good Day." "Breakadawn" sounds and looks just as dreamy. Ice Cube's video and song depicted just that—a dream. For one day, everything went right; no one lost their lives to violence, the police did not pull him over, he played basketball and got a triple-double. Ice Cube presented something removed from the prophecies of the 1992 uprising and the xenophobic "Black Korea" on his *Death Certificate* album. On "It Was a Good Day," Cube adopted the laid-back flow that west coast rappers had started to utilize (a delivery that Rakim, Big Daddy Kane, Erick Sermon, and De La Soul had beaten him in using). Ice Cube's song enjoys legendary and now meme status, as people use clues in the video to try to mark the date the rapper is seemingly referring to.

For De La Soul, "Breakadawn," like "Ego Trippin' (Part Two)" and their future music videos, continued a tradition of producing imaginative visuals. They were the colorful class clowns on "Me Myself and I" and flower-toting, smitten rappers on "Eye Know." "Buddy (Native Tongue Decision)" and "A Roller Skating Jam Named 'Saturdays'" evoke fun and sunny vibes. One cannot help but feel the rush of endorphins as one watches Trugoy spray people with a hose while repeating, "Mr. Sprinkler. Mr. Sprinkler." *Buhloone Mindstate*'s "Ego Trippin' (Part Two)" and "Breakadawn" reflected the group's attempts to call attention to the excesses of rap in the early 1990s. While De La Soul emphasized realism on their albums to follow—with the exception of the *Wizard of Oz*–inspired fantasy of "Oooh"—it is hard not to see rappers who took creativity in their music videos to another level, like Busta Rhymes and Missy Elliott, as descendants of De La Soul.

Like "Me Myself and I," "Breakadawn" sometimes stirred negative feelings among members of the group after its release. Trugoy expressed his displeasure with the song and video. He said to *GQ*,

"I just don't feel it. I just get nothing from it. I think my sentiment somewhere in the back of my mind was 'I am tired of these popcorn radio records that the label is looking for us to do when we have so much more that we can create and that we're about.'" Trugoy recalls, "I remember shooting the video was the worst day of my life. It felt like, 'Gosh, I don't want to do this. I don't like this. I don't feel good about myself. I don't feel good about this music.'" Trugoy's feelings, though, seemed to be less about the song's sound and more about recording singles to satisfy the record company rather than to express their own creativity. He then goes on to remark, "It almost felt like a slave record." This comes back to the group's sampling of *The Five Heartbeats* on "Patti Dooke." "Breakadawn" represented an example of how record labels sought to dictate Black art.

At times, I, too, feel conflicted about "Breakadawn." It was clearly De La Soul's radio single, and we hardcore fans are supposed to like the B-sides and deep cuts. Of course, I want to respect Trugoy's feelings. Nonetheless, it is difficult to deny "Breakadawn." What is inside our minds and bodies shapes how we respond to music. Certain tracks unleash a flood of recollections, endorphins, and/or melancholy. That's what "Breakadawn" did for me. The sample of Michael Jackson's "I Can't Help It" evoked nostalgia in my teenage years. Watching my parents enjoy Michael Jackson's *Off the Wall* is one of my first memories tied to music. I can envision my mom swaying back and forth and happily singing along to "I Can't Help It" with her eyes closed. The song was the ray of light that cut through the group's cloudy rap forecast on the album. "Breakadawn" did what all great songs do for their fans: unlocked dormant memories.

"Bohemian Indulgence"

Like *De La Soul Is Dead*, *Buhloone Mindstate* earned critical acclaim. Brett Johnson awarded De La Soul's third album 4.5 mics in *The Source*'s October 1993 issue, a half mic away from the magazine's perfect score. Critics participating in that year's Pazz and Jop poll ranked it number eight, behind artists like Liz Phair, Nirvana, Pet Shop Boys, and Dr. Dre. Writing in the *New York Times*, music critic Greg Tate called *Buhloone Mindstate* "De La Soul's most consistently danceable album . . . also its most nostalgic and despondent." Tate then punctuated his review with a question about why the album failed to generate the popular reaction of their first album:

> Stauncher fans may wonder if *Buhloone Mind State* doesn't mark a retreat from the dizzying expressionism of the group's earlier work. Do the trio think that the world of hip-hop is too dumb to comprehend their Ebony Tower dispatches? If hip-hop ever needed these high priests of bohemian indulgence, the time is now, when gangster clichés have become the order of the day.

Tate's insights were prescient as De La Soul, and the rest of rap, moved into the mid-1990s, and new rappers, rap groups, and egos began to make their marks on the industry.

While *Buhloone Mindstate* garnered positive reviews, they got lost in context. The record was like the New York Knicks of the rap game in 1993—while not necessarily flashy, the album reflected confidence and skill good enough to contend for the championship. *Buhloone Mindstate* had to contend with two other championship performances, just as the Knicks had to face the Chicago Bulls and would've had to play a sixty-two-win Phoenix Suns team if they had somehow done the impossible and defeated Michael Jordan. A Tribe Called Quest and the Wu-Tang Clan both dropped albums a little more than two months after *Buhloone Mindstate*, on November 9, 1993. And we can't forget the upstart Snoop Dogg, who dropped his debut album, *Doggystyle*, two weeks after Tribe and Wu-Tang Clan! *Doggystyle* further solidified Death Row's and gangsta rap's place in the mainstream. West coast gangsta rap was in prime position to take over.

LIVING IN A D.A.I.S.Y. AGE

Art from the Soul

Even though the egos in commercial rap won out in the 1990s, *Buhloone Mindstate* and the other jazz-infused rap albums like *The Low End Theory* and the *Jazzmatazz* series established this subgenre as a viable lane for hip-hop artists. Jazz-rap fusion flourished well into the twenty-first century, expanding our understanding of the musical parameters of hip-hop culture. Did one always need to rap to be hip-hop? Of course, artists such as Missy Elliott pushed boundaries and deepened our understanding of hip-hop culture by mixing rapping, singing, and using her voice as an instrument. But, what if one sang jazz? What if someone released an instrumental album? Did a rapper always have to rap over jazz-sampled or jazz-infused beats for the music to be considered hip-hop? I am sure that in the 1990s I would have scoffed at calling a jazz record hip-hop. Now, I would not at all. While there are always purists and gatekeepers in any culture, and I can say I was a purist, we tend to forget how much rappers have pushed the boundaries of rap music. De La Soul is a primary example of this.

After *Buhloone Mindstate*, Native Tongues member Queen Latifah expanded what we think is possible for rappers and jazz artists. She dropped two albums covering jazz songs in the 2000s. Rap producer Madlib produced two great jazz albums, starting with Yesterdays New Quintet's *Angles Without Edges*, on which he played multiple instruments under multiple pseudonyms. Then, on 2003's *Shades of Blue*, Madlib "invaded" the Blue Note catalog to produce a great jazz-hip-hop–fused record. Recently, A Tribe Called Quest's Ali Shaheed Muhammad joined forces with instrumentalist Adrian Younge to release a series of records, Jazz Is Dead, along with jazz greats like Roy Ayers and Jean Carne. Coming from the direction of jazz music, composer and pianist Robert Glasper has stretched our understanding of what it means to be a jazz composer. Operating in the tradition of Quincy Jones, Glasper has worked with scores of rappers including Yasiin Bey (Mos Def), Q-Tip, Denzel Curry, Common, and Killer

Mike. Glasper also pays homage to the late Detroit-based producer J Dilla. In fact, Glasper was the reason why I saw De La Soul in concert for the second time in 2024. In fact, the group served as his special guest during Glasper's tribute to Duke Ellington and J Dilla, the former a jazz luminary and the latter a hip-hop legend.

Jazz played a key role in the production of Kendrick Lamar's *To Pimp a Butterfly*, one of the most politically and artistically significant rap albums of the twenty-first century. Similar to a De La Soul project, *To Pimp a Butterfly* can get musically and lyrically dense. Like A Tribe Called Quest and De La Soul, Lamar worked with several west coast musicians and producers who crafted a partly jazzy soundscape (Lamar also pulled from other genres as well, such as funk) like producer Flying Lotus, multi-instrumentalist Terrace Martin, and saxophonist Kamasi Washington.

Of course, André 3000's recent Grammy Album of the Year–nominated instrumental work, *New Blue Sun*, generated discussion about what constitutes hip-hop, partly due to his personal yet somewhat dour views related to rapping and age. He really stoked the debate when he answered questions about his decision to record an album featuring his flute playing by saying he could not imagine what he would rap about at his age. He told *GQ*, "It actually feels . . . inauthentic for me to rap because I don't have anything to talk about in that way. I'm 48 years old." Surely, André 3000 was not trying to comment broadly about middle-aged lyricists continuing to rap, yet again, rappers are competitive, and one cannot blame them for being jealous guardians of their craft. But he decided to record *New Blue Sun* for the same reasons why rappers like De La Soul decided to go left on an album like *Buhloone Mindstate*. Hip-hop, and rap music, as Trugoy, Posdnuos, and Maseo have shown in the thirty years since *Buhloone Mindstate*'s release, are about creating art from the soul, whether one is rhyming over jazz-inspired beats or decides to forgo rapping and blow their flute on a record. Ironically, André 3000 still rhymed on *New Blue Sun*. You just had to settle for reading poetic song titles like "Ghandi, Dalai Lama, Your Lord & Savior J.C./Bundy, Jeffrey Dahmer, and John Wayne Gacy" and "Ants to You, Gods to Who?"

I Be Blowing

One time during what I call my pretentious phase of hip-hop fandom, I ran into one of my older brothers, Jeff, while walking down the stairs at school. He worked as a teacher and as an assistant coach for the basketball team. I was a senior in high school, and by then, some of my friends and I had developed reputations for staying on top of the rap releases and becoming budding rap music critics. Jeff caught me walking down the stairs and started talking to me about music. "As you grow up, you learn to appreciate other genres," he told me. "I've even grown to love listening to jazz." Of course, as a seventeen- or eighteen-year-old rap superfan, I did not want to hear about growing up and evolving into a more diverse listener, not at that time. I was one of those fans who believed that I would always devote myself to hip-hop, from my teenage years to my last days. Hip-hop culture was the first thing I became a true believer of. There was no way age would shake that from me.

But Jeff was right. Over time—in the 1990s and afterward—my tastes evolved. I have never claimed to be a jazz aficionado, but Mom and De La Soul planted the seeds for my enjoyment of that and other genres. Here, I come back to Maceo Parker's interlude, "I Be Blowin'," as a formative song in my jazz fandom. At that time, it was unheard of for a hip-hop group to release a nearly five-minute instrumental song featuring a jazz artist on it, but De La Soul had done it. The fact that I enjoyed listening to Maceo Parker blow his horn on "I Be Blowin'" surprised me at seventeen years old, mostly because I had grown up listening primarily to music with vocals, with some exceptions like Quincy Jones's rendition of "Birdland." But the sound of Parker's horn soothed me. It was the first time I allowed an instrument to guide me through a song. "I Be Blowin'" is the only song on *Buhloone Mindstate* that allows listeners to chill and look outside, so to speak. And as we listen to the song, we also hear a sample of street noise. It's as though Posdnuos, Maseo, and Trugoy decided to take a break from all the angst of *Buhloone Mindstate* and to go outside and watch the kids play on the playground for a while. I learned that jazz and other instrumental music could transport me into another world without the use of vocals or visuals.

CHAPTER 4

Stakes Is High

"This was going to be our Marvin Gaye *What's Going On*."
—Posdnuos

In *We Real Cool: Black Men and Masculinity*, Black feminist intellectual bell hooks criticized the "death-dealing coolness" of many Black men of the hip-hop generation. According to hooks, Black men seemed bent on chasing death or engaging in risky behaviors to maintain their "coolness." Following the critiques of Black elders such as C. Delores Tucker and Reverend Calvin Butts, hooks noted the failure of Black male rappers to produce life-giving art that allowed them to express and listeners to witness the full range of their emotions and to articulate a political critique. She especially took issue with the "keeping it real" ethos present in "patriarchal hip-hop" that, "though entertaining, had, for the most part, no transformative power, no ability to intervene on politics of domination, and turn the real lives of black men around." "If every young black male in America simply studied the history, the life, and work of black musicians," hooks wrote, "they would have blueprints for healing and survival."

hooks, as well as other Black critics of rap music in the 1990s like singer Dionne Warwick and intellectual Cornel West, were not wrong about the genre's and culture's gangsta aesthetic, misogyny, and what scholar Aime J. Ellis called "death-defying" masculinity. One only had to look at the top of *Billboard*'s rap charts in the mid-1990s to see gangsta rap's popularity. By that time, more east coast rappers like

The Notorious B.I.G., Nas, Jay-Z, and Mobb Deep had also risen in status by crafting their own poetic narratives of what the latter called "trife life" and the pursuit of wealth.

However, hooks's criticisms, as well as those of Reverend Butts, Tucker, and Warwick, ran aground when they failed to consider rap's internal conversations and debates about the genre's direction in the 1990s. As De La Soul faded from the center of rap music in the mid-1990s, they led a defiant campaign against the gangsterism, materialism, and death-courting lyricism criticized by activists and intellectuals. While Maseo, Trugoy, and Posdnuos did not present a dissertation on all of Black America's ills in the mid-1990s, they used their art to warn their peers about the limitations of the blind pursuit of wealth and, as hooks called it, a "death-dealing coolness." They also paired their warnings with a critique of the rap industry and US society, especially its racial and economic inequality. And De La Soul was right. In the years after they released *Stakes Is High*, hip-hop culture endured several violent deaths. The murders of rappers Tupac Shakur and Christopher "The Notorious B.I.G." Wallace especially shocked the culture and surely altered its course.

De La Soul articulated their vision of "realness" as a commitment to rap as an art form, sharp lyricism, and the ability to bring the conversation about authenticity down to a grassroots level with folks Maseo and Posdnuos called "everyday people." While Posdnuos, Maseo, and Trugoy never dismissed the realities of those operating in underground economies, they used *Stakes Is High* to highlight that most people did not aspire to live as gangstas or lead lives of material extravagance. With *Stakes Is High*, De La Soul found themselves at the vanguard of hip-hop artists holding the torch for rap's grassroots along with like-minded artists and allies like A Tribe Called Quest, Common, The Roots, and Mos Def. The group's message acted as a lighthouse, helping to direct the next generation of emcees who cared less about getting money and more about maintaining a creative standard.

Like their peers, De La Soul never claimed to be free of contradictions. Maseo, Posdnuos, and Trugoy admitted their shortcomings in interviews and songs. Posdnuos, especially, admitted to engaging in womanizing behavior. De La Soul did not celebrate their messiness, but they did not hide it. The contradictions revealed by letting fans see their flaws would not be enough to eradicate misogyny in rap. But rapping with some honesty could represent the first step toward crafting, as hooks put it, "blueprints for healing and survival."

The King of New York

Rap's landscape in the years between *Buhloone Mindstate* and *Stakes Is High* shifted dramatically. Rap music remained diverse, with albums dropping from artists, groups, and collectives reflecting various styles. Nevertheless, rappers and labels focused on achieving mainstream success and taking control of rap music's marketplace moved to the forefront of hip-hop in the middle of the decade. G-funk, embodied by Suge Knight's Death Row Records; tracks by Dr. Dre, Warren G, and DJ Quik; and Tupac Shakur's intense lyricism occupied the west coast's center of gravity.

On the east coast, Sean "Puff Daddy" Combs's Bad Boy Records and its flagship artist, Christopher "The Notorious B.I.G." Wallace, dropped *Ready to Die* the same day that President Bill Clinton signed the 1994 Crime Bill. Biggie's rags-to-riches story, "Juicy," anchored the album. While rappers like Schoolly D, KRS-One, and Kool G Rap pioneered east coast gangsta rap, Biggie popularized a new version focused on a mafioso-inspired image and storytelling. Puff Daddy played the fly sidekick who often danced alongside the rapper and offered ad libs. Combs narrow-mindedly created a larger-than-life image for his upstart artist and the label. Additionally, the budding superstar executive, like Death Row's Suge Knight, allegedly backed this pursuit with threats and acts of physical and sexual violence against employees.

As Bad Boy Records ascended to the top of east coast rap, Biggie and the NYC-centric rap media began referring to the rapper as the "King of New York," named after a 1990 theatrical mob tale. Soon, other east coast rappers like Nas, AZ, Wu-Tang Clan's Raekwon and Ghostface Killah, Mobb Deep, and Jay-Z released similarly mob-inspired songs and albums. The gangsta aesthetic permeating rap music in the mid-1990s emphasized luxury, tales of mob-style violence, womanizing, and, for some like Mobb Deep and Biggie, a fixation with existential dread and early death on songs like "Hell on Earth" and "Suicidal Thoughts."

De La Soul was backed against the wall before recording their fourth album. While on tour with A Tribe Called Quest, their manager, Lyor Cohen, told the group they needed to buckle up because *Buhloone Mindstate* had not fared as well as their first two albums, and Tommy Boy was wavering on the group's viability for the first time. In an interview with *The Source*, Maseo said *Stakes Is High* was "make or break."

Staring at the potential end of their rap careers, Posdnuos said, "This was the first album where we knew that the title was called *Stakes Is High*. This was going to be our Marvin Gaye *What's Going On*." De La Soul had set a high bar for themselves at the group's lowest commercial point. *What's Going On* is arguably one of the most extraordinary pieces of recorded music in modern history. Maseo, Posdnuos, and Trugoy tasked themselves with responding to the moment—they would address hip-hop culture's limitations and comment on American society.

A Crisis in Black Leadership

Stakes Is High responded to the pivotal and intricate mid-1990s, a crucial juncture for Black Americans. In the words of historian Manning

Marable, it was a "transitional period in which the nation shifted from its liberal reforms on matters of race in the 1960s and 1970s to an increasingly uncertain and unequal racial future." Joblessness, poverty, mass incarceration, and conservative social policy lay at the center of this transition. Although the crime rate reached its height in 1991 and was declining, President Bill Clinton signed the Violent Crime Control and Law Enforcement Act in 1994.

The result of bipartisan calls to address violent crime, the thirty-billion-dollar crime bill included funding for new prisons, it expanded death penalty offenses, and it instituted a "three strike" rule mandating life sentences for a third conviction for violent felonies. The bill also fulfilled Clinton's promise to put a hundred thousand more police onto the streets. The legistlation also bolstered local efforts to crack down on crime, like in New York City, where Mayor Rudolph Giuliani implemented policies based on the "broken windows" theory of policing in his attempts to clamp down on "quality of life" offenses. Nonetheless, as critics claimed, the move facilitated increased police harassment of many New Yorkers, including food delivery workers, street food vendors, and pedestrians. This crackdown also relied upon "stop and frisk" tactics, which disproportionately targeted youth of color. While the 1994 Crime Bill did not *create* mass incarceration, the bill and local policing strategies like those in New York City contributed to the growth of the jail and prison populations over the next several years.

Black politics remained on a conservative path. Legal scholar Michelle Alexander in *The New Jim Crow* writes, "In the early 1990s, resistance to the emergence of racialized social control collapsed across the spectrum." Black intellectuals and scholars like Cornel West decried the "crisis in Black leadership." Reverend Jesse Jackson's insurgent presidential campaigns of 1984 and 1988 were in the past. After being outmaneuvered by Bill Clinton, Jackson made a peace pact with the Democratic Leadership Conference wing of the Democratic Party. More African Americans were elected to Congress in this decade; however, the growing number of Black elected officials failed to deliver economic and social policies to combat structural racism and to lift more people out of poverty. Black mayors pushed Congressional Black Caucus (CBC) members to support the Crime Bill.

Two events in the mid-1990s marked this "crisis" in Black politics. First, the O.J. Simpson double-murder trial captivated Americans. The "trial of the century" initiated a new era of courtroom television, with virtually twenty-four-hour trial coverage on news outlets. The constant coverage accelerated the development of "reality" television, as the court case created new "characters" for watchers to follow like Kato Kaelin, prosecutor Marcia Clark, and Judge Lance Ito. Yet, the O.J. trial, following the Rodney King beating four years earlier, was merely a racialized spectacle. Although many Americans reacted to the not guilty verdict with shock and horror, many Black Americans viewed the trial as a referendum on a racist legal system, even if some thought Simpson murdered Nicole Brown and Ronald Goldman. While the verdicts illustrated historical racial divides, the outcome of the Simpson case did not translate into any more political power for Black Americans nor the ability to transform the criminal legal system.

The Million Man March represented another event that illustrated this crisis of Black leadership. Nation of Islam (NOI) leader Minister Louis Farrakhan arose to fill the vacuum left after Jesse Jackson retreated from presidential politics and the Rainbow Coalition faded as a force in US progressive politics. Farrakhan's resurgence in the 1990s seemed rather unlikely considering his history of antisemitic statements. While his antisemitism made him a pariah in mainstream American political discourse, the NOI leader invested in building relationships with rappers like Ice Cube. As Farrakhan accumulated enough social and political capital, he called for a Washington, DC, mobilization of Black men. Henry Louis Gates quoted former Black Panther Eldridge Cleaver (of all people considering his right turn in the early 1980s) as saying, "'Farrakhan saw that vacuum, saw nothing motivating the people, no vision being projected to the people, and he came up with the defining event for a generation of people, this Million Man March.'"

Farrakhan's call for Black men to attend the mass mobilization sparked controversy because it reinforced patriarchal ideas that Black men were the only ones who could uplift the race. Still, the march garnered attention and excitement among Black men, enough to make some wonder if Farrakhan was the next "Head Negro in Charge." The 1995 march was very different from the protests demanding jobs and freedom organized by Dr. Martin Luther King, Jr., John Lewis, and others in 1963. Instead, hundreds of thousands flocked to listen to Farrakhan's call for more personal responsibility and "spiritual atonement."

Cleaver told Gates that Black Americans in the 1990s "had the worst leadership in the black community since slavery." At the time, I possessed a superficial understanding of racism, party politics, and Black history. But I felt little appeal in or connection to the March, the Democratic Party, or the Black Christian church. I looked to my parents and to hip-hop for guidance. Moreover, I gleaned bits of life lessons from listening to Wu-Tang Clan's *Wu-Tang Forever*, A Tribe Called Quest's *Beats, Rhymes and Life*, and De La Soul's *Stakes Is High*.

The mid-1990s were a violent time, and rappers like Biggie and De La Soul also acknowledged the surge in political violence and terrorism. Biggie immortalized the 1993 World Trade Center bombing on his 1994 coming-of-age track, "Juicy," in a way that wrapped the attack within the struggle for wealth: "Time to get paid, blow up like the World Trade." Two days after the bombing, the FBI began its standoff with cult leader David Koresh, which eventually ended in the deaths of seventy-six Branch Davidians. Then, two years later, anti-government extremist and white supremacist Timothy McVeigh parked a Ryder truck containing ammonium nitrate fertilizer, nitromethane, and diesel fuel in front of the Alfred P. Murrah Federal Building in Oklahoma City. The truck bomb exploded a little after 9:00 a.m., killing 168 people and injuring hundreds more. Angered by the FBI's standoff with Randy Weaver at Ruby Ridge and its handling of Waco's Branch Davidians, McVeigh and his co-conspirators hoped to spark a right-wing revolution.

In eighteen months between 1995 and 1996, more than thirty church arsons and burnings took place across the south. White supremacists have historically targeted Black churches because they have served as meeting places for community building and political mobilization going back to the nineteenth century. (This is what motivated neo-Nazi and white supremacist Dylann Roof to murder nine people at the Mother Emanuel African Methodist Episcopal Church in June 2015.) While federal investigators did not find links to racism in the burnings, the property destruction was reminiscent of the history of racist intimidation and violence many Black Americans lived with during the Jim Crow era. In response, President Bill Clinton signed the Church Arson Prevention Act on July 3, 1996, one day after De La Soul released *Stakes Is High*. Writing for *The Source*, Steve Walker explained, "For many African-Americans, the congressional inquiry and responses to it hint at the last vestige of racial oppression.... Unlike the fire bombings and church fires of the 1960s, [these] acts of violence are not just aimed at activist churches; actually, they seem to have no rhyme or reason."

Time to Take Sides

Meanwhile, the rap industry smoldered with conflict. While the mid-1990s "rap wars" are often reduced to the dispute between Death Row Records' Tupac Shakur and Bad Boy Records' The Notorious B.I.G., rivalries seemed to be brewing everywhere. On a skit on Raekwon's debut album, *Only Built 4 Cuban Linx*, Wu-Tang Clan's Raekwon and Ghostface Killah called out Biggie for copying Nas's *Illmatic* cover on *Ready to Die*. Chicago MC Common Sense, later known as Common, released his biggest song, "I Used to Love H.E.R.," the year before *Only Built 4 Cuban Linx* hit stores, where he lamented rap's pivot away from a genre focused on a commitment to authentic artistic expression. While presenting hip-hop as female still feels like unnecessary objectification, the song appealed to many of us looking for alternatives to gangsta rap. The song earned Ice Cube's ire, and he dissed the Chicago rapper on Mack 10's song, "Westside Slaughterhouse," and later, "Hoo Bangin' (WSCG Style)," appearing on the Ice Cube, Mack 10, and WC Westside Connection collaboration, *Bow Down*, later in 1996. Common responded with the knockout track aimed at Ice Cube, "The Bitch in Yoo," proving that the former N.W.A slayer was indeed beatable in rhyme.

Then, armed men shot Tupac Shakur in a botched robbery at Quad Studios in Manhattan in 1994. Shakur was jailed for sexual assault soon after. *Vibe* magazine began reporting a burgeoning rivalry between LA's Death Row Records and New York's Bad Boy Records. Some believed *Vibe*'s reporting on the beef, especially its later "East vs. West" issue featuring the Puff Daddy and Biggie cover story that came out the same month of Shakur's murder, stirred the pot. Subsequently, Death Row Records CEO Suge Knight raised the stakes at the infamous 1995 *Source Awards* when he took the stage and invited any artists to join his label if they didn't "want their producer all up in their videos," a clear shot at Sean Combs. Snoop Dogg called out east coast rappers for not having "any love for Dr. Dre and Snoop Dogg and Death Row." OutKast also experienced the regional animus when the audience booed the group as they accepted the Best New Rap Group award, provoking André 3000 to famously declare that "the South's got something to say."

It would be a mistake to reduce the mid-1990s rap rivalries to a coastal beef or a dispute between Death Row and Bad Boy. Divisions between more "commercial" and gangster rap and "underground" or "backpack" rap began to surface as well. Posdnuos's references to Big Daddy Kane and Treach on the first track of *Stakes Is High* led Kane and Treach to wonder if Posdnuos had dissed them. Westside Connection, the supergroup comprised of Ice Cube, Mack 10, and WC, dissed A Tribe Called Quest because they thought the group threw shots at them. Jeru the Damaja's *Wrath of the Math* featured tracks blatantly dissing Puff Daddy and Bad Boy Records. Biggie made a joke at Tupac's expense on Jay-Z's "Brooklyn's Finest" and sent shots at Nas on his own track "Kick in the Door."

De La Soul got ensnared in this beef. As mentioned previously, Tupac Shakur believed De La Soul had dissed his "I Get Around" visuals on the group's "Ego Trippin' (Part Two)" video. Consequently, Shakur named De La Soul on "Against All Odds," which appears on *The Don Killuminati: The 7 Day Theory*, one of several attacks on many of east coast rap's heavyweights. On the song, Shakur ridicules the group members for their ages, referencing Larry Holmes, a former boxing heavyweight champion who fought too long. Here, Shakur's decision to name-drop De La Soul in an adlib was meant to be dismissive as he sought to present the group as an afterthought in rap. And while he does not name De La Soul specifically, Shakur later continued this theme of presenting older groups and artists like De La Soul as has-beens on an unreleased track, "Watch Ya' Mouth," where he calls them "washed up" and "jealous" of his success.

I remember thinking, "What did De La Soul do?" after my first listen. "They did not diss anyone," I thought. "They're the good guys." Remember, I was sixteen, and it would be a year or two before I connected "Ego Trippin' (Part Two)" and "I Get Around." I could see Shakur responding poorly to some of De La Soul's messages that appear on *Stakes Is High*, but De La Soul's album came out nearly two months before Shakur was murdered in Las Vegas. This was the point where Shakur's disses began to alienate me as a listener. I remained a fan of some of Shakur's new music, but I also began to sour on the negativity. Although I was a teenager living in a Midwestern rust belt town, I began to take sides as a fan—I now identified more with east coast artists like Wu-Tang Clan, Mobb Deep, A Tribe Called Quest, and especially De La Soul.

LIVING IN A D.A.I.S.Y. AGE

Runnin' Through the Block / Time to Start the Revolution

My taste in rap music and my perspective on hip-hop culture continued to change. As I entered high school, I moved from Ice Cube, Tupac, and gangsta rap to east coast rap like Nas, The Notorious B.I.G., and Wu-Tang Clan. Wu-Tang Clan's first album, *Enter the Wu-Tang (36 Chambers)*, changed my life as the group of ten emcees opened my mind with their slang and raps about growing up on Staten Island, or "Shaolin." RZA's disjointed and jagged production style fit my personality more than Dr. Dre's smoothed-out soundscapes. And the fact that the group boasted an unheard-of ten members allowed my friends and me to bond over learning all of the albums and songs that appeared in the Wu-Tang universe.

We talked more about the music videos we watched and the new songs we heard while walking home from school. I started paying closer attention to the rap industry. I watched BET's *Rap City*'s top ten countdown every Saturday morning. I bought a new *Source* magazine anytime I had some cash. *The Source*, considered rap music's bible in the 1990s, reinvigorated my love for reading and history. Perusing the magazine allowed me to learn more about my favorite artists, find out when they would drop their albums, and understand more of the culture's past. *The Source*'s Record Report introduced me to music criticism. I usually flipped to the back of the magazine to see how many mics their writers awarded albums as soon as I acquired a new issue.

Learning about hip-hop culture and rap music scratched an intellectual itch in ways that going to school failed to do. No disrespect to any of the teachers I had in high school, but I was like many of my peers—I would perform well if I applied myself, but . . . I was too bored to apply myself. My apathy and the fact that I cared more about socializing with friends dragged down my high school grade point average until my junior year, when I decided to focus more on my studies.

Yet I performed the best in my history classes and was still catching my stride. With the exception of the AP History class I took in my senior year, I learned the standard lessons back then. We always started with the founding fathers, and then we might reach one of my favorite subjects—World War II—by the end of the school year. We took some time during Black History Month to discuss some of the most famous Black leaders and figures, such as Martin Luther King, Jr., and Rosa Parks. Yet again, I never took a middle or high school history class that encouraged us to consider other Black leaders and events beyond King, Parks, and the civil rights movement. Malcolm X only broke through because of the hats and T-shirts emblazoned with an "X."

While I loved to play and watch sports, listening to and reading about rap music stoked a self-sustaining intellectual curiosity that never dissipated. Hip-hop culture became my refuge. It offered me a means to understand myself and to express my disdain for the trappings of respectability politics. Like most teenagers, I gravitated toward its expressions of anti-authoritarianism and anti-racism. Unfortunately, also like many teenagers—the boys, at least—I mimicked rap music's misogyny and homophobia. Thankfully, I grew out of articulating these problematic expressions while in college. (Although I would not claim to be pure in any respect, socially and politically. I continue to grow.)

As I nurtured my interest in rap music, my commitment to hip-hop culture as an aspect of my identity grew. So I scoffed when I heard older folks like Reverend Calvin Butts and C. Delores Tucker blaming hip-hop for anti-social behavior. Instead, I took Nas's threats to shoot his foes and "start the revolution" on "N.Y. State of Mind" more seriously. I saw "the revolution" as a statement mocking the lost promise of the civil rights movement. Even if hip-hop artists barely articulated a political alternative to police violence, incarceration, the two-party system, or systematic oppression, hip-hop delivered a critique of my parents' generation, the Black middle class, racism, and an education system that failed to hold my interest.

LIVING IN A D.A.I.S.Y. AGE

A slew of classic releases in 1996 distracted all of us from our studies. Tupac Shakur dropped his magnum opus, *All Eyez on Me*, on the same day in February that The Fugees released *The Score*. Busta Rhymes, the standout rapper from Leaders of the New School and Native Tongues affiliate, unleashed his colorful debut album, *The Coming*, in March. Jay-Z, at the time known more for his connection to rapper Jaz-O, released his debut album, *Reasonable Doubt*. Although *Reasonable Doubt* was not seen as an instant classic, we thought it was a solid record that included a great Biggie feature on "Brooklyn's Finest." Jay-Z's future rival, Nas, dropped his highly anticipated follow-up to *Illmatic*, *It Was Written*, on the same day De La Soul gave us *Stakes Is High*.

"I Guess I'm Gonna Start Looking at Washing Dishes"

Stakes Is High is an urgent and defiant album. The gangsta aesthetic and materialism dominating rap threatened to wash out rappers who failed to get in line. These circumstances pushed Maseo, Posdnuos, and Dave to rethink their relationship to the silly-serious approach they'd employed on their first three albums. (Trugoy started referring to himself by his given name, "Dave," on this album.) De La Soul's and Prince Paul's parting at the beginning of recording *Stakes Is High* was the clearest sign that the group had decided to go in a more serious direction. There was no beef, but Paul sensed there was little room for his creative playfulness, as the group sought to comment critically on the rap game and society. Posdnuos reflected on the group's split with Paul in the 2016 documentary *De La Soul Is Not Dead*, "One of those amazing qualities that Paul brings is the zaniness. . . . There was no time for [it]."

De La Soul abandoned elaborate and comical skits found on their earlier albums and used interludes to underscore their commitment to focus on the everyday struggles their listeners faced.

De La Soul seemed to take the notion of rappers representing "street reporters" literally. Rather than fantasies of gangsta life or the shiny expressions of conspicuous consumption and wealth that we saw in Biggie, Jay-Z, or Nas videos, listeners heard from a group of folks discussing the O.J. Simpson verdict, a racist dismissing rap music, a houseless person talking about their plight before the beginning of the album's title track, and Maseo expressing some frustration while recapping a prior conversation about a club.

Maseo explained the album's skits to *Okayplayer* in 2023. "Man, it was just reflecting on real people's everyday struggles, you know?" Chris Norris distinguished the realism displayed in De La Soul's work from that which dominated performances of gangsta and commercial rap in a *New York* magazine review of A Tribe Called Quest's *Beats, Rhymes and Life* and De La Soul's *Stakes Is High*, "Rather than sirens and gunshots, the audio-verite bits here are street-corner arguments about O.J., a chat with a homeless man, a southern-accented kid saying, 'Rap is just niggers talking'—proof that mundane reality can be way scarier than a florid drive-by skit."

Posdnuos, Maseo, and Trugoy not only looked at the real world to express their vision of realness but also continued articulating the more complicated form of Black masculinity that listeners heard on *Buhloone Mindstate*. Posdnuos acknowledged his limitations in a 1996 *Rap City* interview. "Me, as an individual, I express every level of it. I'm a positive brother. I'm a negative brother. I'm a brother who take care of my daughter. I'm the womanizer who get busted. That's me. And I don't front. I don't front for nobody. I let you see it all." Trugoy, in an interview with *Vibe* in the same year, underscores an authenticity grounded in the everyday. He assured fans, "Since all of this is happening, let's do as we always did. . . . If everybody talkin' about crime, guns, Versace, hoes, and all that, well, I guess I'm gonna start looking at washing dishes, mowing the lawn, kids—stuff like that." De La Soul presented an authenticity that challenged dominant forms of Black masculinity in rap, and offered a reality that both challenged the rags-to-riches stories of songs and music videos like Biggie's "Juicy" and sought to question the authenticity of the gangster and mafioso tales of artists like Raekwon, Nas, Jay-Z, and Fat Joe. De La Soul did not advocate for the abolition of gangster, mafioso, and pop-sounding rap. They sought balance and the freedom to tell a multitude of stories. Other artists could use gangster tropes to talk about their experiences, but the stakes were too high for De La Soul to tell any lies about their lives.

Criminal Minded

"When I first heard *Criminal Minded*."

Upon pressing play on *Stakes Is High*, listeners hear these words spliced together from various folks who responded to the prompt. In the spirit of the group's commitment to the grassroots, what follows is a compilation of answers from relatively anonymous (except for Mos Def, now known as Yasiin Bey) voices detailing the first time they listened to Boogie Down Productions' 1987 album, *Criminal Minded*.

Although bell hooks contended that some male rappers failed to study certain forms of music, Maseo, Trugoy, and Posdnuos were not among this group. It seemed in the 1990s, when producers still relied upon sampling, that possessing a basic understanding of music history was essential. So the real question arising from hooks's critique is, What purpose does music knowledge have? There are exploitative ways to mine history to make money while also endorsing questionable and problematic values like materialism and misogyny. Puff Daddy's sampling pop hits for the sake of creating more hits is one example of this. There are also ways to look at the history of Black music as a model for resistance.

Whether by sampling, through language or rhyme style, or in interviews, De La Soul typically demonstrated their understanding, if not reverence, of the history of popular music and hip-hop culture. But few of their albums are as explicit in their recall of the past. Clearly, the Boogie Down Productions shout out is supposed to remind us of the sound of "real" hip-hop, which is from what many artists and scholars consider rap's "golden age." Yet, by June 1996, many of rap's major acts from the mid- to late 1980s were either gone from the scene, struggling to adapt to rap's new era, or operating on the margins of the genre. In a time of transformation for rap and De La Soul, however, starting their new album by asking people to reminisce about the first time they listened to Boogie Down Productions' classic represented a way for the group to plant their flag in rap's and the music industry's changing landscape.

There were other reasons for citing *Criminal Minded* instead of other notable golden age albums like Run-D.M.C.'s self-titled debut album, Eric B. & Rakim's *Paid in Full*, or even Public Enemy's *It Takes a Nation of Millions to Hold Us Back*. *Criminal Minded* might not have shifted hip-hop's sound, but KRS-One, DJ Scott La Rock, DJ D-Nice, and the other members of Boogie Down Productions brought together various elements of production and vocal performance over boom bap production. *Criminal Minded* included anthems like "South Bronx" and "The Bridge Is Over." But glimmers of KRS-One, the knowledge dropper, pierced through the opening track, "Poetry," where he used his lyrical ability to make the case for rap as art.

What makes De La Soul's choice of *Criminal Minded* ironic is that Boogie Down Productions' first record also contained lyrical and nascent gangster rap elements. KRS-One calls *Criminal Minded* one of the genre's first gangsta rap albums, with the rapper and DJ Scott La Rock posing with guns on the cover. (Eazy-E pointed a gun at the camera on N.W.A's *Straight Outta Compton* cover.) But, it would be a mistake to minimize Schoolly D's contributions, as he's often cited as one of rap's pioneering gangsta rappers. His 1987 album, *Saturday Night! The Album*, is a landmark in the genre.

One also cannot think about *Criminal Minded*'s gangsta elements without recalling Scott La Rock's murder in 1987 while trying to intervene in a dispute involving DJ D-Nice and another man. De La Soul pointing to *Criminal Minded* and speaking on the deadly potential of gangsta rap on *Stakes Is High* raises the specter of Scott La Rock. Of course, no one is blaming gangsta rap performance for La Rock's death. But it was the start of the trend of violent killings of rappers that De La Soul tried to warn against on *Stakes Is High*.

What follows the brief *Criminal Minded* skit on the "Intro" is a demonstration of what to expect from *Stakes Is High*—sharp, complex lyrics over slick boom bap beats. Originally conceived as a remix to *Buhloone Mindstate*'s "Eye Patch," the "Intro" features Posdnuos and Dave engaging in lyrical gymnastics over a slowed-down, Jackson 5–sampled, bass-thumping beat. One of Posdnuos's lines stuck out the first time I listened to this song in 1996: "De La Soul is here to stay like racism." Posdnuos's declaration about their group and racism not going anywhere set the album's tone. I cannot say I was equipped to talk extensively about racism when I first heard this song, but I understood Posdnuos's statement. All I had to do was turn on the TV—the 1992 Los Angeles uprisings, the O.J. Simpson double murder trial, the Black church burnings.

While Posdnuos's line about racism arrested my ears, the rapper's instructions for some fans to "stick to" listening to Big Daddy Kane and Naughty by Nature is what got De La Soul caught up in the mid-1990s rap wars. According to group members, Naughty by Nature's Treach and Big Daddy Kane thought Posdnuos dissed them. Treach and Tupac were close friends, and the latter thought De La Soul dissed him in the "Ego Trippin' (Part Two)" video. Tupac dissed De La Soul in songs afterward. Later, Treach allegedly physically attacked Posdnuos at a concert as De La Soul performed on stage and later settled their differences.

"Long Island Degrees"

While bell hooks seemed to pathologize young Black men in her critique, there were points of convergence between her and De La Soul's critiques of gangsterism. Pos and Dave took rappers' gun talk seriously;

it reflected the changes in rap they'd observed and had become part of the daily realities of young Black and Brown men. Because if gunplay did not seem so prevalent, then why would Pos remind listeners on *Stakes Is High* that "gun control" really referred to how one handles firearms? Dave, however, was more direct in his critique of death-defying Black masculinity on "Long Island Degrees," where he called out The Notorious B.I.G. "I got questions about your life if you're ready to die."

If some rappers drew inspiration from the violence in their immediate surroundings in the mid- to late 1980s, and some earlier in the 1990s viewed jazz as a muse, then it was not hard to find rappers in the mid-1990s who looked to real-life or fictional gangsters and drug dealers like Tony Montana (from the movie *Scarface*), the Gambino crime family, John Gotti, and Pablo Escobar. Raekwon included "Wu-Gambinos" (a favorite song of mine) on his classic *Only Built 4 Cuban Linx*. Nas adopted "Escobar" as his persona during his *It Was Written*, *The Firm*, and *I Am* stretch. Biggie started to call himself Frank White, after the main character from the 1990 movie *King of New York*, in his *Life After Death* era. And while Cartegena is Fat Joe's last name, he adopted "Don," the mafia reference for "boss," for his third album, *Don Cartegena*, released in 1998.

De La Soul's criticisms of gangsterism ranged from general mockery (we will get to Trugoy on "Itzsoweezee" later) to specifically calling out Black rappers for adopting non-Black gangster personas. Maseo added more nuance to this critique later. He argues that he was critical of the "Mafioso ideology" due to the racist violence he experienced at the hands of some Italian youth. He told *Okayplayer* in 2023, "It was heartbreaking because we're talking about Italian mobs who don't like Black people and we've got rappers adopting this Mafioso ideology. . . . This was reality for me," Maseo continued. "I went to school in Bay Ridge. So to go from where I lived to school—going home was tough. It was rough. I got chased home many times by Italian white boys. I got my ass kicked a couple of times, too. It was all part of the premise of just being Black. Like,

'Nigga, get from around here.'" Maseo contended that he saw little wrong with Black rappers adopting the persona of Black gangsters because they were Black.

De La Soul's criticism of this expression of Black masculinity, like Cornel West's and bell hooks's, also bordered on pathologizing rappers. Nothing exemplified this more than the title of Track 14 on *Stakes Is High*, "Down Syndrome." The song is a clever articulation of the problems found in equating authenticity with a Black identity bent on participating in criminalized behavior, gunplay, and pursuing wealth and luxury goods no matter the cost. The group warns in their muffled chorus that all the sales, popularity, and material possessions could not shield rappers from violence or an early death. The song is also prophetic, as the later murders of Tupac Shakur and The Notorious B.I.G. illustrated. The song's title is a rather unfortunate double entendre, superficially referencing the genetic condition where a person is born with an extra chromosome. Nevertheless, in the context of *Stakes Is High*, De La Soul calls young folks' desires to be "down" with violent masculinity and material overconsumption a condition or disease.

Legendary music engineer Bob Power offers some insight into De La Soul's approach to "being down" in an interview in *Frank* magazine that also helps explain the song's meaning. "They didn't have to be 'down,' and the concept of 'down' was a very bizarre and foreign thing to them. [Prince] Paul has made a wonderful career of making fun of being 'down,' and Pos has had some fascinating commentary on that, also."

Again, "Down Syndrome" is very clever, but as scholars of racism and social inequality have argued, it is necessary to understand the role played by structural problems in shaping people's lives and identities. We must continue to pay attention to the decline of 1960s social movements, capital divestment from and economic restructuring of inner cities, the defunding of public education, the federal government's abandonment of anti-poverty policies and social welfare, and the emergence of an organized drug trade and militarized police forces in the wake of these transformations as several factors that help explain the conditions under which death-defying behavior in real life and displayed in art could emerge.

De La Soul would not be the only rappers to diss gangster and mafioso ideology in 1996. The Fugees devoted much of their album *The Score* to calling out gangster and mafioso personas in rap, Pras, Wyclef Jean, and poet and current Newark, New Jersey, mayor Ras Baraka took aim at the gangsters, "gambinos," Corleones, and the "cowboy ass niggas" who did not possess any power in society on the album's introduction. Posdnuos even appears in the Fugees' video for "Cowboys," which continued the group's critiques of hard personas in rap. Two years later, Erick Sermon echoed this criticism on "U Got Shot," which appeared on EPMD's 1999 album *Out of Business*. Delivering the final verse over a hard beat and a vocal Ol' Dirty Bastard sample from "Brooklyn Zoo," Sermon chastised gangster and mafioso rappers, employing some misogyny, for "acting like Sicilians" while "chasin' gold diggers."

As with many trends within rap music, artists developed their own takes on gangsta and mafioso rap. Many artists also articulated their rebukes of this subgenre, seeing it as a path toward rap music's artistic destruction. Yet, it was hard to take Biggie's death-related imagery literally, considering how those around him maintained the rapper looked forward to future tours, business ventures, rap collaborations like the famed Commission group with Jay-Z, and raising his children. However, where the realism of De La Soul's *Stakes Is High* might collide with Biggie's and Tupac's premonitions of death is that living while Black and poor can be exhausting. It is quite conceivable that if you are poor, you do not possess any employable skills in the legalized job market, and you live in an impoverished neighborhood without good public institutions and safe spaces. You might turn to drug dealing and all its death-defying trappings. You could fantasize about going out in a blaze of glory. You might garner some recognition from your peers: many people, especially men, dream of being immortalized. Death is a direct path, whether one is fighting in a war abroad or at home. Like Biggie, you might even consider dying by suicide. And, if you are fortunate enough to record an album, you might name it *Ready to Die* and dramatize your demise.

"The Bizness"

Although De La Soul reserved much of their lyrical barbs for materialistic and gangster rappers, the group did not spare criticism for the rap industry. De La Soul teamed up with Common Sense (now known as Common) to critique the industry on "The Bizness." I first heard this song, or at least the last verse, on the Akron R&B and rap radio station while sitting in Mom's car waiting for her to run an errand. Believing it was some remix, I thought, "What did I just miss?"

Listening to "The Bizness" feels like watching the three rappers in a cypher engaging in verbal acrobatics while expressing their authenticity through high-minded lyrics. The song would have fit in well on a Rawkus Records compilation album. Trugoy distanced De La Soul from rap's growing materialism in his first verse. Common performed a standard verse for himself at the time, including a homophobic reference to gay Olympic diver Greg Louganis. Posdnuos, on the other hand, kicked a battle rhyme questioning the notion of realness, instructing listeners to live "right" with the wisdom of a parent, uncle, or a seasoned rap veteran. In his verse, Posdnuos leaned in to the style of extending "tough love" popularized in rap by artists like Public Enemy's Chuck D.

On the original album, De La Soul started "The Bizness" with a Craig Mack sample from "Get Down." (The streaming version leaves him off.) Interestingly, they sampled Mack, a Bad Boy artist, right after the previous song where Posdnuos name-dropped Puff Daddy. De La Soul's sample of Mack is notable because Bad Boy Records was transforming into the ostentatious label that caught the ire of the underground and those of us looking for a more authentic form of rap. Radio hits like Biggie's "Big Poppa," sampling The Isley Brothers' "Between the Sheets," and R&B group 112's remix of "Only You" with The Notorious B.I.G. and Mase overshadowed the boom bap, grittier production that Craig Mack leaned on for his Bad Boy debut album. While Puff Daddy was on his way to solidifying himself as a hitmaker who led a group of producers who typically crafted big, glossy beats around apparent samples, some who worked with the ascendant CEO claim he ensnared artists like Craig Mack and The LOX in unfavorable contracts and threatened physical violence to maintain discipline within Bad Boy. In the last few years, Combs has emerged as rap's most infamous example of abusive men in the industry. Many women and men have since accused Combs of physical and sexual abuse stemming back to those early Bad Boy years, however he has been acquitted.

"Dog Eat Dog," the last song Prince Paul worked on for De La Soul, bemoans the downsides of capitalist competition in rap. Posdnuos and Trugoy critique narrow individualist pursuits of materialism inside and outside the rap world. "It's a dog eat dog competition," Dave laments over a beat featuring sampled dog barking. Similar to other jeremiads on the state of rap music, like Common's "I Used to Love H.E.R.," Trugoy muses on how the dominance of conspicuous consumption in hip-hop is spoiling his love of the culture.

On the track, Posdnuos compares record executives with pimps, describing the ways they take artists' hard-earned money and redistribute meager royalties back to them. While this critique of record executives and the industry is not novel, it reflected how De La Soul felt Tommy Boy interacted with them since the beginning. But Posdnuos's lyrics also underscored how record executives sought to control Black artists' careers, and this has a long history, extending back to Motown and Berry Gordy seeking to control every aspect of album creation and artist development and also to Prince's protests against Warner Bros. earlier in the decade.

The hook to the song almost seems like a threat to leave rap.

Dave remarks he did not want to stick around. "Dog Eat Dog" could also express acceptance that De La Soul's time in the game might have passed. They are making peace with the fact that gangsta, mafioso, and commercial rap in the mainstream might wash them away. But as Dave told Joe Clair on *Rap City*, "If it ends tomorrow, I got my daughter. . . . If it die tomorrow, I'm alright with that. I'll fly to Haiti and just chill."

"Dog Eat Dog" also reflects on and anticipates the music and rap industry's restructuring during the late 1990s and early 2000s. Recently, Maseo described some of this context in an interview with *Okayplayer*:

> The change in the business was taking place. That was like a first major change for us. This was around the time all the indies was like, "We going corporate." Everybody was doing their mergers. Tommy Boy was kind of the last to do their merger. They closed. They were like, one leg in and out with Warner Brothers. There was things that they would put out with Warner Brothers and there was things they won't. They still had their hand independently in the game for a long time but this was a time where either labels was truly making that transition to go corporate and be a subsidiary of somebody major.

Many rappers who were not part of the Death Row/Bad Boy/Roc-A-Fella/No Limit Records/Cash Money contingent were left in the cold due to restructuring. The Roots and Common eventually became MCA recording artists after the record company bought Geffen Records. An assemblage of labels that Priority Records oversaw eventually disintegrated, leaving artists like those on Rawkus Records including Pharoahe Monch, Mos Def, Talib Kweli, and Hi-Tek looking for new label homes in the mid-2000s. Even De La Soul had to search for new label arrangements after Tommy Boy Records went defunct in 2002.

Sick of Talkin'

Typically, when De La Soul tucks a single toward or at the end of their record, they do so out of spite. But *Stakes Is High*'s penultimate track captures all the group's concerns with rap and society. Although someone skimming the album, or skipping to the song, may not realize it, "Stakes Is High" starts with the album's last skit following "Pony Ride." And De La Soul's social critique on the album could not have been more explicit than in the skit preceding the album's title track. In another moving snapshot of the reality of "everyday people" De La Soul hoped to highlight, a houseless guy describes the physical and mental tumult of houselessness, including not knowing where his next meal might come from. He discusses how he survived by chance, "I don't get a whole lot of good food to eat for a couple days or something like that. . . . But it just gets more depressing and depressing as you go on. . . . And I even start thinking . . . not a hallucination, actually, not a visual or an auditory, but . . . like I'm in a dark fantasy where I even start thinking about that I want to do this to myself."

The houseless man's description of his experience as a "dark fantasy" recalls the first song appearing on Kanye West's 2010 album *My Beautiful Dark Twisted Fantasy*. What is more haunting for a person than the daily struggles and stressors of living without a home in a capitalist society? This person's "dark fantasy" might be a different type of "suicidal thoughts" than the ones Biggie articulated in the concluding song on *Ready to Die*. De La Soul is sympathetic to this houseless person, talking about how poverty has robbed him of individual agency and control over his mental health. Yet, it is difficult not to point to the structural origins of the madness. Capitalism created "the streets," the same streets where Black and Brown youth work in underground economies and seek to earn a living the way their parents did working in factories. Everyone on these streets is trapped, as stated in critiques of "the ghetto" and by

LIVING IN A D.A.I.S.Y. AGE

Tupac on *2Pacalypse Now*. Policymakers and capitalists abandoned the houseless and hustlers, and a lack of money and resources, plus police oppression, keep them contained. Death, unfortunately, becomes a way out of this "dark fantasy."

Of course, most of us would not hear the last skit on the album until we bought *Stakes Is High*. Instead, in the opening scene of the music video, we saw the group sitting on the set of *The Maury Povich Show*. This is how I encountered the video as a teenager. Sitting in my room in my parents' two-bedroom apartment, I gasped when the Ahmad Jamal "Swahililand" sample dropped. (Obviously, I did not know who Jamal was, but I knew who *Jay Dee* was!) Then we hear Maceo Parker's voice sampled from James Brown's "Mind Power"—"Vibe, vibrations."

De La Soul had to play mind games to acquire the Jay Dee–produced beat. Q-Tip played some of his beats for Posdnuos, and, according to him, no one could act excited about a track around Q-Tip because the latter might claim it. Maseo told the story to *Okayplayer*, "'Stakes Is High' came up on the beat. Pos kind of held back. He [Q-Tip] was like, 'What do you think of this beat?' 'Stakes Is High' beat playing and Pos was like, 'It's all right. It's okay,' but then secretly goes off in the corner and calls Dave, was like, 'Yo! This is the fucking beat. This is it right here.'" Pos then went to Jay Dee for the beat without Q-Tip's knowledge. De La Soul got their track.

I had not heard of Jay Dee, later known as J Dilla, by name before A Tribe Called Quest released *Beats, Rhymes and Life* where the producer joined with Q-Tip and Ali Shaheed Muhammad as "The Ummah." I'd heard of The Pharcyde's "Runnin'" and "Drop," but I ignored the fact that Dilla produced those songs. Those songs failed to move me at the time, unlike his other work on The Pharcyde's *Labcabincalifornia*, like "Bullshit," or the tracks that appeared on projects like Common's *Like Water for Chocolate*, Slum Village's *Fantastic, Vol. 2*, and the producer's solo album, *Welcome 2 Detroit*. While there was no way I could have developed a deep understanding of Dilla's contributions to rap production like Questlove has articulated and Dan Charnas illustrates in his musical biography of the composer, *Dilla Time: The Life and Afterlife of J Dilla, the Hip-Hop Producer Who Reinvented Rhythm*, Dilla's work in the late 1990s and early 2000s appealed to my Native Tongues nostalgia. But when I heard that Dilla beat in the summer of 1996, I was hooked.

De La Soul seemed to have faded from my view before I watched the video for "Stakes Is High" for the first time. As a rap fan and budding hip-hop nerd, I was a Wu-Tang Clan devotee who followed all the group members' solo releases. Like many rap fans, I have listened to a lot of "commercial" rap—Tupac, Bad Boy, and Ice Cube.

But, one day, I'm sitting in my bedroom in my parents' two-bedroom apartment watching Maury Povich introduce the song—"How does the music dictate real life, and how much does real life dictate the music? Today on the show, we have De La Soul, to discuss the many ways to keep it real." Then the beat dropped.

"What is this?" I thought.

Then, Posdnuos set off the song.

"The instamatic focal point bringin' damage to your borough be some brothers from the East with them beats that be thorough...."

"Oh my God," I gasped.

Posdnuos's lyrics sounded sharper as he cut through J. Dilla's hard production. Pos was also pointed in another way—he sarcastically critiqued violence and gun policy. Then Trugoy joined Posdnuos in a critique of the rap game at the time. Dave lists all of the elements of commercial rap he was "sick of": "I'm sick of talkin' 'bout blunts, sick of Versace glasses. Sick of slang, sick of half-ass award shows. Sick of name-brand clothes." Dave's verse more aggressively articulates the group's earlier "Take It Off" skit. But the first thing I thought while watching the video was "Yeah! I'm sick and tired of the commercial rap, too!" (Although I still listened to Biggie.) Dave points out the fakeness in the flashy displays of wealth in rap videos and sarcastically questions the mafioso aesthetic in rap—"Seem like every man and woman shared a life with John Gotti," he raps before Posdnuos interrupts him. "But they ain't organized!"

The song synthesizes the group's arguments articulated on the album most straightforwardly: Posdnuos's and Dave's comments on inner-city violence, racism, and rap's turn toward the pursuit of wealth. Like Dave started lines with "Sick of . . ." rhymes, Posdnuos talks about how his generation fell in love with the wrong things—cars, money, sex, guns, wealth, and fame. However, his rhymes about racism might be the most affecting—"A skin not considered equal, a meteor has more right than my people." First, this is because of the meteor/meteorite wordplay. Secondly, while a meteor is not a comet, Japanese astronomers discovered the Hyakutake comet in January 1996, and it was visible that spring. Of course, the discoveries of Hyakutake and the Hale-Bopp comets generated much news coverage and public awe. But, in an echo of the 1969 moon landing, Posdnuos is pointing out how many tend to allow otherworldly events to eclipse issues more important to Black Americans.

"Stakes Is High" was more serious and caustic than most of their other singles, such as "Ring Ring Ring," which playfully dissed aspiring artists who tried to push their demos on the group, or even "Ego Trippin' (Part Two)," which probably served as a precursor to "Stakes Is High" because it threw rocks at the braggadocio rap style of popular artists in the early 1990s. Dave and Posdnuos took aim at a rap game that not only seemed to be going pop, but was also at its breaking point.

The song reflected the group's desire to position themselves as rap's everymen. They felt comfortable demonstrating complex lyricism while also presenting themselves as accessible. Dave is washing and drying clothes at a laundromat. Maseo is riding a lawnmower in the yard, which, if we think about the meaning of their song "Potholes in My Lawn," could mean that he and the group are trimming the rap game, hoping to dispose of those who disrespected it. In any case, it seemed they wanted us to relate to them, while other rappers such as Nas, Biggie, and Tupac spent much time, ink, and money telling us we could not relate to them because of their newfound wealth, mafioso lifestyle, or sheer recklessness.

"Betta Listen"

Even if De La Soul's *Stakes Is High* resisted rap's fascination with gangster culture, conspicuous displays of wealth, and the genre's commercialization, the album was not without contradictions. The group sought to uplift a more populist form of rap but still perpetuated homophobia and misogyny. Common uttered homophobic lyrics to belittle emcees on "The Bizness" (although he has since disavowed these types of lyrics). The group utilized misogynist language to deride wannabe rappers, and Posdnuos also seemed to throw shots at popular women rappers on "Wonce Again Long Island" with his lyrics telling women to "go put on some clothes." Of course, women rappers like Lil' Kim and Foxy Brown come to mind when thinking about these words. Lil' Kim had made a splash the year before as one of The Notorious B.I.G.'s protégés in the rap group Junior M.A.F.I.A. and helped usher in a transformation of how women in hip-hop looked and rapped. Lil' Kim and Foxy Brown presented themselves more like sex symbols and rapped more raunchily than some of their predecessors like MC Lyte. Lil' Kim made an impression with her explicit lyrics and in public, wearing designer clothing (often created by Black women) that left little to viewers' imagination. Looking back, misogynist lyrics would undermine rap's authenticity if we thought of it as inclusive. But this was not the case in 1996. Misogynist language often sat at the center of what it meant to "keep it real" in rap, especially among male lyricists.

But then, *Stakes Is High* features more mature songs about sex and intimacy with "Betta Listen" and "4 More." On "Betta Listen," like "Jenifa," De La Soul presents women who turn the tables on them. The women are assertive in both depictions. A woman turns Dave down, while Posdnuos and his lover consummate their connection that night. The son'g chorus serves as a reminder to men that they should treat women respectfully. One could ask, at least in relation to Posdnuos's admission to engaging in womanizing behavior, are songs like "Betta Listen" manifestations of his conscience? Or maybe the group's art, especially in this case, is aspirational and also a way to deal with any guilt in one's personal life?

De La Soul's approach to women on *Stakes Is High* reflected a form of benevolent sexism where their respect for women appeared conditional—dependent upon male-defined respectable behavior in dress, speech, and emotional comportment. Also, and this is not particular to De La Soul, some songs like "Betta Listen" idealize a certain type of "respectable" woman: "a philosopher," someone into conscious hip-hop music, an independent woman. Yet, the trap of this form of sexism lies in the fact that idolizing these characteristics does not mean that men will ultimately treat women with respect.

"Baby, Baby, Baby, Baby, Ooh Baby" and "4 More" strike as parody, in a way. They are both "I will steal your girl" songs, with Posdnuos rapping in a Biggie-like cadence on "Baby, Baby, Baby, Baby, Ooh Baby." Or, I would clarify by asserting Posdnuos's verses are "I will steal your girl," whereas Trugoy's are more unassuming. I can picture the latter throwing in an "aw shucks" while flirting with someone. "4 More," even if it is one of the album's weaker songs, sounds like an attempt at mid-1990s rap aimed at women. Unfortunately, the track is not like A Tribe Called Quest's clever and sensual "Electric Relaxation." In fact, while some of the songs contained comical metaphors, "4 More" featured the type of cringe-worthy lines I would have written in poems while in college, like "Is it a crime to sex your mind to death?" These songs do not contain any lyrics that would elicit gasps like Phife Dawg's reference to "Seaman's Furniture" on "Electric Relaxation." But maybe this is the point. Posdnuos and Trugoy go through the motions on these songs. And, like "Ring, Ring, Ring," and "Breakadawn," these songs are more about demonstrating that they can construct "playa"-like rap songs, adapt Biggie's cadences, and slick talk, and make it look easy while doing so.

9/13/96

Stakes Is High was prescient. De La Soul tried to caution us. Unfortunately, their warnings of violence on *Stakes Is High* and Tupac's and Biggie's premonitions of death came to pass, throwing the rap world into an existential crisis.

I'll never forget the shock I felt while sitting on the arm of a friend's couch, watching as *MTV News* announced Shakur's death on September 13, 1996, three months after *Stakes Is High* dropped. In March of the following year, we learned Biggie had been shot and killed after a *Vibe* magazine party in Los Angeles. I didn't know a celebrity death could affect me the way these had, but I saw myself as part of a beleaguered imaginary community, or a "hip-hop nation." Hip-hop culture stood at a crossroads after the killings of Shakur and The Notorious B.I.G. Who was the next artist to die? Violence snatched the genre's two most promising artists. Where was hip-hop going? Where was *I* going?

Although I never engaged in any of the activities Biggie rapped about, it became easier for me to share in the collective pain with artists and fans everywhere. Even if I had never stepped foot in New York City, Los Angeles, Atlanta, New Orleans, Houston, or Chicago, I felt an affinity with everyone mourning Tupac's and Biggie's deaths. My love for hip-hop culture and rap music overlapped with my racial identity. I knew what it felt like to be stereotyped based on my race, how I dressed and spoke, and the music I listened to. Consequently, I felt solidarity with the millions of other hip-hop fans and practitioners. I would not feel this way again until I started organizing protests against police violence as a graduate student in Ann Arbor and attended vigils for the killings of other Black people.

The killings of Tupac Shakur and The Notorious B.I.G. haunted hip-hop, and the culture embarked on a search for its soul and identity. I also began my search for identity as a young Black man. Shakur's and Wallace's deaths brought me closer to groups who aspired to affirm those of us who wanted to participate, but without having to adopt an unreachable and unreasonable masculine hardness preoccupied with death. That just wasn't my real life. Thus, while I remained a committed Wu-Tang fan, I gravitated back to A Tribe Called Quest and De La Soul. I also connected with underground artists who built on De La Soul's anti-corporate legacy, like Mos Def and Talib Kweli, Apani B Fly, Common, The Roots, Pharoahe Monch, Company Flow, and Dilated Peoples.

Yet, even as I gravitated away from gangsta rap, I felt the coldness of the genre's biggest stars going dark. They were our ambassadors to the mainstream, for better and for worse.

Shiny Suits and Superpredators

While De La Soul won me back over with *Stakes Is High*, they and other like-minded artists like Common, The Fugees, and A Tribe Called Quest did not entirely win the argument over the direction of rap music. The deaths of Tupac Shakur and Biggie might have placed the intra- and interregional conflicts on ice, but rap's materialism and gravitation toward more pop-oriented music continued apace. The "shiny suit era," characterized by Puff Daddy and Bad Boy's glossy rap videos featuring artists wearing shiny suits, emerged out of the turmoil. While some of us grew tired of rap songs conspicuously sampling pop and rock songs, other artists and producers like Missy Elliott, Timbaland, OutKast, Goodie Mob, and Lauryn Hill pushed rap music in diverse creative directions.

Public policy also helped facilitate rap's move into pop culture's mainstream. In early 1996, Congress passed the Telecommunications Act, deregulating the industry. The bipartisan legislation was intended to allow more competition in communications. However, this bill created the conditions for corporate consolidation. As historians Nelson Lichtenstein and Judith Stein write about the telecommunications law, "It was to be a game not of continuous competition but of winner take all." Soon, corporations like Clear Channel began gobbling up radio stations. According to historian Katherine Rye Jewell, Clear Channel owned forty stations in 1996 and increased its holdings to over 1,200 in several years. Mass layoffs and the establishment of corporate-controlled and standardized music playlists followed. Radio stations played fewer songs, and the rap industry adjusted. The narrowing of playlists encouraged trend-chasing among artists and producers. "Whereas saying and doing something original in rap was once a main goal," S. Craig Watkins explains in *Hip Hop Matters: Politics, Pop Culture, and the Struggle for the Soul of a Movement*, "in the era of big radio the mimicking of already established styles and trends meant more." It seemed De La Soul's criticisms of corporate music had come to fruition. The telecom act underscored the group's critique of the merger of corporate music and materialist, violent rap. The law would have long-lasting ramifications for the music industry, helping lay some of the groundwork for the popularization of the internet and the digitization of music.

Meanwhile, President Clinton and the GOP-controlled Congress continued their regressive policies directed at poorer people. A little more than a month after De La Soul released their fourth album, Bill Clinton signed the Personal Responsibility and Work Opportunity Reconciliation Act. PRWORA abolished the Aid to Families with Dependent Children program, which provided poor families with almost $8,000 a year. "Welfare reform" instituted the Temporary Assistance for Needy Families program, which limited the duration of welfare payments to two years and forced recipients to find employment. The bill generated so much anger within the Clinton administration that three assistant secretaries at the Department of Health and Human Services resigned in protest.

And as the jails and prisons filled with Black youth amid the decline in crime, some in the Clinton administration adopted a new name to describe violent youth—"superpredator." Princeton professor John J. DiIulio, Jr., coined the racist and classist term in a 1995 *Weekly Standard* article. This new class of youth, according to DiIulio, roamed the streets like "wolf packs," committing violent crimes indiscriminately without any regard for humanity. DiIulio helped spark a media panic as news outlets used the term hundreds of times after the article's publication. The term caught on so much that Oprah Winfrey and Hillary Clinton used it.

Amid debates around welfare reform, there was less appetite for structural alternatives to addressing concentrated poverty. "Superpredators" could not be rehabilitated, only locked up and warehoused. It was not a coincidence that much discourse about rap music and the "hip-hop generation" mirrored pathological explanations and panics about this subset of American youth. (Although DiIulio later renounced his use of "superpredator," it was his term others continued to use to dehumanize youth of color.)

"Apologies Are in Order"

Stakes Is High might be one of De La Soul's most critically underappreciated albums. At least it seemed that way when it came out. *The Source* and Robert Christgau scored *Stakes Is High* rather highly (four mics and a B+). Yet, compared to their first three albums, some reviewers criticized De La Soul's fourth effort more negatively. *Rolling Stone*'s David Sprague awarded the album two stars, stating that the group "opts to wax old school rather than return to the Daisy Age sound that inspired spiritual descendants like Fugees." Jeff Salamon panned the record's beats—"De La Soul have settled for a series of serviceable, midtempo grooves"—and lamented Prince Paul's departure in his six-out-of-ten review for *SPIN* magazine. *Entertainment Weekly*'s Ethan Smith wrote of the group's tone on the album, "And while they've always had a cynical streak, Posdnuos, Trugoy, and Maseo now frequently verge on utter joylessness." While Robert Christgau hardly ever grades the group lower than an A-, he justified his B+ rating by stating, "It's a relief to have them back. But it's never a revelation."

Although reviewers still wanted De La Soul to do something they said they'd never do, which was to go back to 1989, 1991, or 1993, *Stakes Is High* has garnered more appreciation over time. Jack Hamilton, writing on the album's twentieth anniversary for *Slate*, confesses, "*Stakes Is High* holds a singular place in my heart, one of those musical works that sounds perfect to me every time I hear it even if it doesn't always to others—especially if it doesn't to others." Hamilton proceeds to call De La Soul's fourth album, "a ferociously intelligent record." Eddie "STATS" Houghton of *Okayplayer* called *Stakes Is High* "seminal" in the website's 2023 oral history of the album. Blake Gillespie, in his twenty-year retrospective for *Vinyl Me Please*, declared, "Apologies are in order as 20 years later *Stakes Is High* is secretly a catalyst album that influenced an entire generation, for better or worse. . . . Quite inadvertently, it fostered a generation of junior curmudgeons and the next indelible generation of Native Tongues."

What reviewers did not seem to pay attention to in 1996 was that the album, song, and video for the title track became a calling card for many fans, especially African Americans. De La Soul might have told Black youth that it was okay to not fit in and to be intelligent and complicated on *3 Feet High and Rising*. But none of their first three albums, nor any afterward, has represented more for conscious rap and rap fans who desired to elevate their consciousness. *Stakes Is High* helped introduce me to hip-hop criticism, and the song and album made me believe rap and hip-hop contained meaning beyond materialism and gangster-inspired culture. De La Soul reminded us again that rap was for everyone, not just gangsters, hustlers, and the wealthy. One could be a student, an activist, or a parent doing chores around the house and still be hip-hop without reservation.

Over time, *Stakes Is High*, whether as a phrase, slogan, or mantra, has taken on a life of its own. Scholars and activists such as Marc Lamont Hill, Gloria Ladson-Billings, Ruha Benjamin, and Mychal Denzel Smith have either cited or were inspired by De La Soul's *Stakes Is High* in their writings. In her book *Viral Justice: How We Grow the World We Want*, Ruha Benjamin, an activist and Black studies professor and a scholar of race, technology, science, and medicine, lists De La Soul's album as one of several hip-hop records (including Poor Righteous Teachers' *Holy Intellect* and Queen Latifah's *Black Reign*) that contributed to her education and politicization. Professor, activist, and TV host Marc Lamont Hill titled the first chapter of *Beats, Rhymes, and Classroom Life: Hip-Hop Pedagogy and the Politics of Identity*, his book theorizing "Hip-Hop-Based Education," after De La Soul's *Stakes Is High*. Citing the album title and cultural theorist Stuart Hall, Hill explains the need to adopt a teaching method relevant to students because "the cultural, political, and economic exigencies of the day are far too urgent." It is important, Hill argues, for instructors to utilize culturally relevant sources, in this case, "Hip-Hop Lit," to educate youth, especially those from marginalized backgrounds. Mychal Denzel Smith called his latest book, exposing our delusions around democracy, national unity, justice, progress, and upward mobility, *Stakes Is High: Life After the American Dream*. De La Soul and Denzel Smith shared the same lessons in different contexts and scales—they must tell the truth because the stakes are too high to ignore. For De La Soul and Denzel Smith, America needs to pay attention to those left behind—the poor and Black folks trying to survive the everyday struggle, as Biggie put it on *Ready to Die*. In our time, Denzel Smith is issuing a warning as did previous Black radicals like incarcerated activist George Jackson, who speculated on the rise of fascism in response to Black-led social movements. If we do not tell and learn the truths of the past and present, we might be heading toward an unspeakable national catastrophe.

To *the Source*

Stakes Is High inspired me to go back to rap's past to enjoy the music we missed and try to understand its history as we sought to build more credibility among our peers. My friends and I responded to the Shakur and Biggie murders by distancing ourselves from "commercial" rap and deepening our engagement with hip-hop culture. We did not rap, produce, or dance. We tried graffiti art for a while but decided to put down the spray cans after we learned in the local newspaper that residents and law enforcement noticed the buildings we tagged and had been investigating. "Police at least are reassured that the graffiti does not seem much more than the work of some bored, somewhat artistic community members," the Mansfield *News Journal* reported.

After our failed attempts at impressing each other as street artists, I decided I would stick with listening, reading, and arguing about rap music with friends. The publication of *The Source*'s one hundredth issue in January 1998, with LL Cool J holding five microphones on the cover (five mics was the magazine's top rating), became our historical guide for our discussions and debates about hip-hop. We read about the classic albums that earned the magazine's approval and sought to acquire and listen to the albums that appeared on the magazine's 100 best rap albums list. Luckily, several of my friends worked at a locally owned music store, CD Jungle, and two of them used their access to the store's distributor to order many of the records.

Going back and listening to older rap albums and discussing them reintroduced me to the genre and, most important, to thinking historically. Boogie Down Productions' *Ghetto Music: The Blueprint of Hip Hop*; X Clan's *To the East, Blackwards*; and De La Soul's *De La Soul Is Dead* became our primary sources. Instead of just reciting offensive rap lyrics, I honed my critical thinking skills as we interpreted and evaluated the merits of rap albums and songs as texts. We argued about album ratings in school and at parties. I began to piece together my understanding of "real hip-hop." We debated what real hip-hop was among ourselves and with other friends. We chastised others for listening to "commercial shit" (even as I continued to sneak in listening to some Biggie, Jay-Z, Tupac, and Nas on the side). We went from listening to rap and mimicking the style and slang of our favorite artists to building knowledge.

Stakes Is High and later Wu-Tang Clan's *Wu-Tang Forever* and Gang Starr's *Moment of Truth* became blueprints for me in the last three years of high school. Posdnuos and Trugoy rapped about life in a way my friends and I could relate to. The album also inspired me to return to De La Soul's catalog and appreciate some lessons from *De La Soul Is Dead* and *Buhloone Mindstate*. Finally, I understood how the group's 1990s albums allowed young people like myself to be complicated individuals. I could put my nerdiness to use and learn more about hip-hop culture. And like De La Soul, I could be other things, too—I could be athletic, I could develop my aesthetic, I could also perform well in my classes, I could be more vulnerable, and none of my friends would see any of this contradictorily.

While "Stakes Is High" is the album's socially conscious anthem, we should not forget that Dave's solo track, "Itzsoweezee (HOT)," embodies the record's critical ethos and its appeal to positive change. On the song, Dave laments hip-hop's apparent shift from artistry to getting money. After shouting out allies and acknowledging his Haitian background, Trugoy sings about how we need to transform our values. Love, instead of money, Trugoy sings, should govern how we interact in the world. This is another moment where De La Soul reminds me of Dr. Martin Luther King, Jr., and his calls for Americans to abandon materialism (King cited materialism, militarism, and racism as the "evil triplets") in the years immediately preceding his assassination. In his last book, *Where Do We Go from Here: Chaos or Community?*, King asserted, "Violence has been the inseparable twin of materialism." To address materialism, as well as racism and militarism, Dr. King called for a "revolution of values" grounded in principles of love and the presence of economic and racial justice.

Trugoy's message on "Itzsoweezee" and the group's message throughout the album, in a small way, are consistent with King's arguments for a revolution of values.

"Itzsoweezee" is ironic. De La Soul samples the "Happy Days" theme song as background for the mellow, if not somber, track. Dave's lyrics are timely, with references to David Koresh and the siege in Waco (with someone in the music video reading the May 3, 1993, issue of *Time* magazine with Koresh on the cover in case you didn't get the reference). But most importantly, he admonishes rappers who adopted mafioso personas, maintaining that they do not run with any real gangsters and drug traffickers from Cuba or Colombia.

Trugoy's raps demonstrate a maturity, an understanding of one's priorities amid personal growth, including demonstrating success by means other than conspicuous wealth and consumption within a battle rap. He might be among the first rappers to brag about owning land outside the United States or, in his case, in the Caribbean, where he and his family share Haitian roots. Dave continues to reprimand rappers for their materialism, claiming they worshipped expensive cars instead of God.

The song's video is sunny. It also illustrates De La Soul's ability to produce art that presents the group's silliness while addressing serious topics. The group juxtaposes Dave's lament and call for change in rap with school hijinks. We all sat in class with De La Soul while others heckled and bullied them on "Me Myself and I," and the group crashed a school performance in "Fallin'." In "Itzsoweezee," De La Soul appears to be among the top of the rap class. Some Native Tongues make appearances—Monie Love serves as a hype woman. We also see Prince Paul and the Jungle Brothers sitting in a cafeteria. I also recognized Young Zee from the Outsidaz, Kid Capri, The Roots, Lords of the Underground, Pete Rock, and Organized Konfusion. Dave is the center of attention in the cafeteria as the others are socializing, putting "kick me" signs on the principal, some getting caught smoking in the bathroom, and mocking the cheerleaders trying to hold a bake sale.

If "Stakes Is High" was like De La Soul showing the Bat-Signal for the rest of the Native Tongues, then "Itzsoweezee" is a celebration of community. Everyone in the video seems to share a similar philosophy of hip-hop—refraining from the dominant commercial form of rap music. The viewer will not see any dramatic displays of wealth, conspicuous consumption, models, or gangster expressions.

Instead of a rap battle or a shootout, the video ends with a food fight among everyone in the cafeteria. Rather than engaging in mean-mugging, issuing threats, and bragging about their realness, wealth, and sexual prowess, everyone is having fun again. Dave reminds everyone of one of hip-hop's original mottoes—peace, love, and having fun.

While I call the song a lamentation, Dave also ends the chorus with a call for change—"We gots to rearrange that"—after remarking on how money and success can change people for the worse. He also punctuates the chorus by stating, "Gotta change how it's going down." One can glean what kind of change De La Soul would like to see in rap—creative artistry instead of music that is simply about chasing money. And, of course, rappers should be able to produce art with little to no interference from their record labels. Dave presents the problem and his call as a riddle. He states the problem when he sings, "If money makes a man strange," then he declares a restructuring of priorities within rap. But then he asks: What would drive the world if money, as a tool, would not? For Dave? Love, of course. But love wasn't the tool that drove the culture then; it was money, whether it was through conspicuous consumption or corporate drive for profits, which one could argue fueled the mid-1990s rap wars. As Wu-Tang Clan famously chanted, "Cash rules everything around me."

So, in a way, Dave's performance and the video illustrate his and De La Soul's utopian thinking regarding rap artistry. Years after the sampling controversies surrounding the group in the late 1980s, Dave often called for creative freedom in recording. Also, Maseo, Dave, and Posdnuos devoted songs on many of their albums to arguing for the old hip-hop ethic of peace, love, and having fun. But of course, De La Soul operated in a capitalist economy where money was the primary tool for wealth, capital, and power accumulation, consumption, and exploitation. There seemed to be no escape in the mid-1990s, especially with labels like Bad Boy taking over the airwaves and with the political economy of radio changing following Clinton's signing of the Telecommunications Act. As many rappers continued to chase money, De La Soul did what they did best—used their art to challenge the mainstream and to create new artistic and communal possibilities. "Itzsoweezee" reflected how *Stakes Is High* represented a model for more than healing, it was a blueprint for hip-hoppers to engage the world.

CHAPTER 5

Guidance for Change

"The art that we do is official . . . and we're not afraid to embrace the intelligence in what we do."

—Maseo

After dropping their statement album, *Stakes Is High*, De La Soul desired to return to their fundamentals. "I think we did all the complainin' on the last album," Maseo told Letisha Marrero in the September 2000 issue of *The Source*. "[*Mosaic Thump*] reflects a confidence, comfortability, just . . . us feeling good about where we're at this stage of our lives."

It had been four years since De La Soul dropped the defiant *Stakes Is High*. De La Soul's fifth album, *Art Official Intelligence: Mosaic Thump*, celebrated hip-hop culture. *Mosaic Thump* was a record full of sharp lyricism but with more fun and danceable tracks. Maseo's comments about confidence also underscored another theme for De La Soul as they entered the twenty-first century—they had built a legacy. They were on their way to creating a more sustainable career as rap royalty.

Not every rapper or rap group is fortunate enough to earn a living as a hip-hop artist in their thirties. The goal for them, as well as many artists, was to survive and persist. Maseo later said in a recent interview commemorating their May 16, 1996, concert at Tramps nightclub in New York City, "Once you're by your third album, you can pretty much see a decline in all the artists that put out records. And then some of them had another growth spurt. Out of the few artists that had a growth spurt, we were lucky to have one, and that was *Stakes Is High*." Consequently, the group took advantage of what they thought was their second lease on their careers. De La Soul pursued a "working-class" path in the industry. In addition to recording and dropping a few albums throughout the 2000s, they became one of the best live acts in rap. They continued to mentor younger artists in person and through their music. They sought to chart a more independent path in entertainment. Most importantly, De La Soul stayed the course creatively, keeping true to their ethos while demonstrating personal growth and more vulnerability in the face of the transformation of rap and the music industry.

"Real" Hip-Hop

Following *Stakes Is High*, the rap music landscape transformed immensely. The regional rivalries of the mid-1990s were no more after the traumatic murders of Tupac Shakur and The Notorious B.I.G. The rise of southern rap, following the popularity of OutKast, Master P's No Limit Records, and Cash Money Records, powered much of this new collaborative spirit. A new generation of rap artists and producers emerged in the late 1990s to modernize hip-hop's sound. No Limit's Beats by the Pound, Cash Money's Mannie Fresh, Ruff Ryders's Swizz Beatz, and Virginia-based artists like rapper, producer, and songwriter Missy Elliott, producer Timbaland, and The Neptunes forged sounds distinct from the sample-based boom bap tracks that dominated much of the 1990s. Even boom bap beat makers like DJ Premier began collaborating outside of rap, composing tracks for pop star Christina Aguilera and rap-rock band Limp Bizkit. Dr. Dre produced songs featuring former No Doubt singer Gwen Stefani. Yet, the transformation in rap's sound did not mean that beat creators abandoned sample-based production altogether. Producers J Dilla, Madlib, Kanye West, and 9th Wonder became staple producers for artists seeking an updated version of soulful boom bap.

The dissipation of the regional rap beefs did not resolve all divisions among rappers. The Native Tongues remained distant from one another. Although Posdnuos declared that the collective was back on "Stakes Is High," the Jungle Brothers were the only group to release music featuring members of De La Soul and A Tribe Called Quest. Q-Tip and De La Soul appeared on the track "How Ya Want It, We Got It" on Jungle Brothers' 1997 album *Raw Deluxe*. Then, in October 1998, I picked up a copy of *The Source* announcing that A Tribe Called Quest was breaking up after the release of their fifth album, *The Love Movement*. According to the group, they had grown apart and could not reconcile their creative differences. Q-Tip, Phife Dawg, and Ali Shaheed Muhammad would continue their music careers either as solo artists (Q-Tip and Phife Dawg released albums in 1999 and 2000) or in collaboration with others. Muhammad joined with singer and producer Raphael Saadiq, formerly of Tony! Toni! Toné!, and vocalist Dawn Robinson, former member of En Vogue, to form Lucy Pearl.

Also, another battle over what constituted "real" hip-hop ensued following Tupac's and Biggie's deaths. Some in hip-hop media perceived a chasm between hip-hop's commercial rappers and the culture's underground in the late 1990s and early 2000s. Following De La Soul's lead on *Stakes Is High*, rap artists on both coasts began releasing music criticizing commercial rap for its materialism and perceived lack of lyrical skills. Yasiin Bey (known then as Mos Def) mocked Puff Daddy's conspicuous sampling of songs on his rendition of Slick Rick's "Children's Story," appearing on *Mos Def and Talib Kweli is Black Star* album in 1998. After releasing their debut album on Rawkus Records, Company Flow broke up, and rapper and producer El-P founded the record label Definitive Jux, which declared itself "independent as fuck." This perception was my reality as many of my friends and I outwardly embraced "underground" rap artists and groups like those artists signed to Rawkus Records (co-founded by one of Rupert Murdoch's sons) like Mos Def, Talib Kweli, Pharoahe Monch, and Company Flow. I listened to other independent artists like J-Live and west coast groups such as Jurassic 5, Dilated Peoples, Blackalicious, Zion I, and People Under the Stairs.

These artists responded to this moment of excess and bloat in rap music. As artists felt compelled to fill space on CDs, albums got longer. Following Tupac Shakur's lead, Biggie (posthumously), Bone Thugs-N-Harmony, Wu-Tang Clan, Master P, and Jay-Z all dropped double albums between 1997 and 2002. Instead of allowing a few guest appearances, artists stacked their albums with tons of guest artists and posse cuts. Displays of wealth in rap videos, in photo shoots, and at awards shows grew more extravagant. And, to the dismay of many rap fans, including myself, rappers and producers made those "shiny suits" commonplace in their million-dollar videos.

Rap's underground continued the culture's tradition of organizing against racism. On February 4, 1999, four plainclothes NYPD officers shot and killed twenty-three-year-old Guinean Amadou Diallo as he returned home from getting food. The officers, members of the NYPD's Street Crimes Unit—Sean Carroll, Edward McMellon, Kenneth Boss, and Richard Murphy—shot at Diallo forty-one times, hitting him with nineteen bullets. The officers, of course, claimed Diallo was an armed rape suspect who pulled a gun. However, Diallo, like many persons of color killed by police, was unarmed. After killing Diallo, they discovered he had reached for his wallet.

The older I grew, the more these instances of police violence affected me. While watching the LAPD beat Rodney King was horrifying, I still felt distant from his experience. I was ten years old at the time. Diallo's killing was the first I learned of an instance of police brutality and thought, "That could be me." I was at that age where I understood I was more vulnerable to police harassment and bruality. Mom's advice about moving in the world grew more specific—"Always be aware of your surroundings and who you hang out with," she told me. "Make sure you follow their instructions if the police approach you. Do not do or say anything. Your father and I will handle any situation with the police for you. You just have to be safe," she'd tell me. Mom also pleaded, "Remember, if you're around a bunch of white folks, the police will most likely focus on you. Please be careful."

I was eighteen years old when the NYPD killed Diallo, and it illustrated why Mom and Dad always told me to "be careful" every time I left the house. At the time, I thought Diallo wasn't doing anything wrong. The twenty-three-year-old was doing something many of us his age do; he was going to get some food to eat. How often did I leave the house late at night to go to the store? But the police suspected him of criminal behavior because of his appearance, and they killed a young man who was afraid of a group of men stopping him near his place in the middle of the night. This is why my parents told me to be careful. As a Black man living in America, you never truly know if you could be the latest casualty in the ledger of police killings.

Rawkus artists Talib Kweli and Yasiin Bey (formerly known as Mos Def) organized an effort to bring rappers and producers from all over the United States to record a four-song EP, *Hip Hop for Respect*. *Hip Hop for Respect* reflected the genre's new spirit of cross-regional collaboration permeating rap in the late 1990s and early 2000s. Kweli and Bey brought together Atlanta-based producers Organized Noize; Common, out of Chicago; Detroit's Invincible; Ras Kass, representing California; Florida's Dead Prez; as well as several east coast artists including Posdnuos.

Posdnuos appeared on the project's first single and video, "One Four Love Pt. 1." The title (One Four) reversed the number of times Diallo was shot at (forty-one) in a call for love and unity in the face of police brutality against Black people. Yet, the artists on the track—Shabaam Sahdeeq, Common, Talib Kweli, Kool G Rap, Rah Digga, and others—expressed little love for law enforcement. Shabaam Sahdeeq issued a warning that could have applied in 1989, 2000, or

2020, telling us that the police will keep killing Black folks. Sahdeeq then ended his verse with the question many Black Americans might still ask today—I am paraphrasing—Are the police killings of Black people by design?

Posdnuos closed the song with the same wit and tone he used on tracks like "Stakes Is High." He focused his verse on "everyday people" as he addressed poverty and police violence. I nodded my head as I watched Posdnuos rap about police "clapping" their guns more than fans "clap their hands" in the music video. And I paraphrase again, Why do the police keep killing us?

Rawkus Records released *Hip Hop for Respect* in April 2000, two months after a jury found Boss, Carroll, McMellon, and Murphy not guilty of Diallo's killing. Of course, the verdict spurred more protests. The single, "One Four Love Pt. 1," got some radio and airplay on MTV and BET. It also appeared on the *Billboard* music charts. Yet, the song and EP did not spur a larger movement against police violence among notable rap artists.

"If De La Were to Do That It Would Have to Be a Triple-CD"

Going bigger and dropping a double album seemed to confirm a rapper's or a group's status in the genre. And, in De La Soul's typical fashion, they wanted to one-up the competition. Instead of dropping a double album, Posdnuos, Dave, and Maseo would record and release a triple album. Dave told *Billboard* in July 2000, "The idea of doing a three-CD series was a joke at first." He continued, "At the time we began recording, a lot of artists were releasing double-CDs, and someone said that if De La were to do that it would have to be a triple-CD. So it became a challenge to us. And we love challenges." But Tommy Boy Records CEO Tom Silverman and the group thought releasing three separate albums over the year was a more financially sustainable plan for their new series.

De La Soul named their new series *Art Official Intelligence*. Maseo explained to the *New York Times* that the series' title reflected the group's creative ethos: "The art that we do is official. . . . And we're not afraid to embrace the intelligence in what we do." Dave told *Billboard* that the name referenced the turn of the century. "Regarding the series title," Dave said, "we wanted that new-millennium feel. . . . We didn't want to be gimmicky, but it was a great play on words." The first installment, *AOI: Mosaic Thump*, signaled a shift in theme and sound. The "mosaic thump" described the album's party vibe. "This album isn't what people will expect from De La Soul, but it's real catchy," Dave reported, adding that "Mosaic Thump" signaled that the group would combine their intelligent lyricism with undeniably bumping beats. It was a similar formula to A Tribe Called Quest's on *Low End Theory*. What do we remember when we think of *Low End Theory*? Phife's and Q-Tip's insightful rhymes over bass-driven, thumping beats.

Naturally, *Art Official Intelligence* plays on artificial intelligence. When we think of artificial intelligence, or AI, as we now call it, we typically think of the future, usually dystopian as portrayed in movies like *Blade Runner*, the Terminator franchise, and *The Matrix*. For De La Soul, *Art Official Intelligence* referred to the group's creativity and commitment to creating authentic, sonically innovative, and lyrical rap music. De La Soul produces music that's artistic, official, and intelligent.

"Seeing More of Your Kind"

I graduated with a 2.4 GPA average from Mansfield Senior High School in June 1999 amid these transformations in rap music. I joined my friends in enrolling at the local branch of The Ohio State University and prepared to attend college. Honestly, I just went to college because my parents had preached that as my destiny throughout my teenage years. Mom and Dad worked in factories in the 1990s and always expressed wanting me to do something "better than them." My parents' desire for me not to "end up working in a factory like us," as Mom and Dad often put it, reflected their beliefs in the American Dream. For me to become a professional meant even more to them as Black baby boomers than to me at first. I was pretty aimless. I didn't know what I wanted to do with my life. Maybe I wanted to teach high school? I did not have any clue. "But also, how many of us knew exactly what we wanted to do at eighteen?" I thought.

One day in my senior year of high school, a friend asked, "Austin. Would you ever try to work in the music industry?"

I said, "No."

"How would I?" I thought. I didn't rap or produce, nor did I have any desire to. I lived in Mansfield, Ohio, not New York City, Chicago, or Los Angeles. Although location did not stop some of my peers from trying to pursue a career in music.

As I began college, I did what many of my peers did—I enjoyed my newfound freedom. This mostly included keeping up with rap music—buying *The Source* and *XXL* magazine issues, attending concerts, and listening to and processing the latest releases with friends. Hip-hop culture excited me much more than anything else happening in my life.

But, one of my best friends, who was white, began the process of disrupting my complacency. After my first day of classes, he asked, "How do you feel about not seeing more of your kind?"

"What?" I responded.

"Yeah, um, there aren't too many other Black students. How do you feel about that?"

I felt ashamed because I did not have an answer. "How could he notice this while I didn't?" I asked myself.

It would still take me a few years of goofing off before I rediscovered my love for history. However, my friend's inquiry planted a seed that professors and I would water until it inspired my engagement in campus and community activism.

"What the Hell Is an MP3?"

I began my time in college as society approached the precipice of a technological revolution in media and music. In the same month as my high school graduation, nineteen-year-old Shawn Fanning released an early version of Napster as the first public peer-to-peer file-sharing network. Napster was accessible to novice computer users like me—all one needed was internet service to download the program and set up an account. From there, users could download various digital files, especially video and sound files like MP3s. Our hard drives captured these files and served as a repository for others to download. Consequently, users found ways to download pirated copies of artistic and cultural materials—music, movies, and television shows. Little did I know how revolutionary this development would be for myself, other music fans, and for the media industry.

I learned about MP3s for the first time after reading an issue of the *College Media Journal New Music Report* magazine sometime in 1999. I picked up the issue because of Neil Drumming's cover story discussing the emergence of underground rap. Then, I noticed a short profile of Public Enemy written by journalist Brian Coleman.

"Wow, Public Enemy is about to release another album," I thought excitedly.

Yet, that was not the most intriguing piece of information. Coleman's article contained the announcement that Chuck D and Public Enemy had signed a new deal with Atomic Pop, which was "a full-service company whose online home (www.atomicpop.com) not only represents the record label, but also includes an online CD store" and that they would not just sell copies of Public Enemy's new album, *There's a Poison Goin' On* . . . on CD, but also "non-traditional formats as A2B and MP3, which allow the music to be downloaded digitally, and zip disks, 100-megabyte 'floppy' discs playable on your computer."

"What the hell is an MP3?" I asked myself.

GUIDANCE FOR CHANGE

According to Jonathan Sterne in *MP3: The Meaning of a Format*, the file is the third version of the MPEG-1 sound file. It's a compressed .WAV file. The terms "A2B" and "MP3" seemed foreign to me. Nevertheless, Chuck D's explanation of the impact of digital music intrigued me. He believed artists' ability to sell digital music copies could be revolutionary. Coleman quotes Public Enemy's front man: "The [internet] allows a kid who has a .8 percent chance of getting signed to become their own record company and get into the game." Chuck D then declared, "You have to overstand the system to overthrow it," and Coleman elaborated, "With Public Enemy leading the way in online music distribution, that artistic coup d'etat may take place sooner than the major labels want to admit." The revolution might not be televised, but it would be digitized. I was excited for this.

As technological change in music bubbled beneath the surface, De La Soul released their fifth album, *Art Official Intelligence: Mosaic Thump*, on August 8, 2000, a few weeks before I entered my second year of college. Unlike their two most recent albums, *Mosaic Thump* did not feature a guiding theme besides making listeners groove to sharp lyricism over bouncy beats. Like many albums released at the turn of the century, the group worked with more artists on this project than any other. De La Soul's fifth album offered a new sound due to collaborating with producers like Rockwilder, J Dilla, and Supa Dave West.

Keeping with the theme of heavily featured albums, De La Soul presented a record celebrating hip-hop's past and present. The record boasted features from the Beastie Boys, Xzibit and Tha Alkaholiks, Pharoahe Monch, Black Thought from The Roots, and fellow Native Tongues affiliate Phife Dawg, formerly of A Tribe Called Quest. They also recruited legendary soul singer Chaka Khan for a track.

Again, *Mosaic Thump* was about having fun. The album included feel-good tracks like the aspirational "U Can Do (Life)" and the romping Dilla-produced "Thru Ya City." De La Soul connected with fellow 1980s veterans Mike D and Ad-Rock from the Beastie Boys on the old-school and b-boy–inspired "Squat." Of course, *AOI: Mosaic Thump* appeared at the end of the "shiny suit" era, and De La Soul made their commercial splash with their lead single, "Oooh." Produced by longtime De La Soul collaborator Prince Paul and featuring Redman on the hook, the song showcased the group's return to their more playful selves. Dave and Posdnuos punctuated the lyrics with a shot at the "shiny-suit rappers and flossin' emcees." In contrast with the extravagant rap music videos featuring rappers showing off their luxury vehicles and jewelry, throwing money around, and pouring alcohol on women, De La Soul spoofed *The Wizard of Oz* in the song's video. Maseo, Dave, and Posdnuos played the Cowardly Lion, Scarecrow, and the Tin Man as they accompanied Rah Digga's Dorothy on her journey to finally get into "Brick City," a club in the video, but also the nickname for Newark, New Jersey. The video also featured Redman playing Oz and comedian Dave Chappelle, who played the club's doorman.

On the last two tracks, De La Soul returned to their own experiences to offer some cautionary tales about dealing with or escaping violence. In "The Art of Getting Jumped," the group recounted various times they'd encountered violence. Posdnuos referenced the attack he'd suffered at the hands of Naughty by Nature's Treach while performing. At the end of the song, Maseo recounted how he got jumped by a racist Turkish gang while on tour. Rapper Freddie Foxxx joined Maseo on "You Don't Wanna B.D.S.," the lone song Maseo raps extensively on, where he, as a hip-hop elder, sternly warns other rappers of the perils of resorting to the deadly violence that plunged the culture and genre into darkness only a few years prior. From *De La Soul Is Dead* to *AOI: Mosaic Thump*, De La Soul went from the young aggressors trying to demonstrate their hardness to seasoned veterans who might still defend themselves but had outgrown the fisticuffs.

Mosaic Thump and its follow-up, *AOI: Bionix*, responded to the emergence of neo-soul music. Artists like Erykah Badu, D'Angelo, and

Jamiroquai helped fuel the resurgence of soul music at the end of the twentieth century. Within a few years, this style matured into a form that reflected a bohemian connection to 1960s and 1970s soul music. Neo-soul artists also collaborated with rap producers like Questlove, DJ Premier, and J Dilla, and lyricists like Common, AZ, Redman, and Method Man.

The Soulquarian movement personified the neo-soul tendency. This collective included The Roots, Erykah Badu, D'Angelo, Bilal, J Dilla, Common, as well as instrumentalists like Roy Hargrove and James Poyser. While many of these artists had either built or were building thriving careers in music, they began collaborating on each other's albums while recording at Electric Lady Studios in 1997. The Soulquarians were probably the closest to the Native Tongues in tone, aesthetic, and sensibility. They drew from Black diasporic style and literature and sought to push boundaries in R&B and rap.

De La Soul were not members of The Soulquarians, but with the help of producer Supa Dave West, De La Soul crafted a sound somewhat resembling neo-soul. The group still utilized samples, but some tracks on *Mosaic Thump* like the Dave West–produced "U Can Do (Life)" and "Copa (Cabanga)" featured a bounce not heard on previous albums. It is true that "Ring Ring Ring" took elements from the popular R&B sounds of the early 1990s, but their later songs like the Chaka Khan–assisted "All Good?" as well as "Held Down," featuring Cee-Lo, and "Am I Worth You?" from their second AOI installment, found De La Soul going to the soul and R&B well more than they had before.

"A Deck of Cards"

The political events of the early 2000s were enough to erase the political naivete with which I entered college. I voted in my first presidential election a few months after De La Soul released *Mosaic Thump*. Until this point, my political consciousness centered more on antiracism than anything else. I paid only cursory attention to party politics toward the end of the 1990s. Unfortunately, the 2000 presidential election changed this.

I was infuriated when the Supreme Court decided the outcome of the electoral contest between Vice President Al Gore and former Texas governor George W. Bush in the latter's favor. I held a vague understanding of the electoral college, but my twenty-year-old mind kept thinking, "How was this fair and democratic? Gore earned more votes than Bush." I did not think about it any more profoundly than that. I knew some of my friends had voted for Ralph Nader, but I never blamed them. Bush would have won Ohio no matter what. And they did not possess more power than the five Supreme Court justices who decided to stop the recount in Florida. Something, to me, was amiss with our political system.

Then came the morning of September 11, 2001.

I usually slept with my television turned on. The television's sounds always distracted my brain enough to allow me to sleep. While many Americans watched scenes of planes flying into the World Trade Center that morning, I remember waking up, seeing and hearing something about an attack on the TV, and thinking I was dreaming. I went back to sleep. Then I woke up and realized what I'd seen and heard was all too real.

Growing up, I'd learned to be skeptical of US foreign policy because of my mother's conversations about international relations in her Air Force days. That morning, I walked upstairs to find them talking about the attack. Mom was never a jingoist. She and Dad expressed sadness for the lives lost, but she also retained her critical perspective. She intimated that the United States was not as innocent as it presented itself to be. As the news of the terrorist attacks roiled on, I jumped in my car and drove to the local independent music store, CD Jungle. It was Tuesday, and I needed to get Jay-Z's and Killarmy's latest albums.

The September 11 attacks did not provoke any patriotic expressions or reflections from me. I was not raised that way. And while I had not developed any intellectual framework for understanding

US foreign policy, a friend and I considered there had to be more to the attack than "they hate our freedoms." Of course, I did not think of 9/11 as some "inside job" or anything like that. That seems preposterous. But in a phone conversation with a friend later that day, we both expressed skepticism of the idea that we were attacked by essentially evil forces. Rather, we speculated that these attacks were probably a response to the political and historical context of the region where US and foreign meddling was central.

President George W. Bush responded to the attacks by invading Afghanistan and launching the "War on Terror," taking aim at al Qaeda, a non-state organization with its roots in the Soviet-Afghanistan War in the 1980s, as well as Saddam Hussein's regime in Iraq. The US War on Terror initiated the longest ground war in US history and the invasion of Iraq, which turned out to be a strategic mistake for the US forces.

The September 11, 2001, attacks changed US foreign policy and shattered American innocence, as it was the largest attack on the country since Pearl Harbor. The US response to the strikes intensified Islamophobia in US politics and law enforcement. It also derailed the burgeoning leftist anti-globalization movement that had disrupted the 1999 WTO meetings in Seattle, Washington. The attacks legitimized a neoconservative approach to foreign policy emphasizing preemptive military action and openly advocating for regime change instead of relying on Cold War–era clandestine military and intelligence strategies to prevent democratic movements and communists from taking power in other countries.

Rappers acknowledged the attacks on the World Trade Center on September 11 and the War on Terror in their music. Some, like Paris, Immortal Technique, Dead Prez, and Nas, responded by criticizing President Bush and US foreign policy. Others, like Ghostface Killah, responded more in tone on songs like Wu-Tang Clan's "Rules," emphasizing pride in New York City as their hometown rather than wrapping themselves in the flag.

Yet, September 11 did not stop capitalism. Weeks after the attack, President Bush tried to convince a scared American public to participate in the economy. "Get down to Disney World in Florida. Take your families and enjoy life the way you want it to be enjoyed," he urged in a September 28th speech. American businesses also sought to encourage a "return to normalcy" after the disaster. General Motors and Ford Motor Company offered interest-free financing for their vehicles. Sony Music rushed to produce a patriotic-themed compilation album. Steve Madden partnered with actor Denis Leary to produce American-themed shoes to help the families of firefighters who died on 9/11. However, journalists David Barstow and Diana B. Henriques questioned whether the effort was a ruse since none of the families saw any money. The shoe company kept more than $400,000 in profits. In response to questions about the sneakers' proceeds, CEO Jamie Karson responded, "The most patriotic thing we can do . . . is make money." Eventually, Steve Madden donated a portion of its profits to Leary's foundation.

Nearly a month later, Apple CEO Steve Jobs delivered a presentation that revolutionized the tech and music industries while greasing the skids for consumption after 9/11. Wearing his signature black turtleneck, Jobs paced the stage explaining Apple's next technological wonder. He explained, "Music is a part of everyone's life. Everyone. Music's been around forever; it will always be around. This is not a speculative market. It's a very large target market all around the world." He then showed the crowd a white object the size of "a deck of cards" that could hold more music than anyone could imagine. The iPod weighed less than seven ounces but held five GB of storage. Instead of rewinding cassette tapes in our Sony Walkmans or trying to keep our Discmans from skipping, we could store hundreds of albums on one device. I was unaware of Jobs's announcement at the time, but I would've recognized it as a game changer if I had known about it. Still, I continued to carry my CD player for a year or two longer.

The iPod not only accelerated the disruption of the music industry brought on with the availability of "free music" created by the advent of Napster and CD/DVD burners, but Apple getting into the music game cracked open the door for tech companies and eventually record labels to create an alternative to music piracy. As capitalist corporations always seek to do, they tried to absorb aspects of an underground economy they could profit from, especially when criminalizing all participants became costly and futile. Two years later, Jobs and Apple announced the creation of their music store and software—iTunes. Apple would sell digital versions of albums that record labels licensed. We were on our way to separating the sound of music from its materiality—from the cassette tape, vinyl record, compact disc, and other tangible aspects of physical media that historically made some music panoramic pieces of art.

Trying People

AOI: Bionix arrived months after the September 11 assault and Jobs's announcement. The follow-up to *Mosiac Thump* was the group's most mature and spiritual album. Maseo, Dave, and Posdnuos produced a "grown man rap" album a decade and a half before Jay-Z released *4:44*, Nas dropped his *King's Disease* and *Magic* series with producer Hit-Boy, and Phonte gave us the second of his two solo albums. On *Bionix*, De La Soul continued an honest exploration of themselves, their spirituality, and maturation, which coincided with one of the most existential events in US history.

While De La Soul's AOI albums were in dialogue with the neo-soul movement, they also stood apart from the trends coursing through rap at the time. Of course, one would not call the group commercial, but they also resisted being labeled "underground" or "backpack." Posdnuos brags on the opening track, "Bionix," that the group appealed to everyone, not just underground fans who desired complicated rhymes. As Posdnuos declared on the track, De La Soul did not have anything to prove to any super lyrical rapper; they were among the first to set new trends in rap. Posdnuos did not necessarily criticize much of the dense, heady, lyrical rap one would hear if they attended independent rap showcases like Lyricist Lounge or Los Angeles's Good Life Cafe. Still, he reminded listeners how De La Soul sought to appeal to all rap listeners' senses—by crafting songs featuring clever, playful, and thought-provoking lyrics and laying them over creative, soulful beats. For De La Soul at the turn of the century, rap was not just about impressing cipher spectators in Washington Square Park; it was about making good music, period.

De La Soul did not abandon the celebratory and playful tone of *Mosaic Thump*. "Simply" and the Beatles-inspired "Simply Havin" are infectious party tracks. On "Peer Pressure," Cypress Hill's B-Real, producer J Dilla, Dave, and Maseo try to convince Posdnuos to smoke weed.

The album's first single, "Baby Phat," with Devin the Dude, mobilizes the Native Tongues's playfully flirtatious approach in the group's body-positive ode to women. In what could be seen as a more mature version of "Buddy," Posdnuos and Dave articulate their acceptance and appreciation of women without body shaming them. Posdnuos approaches the topic with a sensitivity we had not heard from him before, as he assures women that he does not care about the weight of his lovers. Dave even admits to having a larger frame himself. And while he and Posdnuos exchange verses about the diversity of bodies and images of beauty, they sensitively ground their lyrics in the acknowledgment of the pressure that patriarchal society places on women to be thin. Dave assures women that it's okay for them to pursue the body image they desire.

The video is probably the group's best example of reflecting contemporary trends. The visual features the group dancing in a club among women of various sizes. Posdnuos, Maseo, Dave, and everyone else in the video are wearing designer clothes. Of course, the song and video contain contradictions in De La Soul's inclusiveness—there's a scene where the club bouncer lets a woman know she might be too thin to get in while women of various sizes and racial and ethnic backgrounds are dancing inside. Where is the line between objectification and acknowledging the diversity of women's bodies in a patriarchal society? Honestly, I do not have an answer. Yet, no one would argue that we live in a society that is not just obsessed with thinness as a reflection of beauty, but that is organized structurally around it, from narrow plane seats to blood pressure cuffs that are too short to job discrimination. In other words, we live in a fat phobic society, and De La Soul tried to address fat phobia in their own way.

It is important to note, however, that De La Soul's approach to women was always mixed. While Dave and Posdnuos rap about body positivity on "Baby Phat," *Bionix* also features "Pawn Star" and "What We Do (For Love)" with Slick Rick, which are horny, like many of De La Soul's songs. But both tracks come off as awkward as the group offers raunchy imaginings of partners as porn stars.

Bionix also features some of the group's most pensive and existential songs. On his reflective solo track "Held Down," Posdnuos returns to the themes of individuality and extending "tough love" to rappers found on *Stakes Is High*. Assisted by Goodie Mob's and Gnarls Barkley's Cee-Lo Green, Posdnuos dedicates his first verse to the individuality cultivated in the "not-so-ideal" environments of working-class Black and Brown youth. He laments how his life decisions and pursuit of his artistry may have stirred jealousy and back "stabbin'." In the next two verses, Posdnuos tries to articulate the struggles of staying on the right path—dealing with failed friendships and personal indiscretions. What's interesting about "Held Down" is that it continues themes the group rapped about on their first three albums—individuality and ego—but Posdnuos turns these ideas onto himself. In another mark of maturity, rather than critiquing other rappers' egos, he turns the song into a lesson of how his ego might have contributed to the struggles he experienced and the baggage he accumulated. Posdnuos flipped the group's critique of egos on *Buhloone Mindstate* onto himself.

Cee-Lo's chorus punctuates Posdnuos's ode to charting one's own path. The singer-rapper laments about a long-standing theme in Black music—how one needs to beware of the jealousies of those closest to them. Friends and former associates might be the ones to "bring you down." The chorus also harkens back to the dilemma regarding "being down"—that some would try to hold you back, to remain in your orbit, because if one ascends too far, then, to paraphrase Benny the Butcher, not everyone can go. The chorus also continues De La Soul's critique of the emphasis placed on "being down" found on songs like *Stakes Is High*'s "Down Syndrome."

De La Soul organized *Bionix* with "Trying People" as a culminating point. The Fifth Dimension sample that forms the beat for "Trying People" is actually previewed in the album's "Intro" and before "The Sauce." "Trying People," like many of De La Soul's singles, appears on the back end of the album. It starts with a phone message from an associate asking to hear the track because of how highly Maseo spoke of it. Their friend ends the message sighing with anticipation.

"Trying People" exemplifies De La Soul's vulnerable masculinity during national crisis and personal reckoning. The track is a lesson in dealing with the realizations of aging, experiencing change, and facing one's mortality. The beat is good but not overpowering. Dave's and Posdnuos's lyrics form the song's centerpiece.

If Posdnuos stole the show on "I Am I Be," Dave shines on "Trying People." For a man in his early thirties, he sounds more like a weathered veteran as he asks some of the existential questions we ponder as we grow older and move into middle age. Dave wonders whether he has peaked and if the rap game has passed them by. Dave's verse on "Trying People" is about time—the struggles of aging; the desire to travel back in time to correct mistakes; the fear of missing out, or FOMO; how time moves quickly as one gets older; and how one wants to be remembered when they are gone.

GUIDANCE FOR CHANGE

Dave answers the question of what he wants his legacy to be in his moving verse—he wants everyone to know that he developed his art, performed, and served as a leader in hip-hop "for us."

In "Trying People," Dave says something in his verse that was difficult for many men, let alone Black men, to express openly, especially in rap. He raps about crying. And he admits that he wanted to embed himself in loving relationships. "Trying People" was unlike LL Cool J's "I Need Love." Do not get me wrong, "I Need Love" is an important example of a macho rapper willing to risk credibility to show his vulnerable side. But "Trying People" was bigger than that. Rather than lament the loss of love within hip-hop culture like he did on "Itzsoweezee," Dave admits it was time to address the lack of it in his life. Therefore, he declared he was willing to take the plunge.

Many of us are part of loving communities, partnerships, and friendships. Some of us straight men not only have a hard time admitting it, but we struggle to change our behaviors so that we align ourselves with that goal. Hence, De La Soul asks themselves, us, and the kids participating in the hook, "People, are you ready?"

In his verse, Posdnuos continues his confrontation with his limitations as a father and partner that he articulated on "Held Down." He references the loss that often accompanies aging, making mistakes, and losing relationships, romantic and otherwise. Posdnuos uses the song to process how he grew apart from friends as his career progressed. Posdnuos continues letting listeners into his personal life as he describes a major contradiction in his life at the time—he, Dave, and Maseo could travel the world to play to thousands of adoring fans, while his significant other was not one of those fans. His rap career strained his partnership past the point of repair. Working as a professional hip-hop artist gives and, in Posdnuos's case in the early 2000s, it had taken away.

Posdnuos's verse is rife with references to a struggle for balance—how experiencing professional success and a degree of socioeconomic mobility can strain relationships and friendships; the desires to maintain their artistic ethos, and the necessity of producing music and touring for money; and the pressure of needing to balance work life, especially a career dependent upon touring, and a life at home with a partner and children.

I often identified with Posdnuos's verse, but not necessarily because I thought I dealt with interpersonal strife with friends. I would be foolish to insinuate such a thing. Even so, we all know what it feels like to grow apart from longtime friends. We all take different paths—some pursue careers and build families sooner. I decided to work toward earning a doctorate in history. And I pursued this goal single-mindedly, sometimes to the detriment of family relationships, friendships, and romantic relationships.

But at times, I understood Dave's desire to start charting my own path. A health emergency in early 2002, during my third year of college, shocked me further out of my complacency. At the end of the winter quarter, I contracted mononucleosis. I remained functional, or at least I thought. I continued going to class and working because I grew up in a household where my parents went to work every day—no matter what. I thought I was doing the same. Soon after my diagnosis, I started experiencing intermittent stomach pains. My discomfort grew so bad that I went to the doctor. He told me that I suffered from an "inflamed abdomen." I didn't understand what that meant, nor did he really offer any advice to treat it.

Then, during finals week, I woke up feeling ill. I thought I had just contracted a cold or the flu. I dragged myself to the bus stop to attend my Native American History exam. Later, I felt nauseous as I struggled to answer exam questions. I even got up to go to the bathroom because I thought I was on the brink of vomiting. I completed the exam and then dragged myself back to the bus stop. "I can't wait to go home and take a nap," I thought. I did just that.

Then, I woke up in the most excruciating pain. My stomach hurt so bad that I could not stand straight up. I crawled to my housemate's room and told him I needed to go to the hospital. He drove me to the emergency room, and we waited for what seemed like hours. Eventually, the doctor told me that my appendix had ruptured, and I would need surgery as soon as possible. "Whatever," I told him. I just wanted the pain to end.

Mom arrived as I sat up in a hospital bed in intense pain and vomiting all over the place. I forget how she found out I was sick, but she left work and drove an hour to the hospital. Eventually, Dad and my sister, Brandenn, visited. Then, after I got out of surgery, my girlfriend at the time and some of my friends came through. I never cussed around my parents, not even after I entered my thirties, but apparently, I was in so much pain that I cussed out everyone until the doctor prescribed me a morphine machine.

While hospitalized, I learned a tough lesson about staying the course. I spent nearly a month in the hospital, walking around the floor and pondering what I wanted to do. After finally getting out, I returned to Mansfield to complete my bachelor's degree in History. It was probably my best decision, leading me to become a historian and activist.

As I reignited my love of history, my understanding of the past, the present, the United States, and the world expanded. I spent more time reading, researching, writing, and talking about theory and historical phenomena like capitalism, socialism, colonialism, racism, feminism, and classism with my graduate student friends, peers, and professors. Yet, the more I engaged in intellectual work and activism, the further away I grew from my working-class upbringing in Mansfield. My community shrank. Pursuing a life of the mind gets lonely.

Although somber, "Trying People" continues De La Soul's commitment to adapting. Yet, instead of the self-deprecation of "Me Myself and I," or the self-righteousness of "I Am I Be," De La Soul crafts "Trying People" as a confessional and motivational song encouraging listeners to "try" to change. The song is a sonic mark of maturity. The song is about change. "Trying People" refers to those who seek to confront their limitations, fears, and desires with honesty. To try, for Dave, Posdnuos, and Maseo, means to express a willingness to change. And it is okay if we do not fully get there because the point is to try. "Trying People" refers to the people who persist, those who refuse to allow the world just to pass them by. "Trying People" is about those who approach life with more grace.

A Taste of Freedom

As De La Soul prepared the third AOI album, Tommy Boy Records ended its nearly twenty-year partnership with Warner Music Group. CEO Tom Silverman announced that he'd started a new venture, Tommy Boy Entertainment, focusing more on dance and electronic music, and singles. De La Soul's fate and that of Handsome Boy Modeling School, Prince Paul's and Dan the Automator's group, were now in limbo as Warner allowed its labels to court them and other Tommy Boy rap acts they retained.

Posdnuos told rapper and podcast host Noreaga, in a May 2019 episode of his *Drink Champs* podcast, that Elektra Records expressed interest in bringing in De La Soul. The group met with Sylvia Rome and began discussing a possible partnership. However, Posdnuos and the rest of the group realized that they would most likely cede creative freedom if they signed with Elektra or any other major record label. "Rome wanted Timbaland to produce all of our next project," Posdnuos told Noreaga. A Timbaland-produced De La Soul album is an interesting what if, considering the group would be working with one of rap's top commercial producers. Nor was such a collaboration too out of the box, considering that the Virginia producer worked with Slum Village, the Detroit-based descendants of the Native Tongues, on the remix to "Disco." Yet, what would signing to Elektra and working with Timbaland cost De La Soul? At that time, fans and critics might have interpreted that decision as a compromise in the group's principles. For Posdnuos, Maseo, and

Dave, it seemed that if they allowed a record label to determine who they would work with, the group would be giving up their creative freedom, which was a hallmark of all of their projects.

Since De La Soul was unwilling to compromise on their artistic and creative principles, they were left without a label home. Still independence is what De La Soul desired and wanted. It was a logical outcome of their careers. Instead of having to deal with Tommy Boy or another label pressuring them to produce hit songs, another "Say No Go" or "Me Myself and I," De La Soul could now control everything financially and creatively—the production, who appears on their records, and the singles. "[Going independent] was the best thing that ever happened to our career," Dave confessed.

"Out Here Plowin' the Fields"

The Grind Date was De La Soul's seventh, and first post–Tommy Boy album, released on October 5, 2004, a month before George W. Bush won reelection and as the music industry remained in the doldrums. They signed a label deal with Sanctuary, owned by Beyoncé Knowles's father, Matthew, and created a subsidiary label, AOI, named after their previous two albums. With the help of producers Supa Dave West and J Dilla, and with features from Common, DOOM, Flava Flav, Ghostface Killah, Yummy Bingham, Butta Verses, and Carl Thomas, De La Soul returned to familiar themes on *The Grind Date* such as personal growth, demonstrating their lyrical prowess, and critiques of materialism. Dave, Posdnuos, and Maseo also focused on securing their legacy.

The album's title references grind culture or the belief that one must constantly work to get by. Hip-hop culture always trumpeted grind culture as many songs centered on hustlers staying up all day and night to make money. The Clipse popularized grind culture by releasing "Grindin'" in 2002. Lyricists Pusha T and No Malice (formerly known as Malice) defly used metaphors referencing stereo speakers, nursery rhymes, and windmills as they rapped about selling crack cocaine over The Neptunes's stripped-down, cafeteria table–pounding beat.

In De La Soul fashion, they emphasized the working-class aspect of grinding, at least in the context of the music industry in the 2000s. As record sales declined over the decade, rap stars such as Dr. Dre, Diddy (formerly Puff Daddy), Birdman, and Jay-Z, who all ran or oversaw major rap record labels, were on their way to becoming the genre's first moguls. The mid-2000s was the era of "get rich or die tryin'." Rappers made major moves. Artist 50 Cent made news after earning a 100-million-dollar payout when Glaceau sold vitaminwater, a product the rapper endorsed, to Coca-Cola. Jay-Z sold his clothing company, Rocawear, to Iconix International for 204 million dollars. Dr. Dre and Jimmy Iovine founded a headphone company, Beats by Dr. Dre, which eventually grew the former N.W.A member's net worth by hundreds of millions. *Forbes* started tracking rappers' wealth in 2007 as hip-hop created more multimillionaires. Lyricists like Eminem, Snoop Dogg, and Kanye West soon joined the annual *Forbes* list of wealthy rappers. Consequently, groups like De La Soul had to grind to earn a living—record and sell music, peddle merchandise, secure endorsements, and most importantly, fill up their calendar with shows, which required nonstop travel.

Of course, Dave, Posdnuos, and Maseo probably earned more than most working-class people, but in the context of the music industry, De La Soul were "working" artists—they were not part of the top ten percent of rap artists who consistently sold millions of albums and raked in millions more in tour revenues and endorsements. De La Soul, like other artists such as The Roots, Dilated Peoples, KRS-One, and Curren$y, relied upon a combination of releasing more albums, touring constantly, doing endorsement deals, and finding other streams of revenue to make a living off their artistry.

Like all their releases, De La Soul's album packaging tells *The*

GUIDANCE FOR CHANGE

Grind Date's story. The album booklet is a twelve-month calendar documenting the group's obligations—photo shoots, concerts, interviews, and studio and other appointments. The calendar illustrates the taxing nature of a performing artist's agenda, with the group traveling throughout and outside the United States. Of course, the absence of off days underscores De La Soul's grueling schedule.

The title track is a monument to working-class life. Rapper Chaundon's spoken-word introduction captures one of the basic tenets of capitalism—the system compels people to work to support themselves and their families. One did not have to like the work, but they had obligations to fulfill. "People gotta go out there and bust they, bust they ass for a job. I mean, my dad got five kids. . . . He hates drivin' a bus, but he loves [his] five kids," Chaundon explains. Posdnuos deploys working-class metaphors comparing rapping to farming, "Keep my John Deere out here plowin' the fields," to describe his devotion to earning a living through his artistry. Posdnuos also addressed the state of De La Soul's relationship with Tommy Boy Records in sexually graphic terms, stating that the group had "got jerked by Tom and his boys. Came on my land, seized my cattle, and catalog." The group's Tommy Boy catalog of music, from *3 Feet High and Rising* to *AOI: Bionix*, could have been primary sources of income for them had it not been for industry restructuring. Posdnuos's reference also foreshadowed the group's struggle to control their music in the next decade.

De La Soul historically had a tenuous relationship with Tommy Boy Records. But, *The Grind Date* might have been the first time the group addressed the situation surrounding their catalog through their music. The group failed to secure their master recordings upon leaving since they got tied up in Tommy Boy's sale and absorption into Warner Music. De La Soul might have achieved label freedom, but as Posdnuos's critique of Tommy Boy illustrates, the group had not entirely escaped their masters.

In discussing the grind, Dave devoted his verse to outlining what it took to achieve longevity in rap. Dave and the group started learning about the trappings of the music business from their first recording contract. Dave also nods to "Potholes in My Lawn" and his early career experiences learning about the industry. The rap game was the neighborhood in which De La Soul lived, and other rappers would defecate on their lawn. Dave raps about how labor under physically punishing conditions ages a worker, even rappers who must keep up a taxing schedule.

De La Soul's *The Grind Date* spoke to my working-class upbringing and reality. I never aspired to be a recording artist, but I could relate to having a demanding schedule, especially as a college student. Holding down multiple jobs that might have added up to a full-time job, or grinding, was a way of life. Most often, I held two or three jobs at a time during the school year. On campus, I worked in the Student Union and as a tutor in the Writing Center. Off-campus, I labored part-time at the YMCA. I also finally got the call to work at CD Jungle. (They never took applications for new hires.) I also worked full-time at a drug and alcohol treatment facility for teenage boys. I performed this job while pursuing a master's degree in African and African American Studies at The Ohio State University. This was a way of life, at least, until I could earn a degree and hopefully start a career, which is what my parents always wanted. As a teenager, I'd learned that I could never identify with artists like Nas, Jay-Z, Lil' Kim, Tupac, or Biggie because I never envisioned myself chasing wealth. But I could identify with working-class artists like The Roots, Little Brother, People Under the Stairs, and De La Soul.

While I went to school and worked multiple jobs, I never had it as difficult as my parents, working day in and day out in factories while trying to care for us. The toll this type of physical labor took on my parents and workers in general became real the night of December 19, 2003. I was sitting on a desk talking with my friend Darrick when I received a frantic phone call from my sister.

"Mom collapsed. We had to call the ambulance. We're going to the hospital."

GUIDANCE FOR CHANGE

"Oh shit."

I jumped into my car and drove to the hospital as fast as I could.

When I got to Mom's room, it was like a family reunion; everyone from her side of the family was present—her mother and her siblings. I believe our older brother, Jeff, was also in the room. I'll never forget hearing Mom screaming in pain. She vacillated between yelling in agony and saying, "I don't want to die." She even started talking as if she was at work on the assembly line. The doctor told us she had suffered a ruptured cranial aneurysm, and she would have to have surgery right away. "She may not be here tomorrow," the doctor said bluntly. "She has about a fifty/fifty chance of survival." My brother and Dad were angry at the doctor's blunt, matter-of-fact tone. "How could he talk about another human being like that in front of their family," we said, gasping in shock.

Unable to process what was happening, I retreated to my car. I sat there in the parking lot, thinking about how terrible capitalism was. "Mom was about to die, and her mind took her to work," I fumed. Her delirium did not bring her comfort. Capitalism consumed her bleeding mind. Some conservatives try to blame "Marxist" professors for "indoctrinating" us into anti-capitalist and socialist philosophies. Watching my mother talk about work while writhing in pain converted me. That experience planted the seeds for me to become more of an activist and labor historian.

Mom survived the surgery but remained in the hospital for more than a month. Dad and I did not always have the easiest relationship. However, Mom almost dying and our having to keep all of the bills paid started us on the path toward smoothing everything over. Dad also contracted pneumonia and had to be hospitalized while Mom recovered. I will never forget the time my sister and I went to visit both of my parents in the hospital. Mom had someone wheel her over to Dad's room, and the image of them talking to each other while wearing hospital gowns never left me.

I talked with Mom about my future as soon as she was well

enough to interact with people and function more normally. While sitting in the hospital cafeteria, I asked: "Hey, Mom. Maybe I should take off from school to help around the house so you can focus on your recovery?"

Mom was not having it.

"No. You do not quit school. I will be fine. I worked too hard for you to do that."

I sat beside her in disbelief while she ate, but Mom truly believed that it was her duty to sacrifice herself for my sister and me. Consequently, I started earning the best grades I had ever received in high school or college and resolved to pursue graduate school. As hip-hoppers said then, I got back on my grind.

Church

On *The Grind Date*, De La Soul continued the mature themes found on the AOI albums. They offered spiritual counsel to their peers and listeners on a track aptly titled "Church." After an introduction from director Spike Lee, who informs us that the alternative song title is "It's Reality," the group raps about the perils of materialism in hip-hop over a soulful 9th Wonder beat. "Church" builds on many of the themes found on *Stakes Is High*. Dave and Posdnuos advocate for creative individualism in their shared voice, urging them to cultivate and use their unique voices. But as Dave uttered on the *Stakes Is High* track "Long Island Degrees," where he admitted there was nothing wrong with rappers spending a little money, in "Church," he advises his peers and listeners not to let the cash blow up their egos, using a reference to Jesus Christ feeding the 4,000 with seven loaves of bread and a few fish.

Following the album's labor theme, Chaundon punctuated "Church" with an economic analysis of rap music. "You know what I mean? Rap outsold crack," Chaundon declared. He then proceeded to echo a Busta Rhymes speech where the latter advanced

GUIDANCE FOR CHANGE

an ironic argument about the genre: "Busta was the one that came out on—on the award show and said that hip-hop is the only thing that provides jobs for people that don't even love the shit." I have yet to find the exact source of the quote, but the substance and Chaundon's parting words were salient in the mid-2000s. Rap music had long become the best-selling genre in the United States, helping to sustain the music industry. Seeing rap and hip-hop culture become more acceptable and immensely profitable, corporate America began enlisting its aesthetic in its advertising and marketing of all types of products—primarily fast food, technology, clothing, sneakers, fragrances, and vehicles. And as rap music became ubiquitous, De La Soul defended hip-hop's artistic integrity.

In their efforts to carry the torch for boom bap rap, De La Soul offered two of their signature songs, demonstrating the group's commitment to making serious head-knocking music, and also that there are times when a producer crafts a beat so well, it threatens to outshine the artists' performance. J Dilla's sped-up flip of L.T.D.'s "Love Ballad" on "Much More" and Jake One's "Rock Co.Kane Flow" are examples of those types of tracks. Still, Posdnuos and Dave are not the type to be outdone by a producer. After a DJ Premier introduction on "Much More," Dave drops on a dime, "Yo! It's been instilled in me since infinite, y'all." Both Dave and Posdnuos rap about De La Soul's contributions to rap music. In fact, the sampled and sung hook references how the group had given listeners "much more than they can see." De La Soul's contributions to hip-hop culture were outsized yet often overlooked if one is only judging by album sales and what was hot at the time. The group revolutionized album construction, blended genres, popularized skits and aliases; positioned themselves at the vanguard of one of rap's most creative collectives; and boosted some of rap's biggest artists, like Mos Def and Common, who became stars.

In the video for "Much More," filmed during their appearance on Dave Chappelle's hit show *The Chappelle Show*, the group continues their working artist theme—Posdnuos, Maseo, and Dave enter a tour bus with Chappelle and Yummy Bingham. Dave steps onto the tour bus like a superhero, wearing an Incredible Hulk arm (because he started referring to himself as Dave Banner), rapping his verse with Chappelle, nodding and vibing to the track.

"Rock Co.Kane Flow," with DOOM (formerly known as Zev Love X and MF Doom), features Posdnuos, Dave, and DOOM rapping over a Jake One–produced track. In the era of early 2000s "coke rap," the three veteran emcees possessed the skills to spit rhymes as addictive as the purest dope. Each lyricist punctuated his verse by rhyming on the beat of Jake One's chopped sample of the electronic group Space's "Deliverance." "Now quit now before we pour that sure shot pure rock cocaine flow," Posdnuos warned at the end of his verse.

While "Rock Co.Kane Flow" represented De La Soul's first collaboration with the mercurial DOOM, their careers ran parallel. They were also kindred spirits. Daniel "DOOM" Dumile was born in London, and his family migrated to Long Island. He and his brother Dingilizwe formed K.M.D. in the late 1980s. Performing as Zev Love X, Daniel appeared on rap group 3rd Bass's single "The Gas Face," featured on their 1989 album, *The Cactus Album*. K.M.D.—Zev Love X and DJ Sub-Roc—released their debut album, *Mr. Hood*, two years later, a day after De La Soul dropped *De La Soul Is Dead*. Tragedy struck the Dumile family as K.M.D. neared completion of their follow-up album, *Black Bastards*, when DJ Sub-Roc was killed after a driver struck him with their car. Sub-Roc's death and Elektra Records' decision to drop the group drove Zev Love X out of rap for a few years. Daniel, like De La Soul, responded to life's challenges by reinventing himself and leaning into otherworldly creativity. Daniel changed his life, and hip-hop, when he donned a metal mask and popped back up on the scene as MF Doom, named after the Marvel Comics character Doctor Doom. DOOM embarked on a more than two-decade

GUIDANCE FOR CHANGE

legendary run of rap projects starting with *Operation: Doomsday* in 1999. DOOM appeared on *The Grind Date* before releasing an underground classic, *Madvillainy*, with producer Madlib.

DOOM deployed his signature flow and his clever use of metaphor in his verses, acknowledging his overlooked longevity, letting rappers know that he's been in the game since they were popping wheelies. DOOM employed the type of food metaphors he organized on his forthcoming *MM . . FOOD* album in his second verse, as he referenced Fruit Loops and eating rivals for breakfast.

Posdnuos's last verse touches on various themes related to aging, death, and the stresses of carrying on a long rap career. Posdnuos's first line hits hard with its realism. I did not want to think about anyone from De La Soul passing on or the group breaking up, especially several years after A Tribe Called Quest's split. However, Posdnuos deftly outlines what he believed was necessary to obtain longevity in rap—a willingness to sharpen their rough edges lyrically and physically after *3 Feet High and Rising*, never chasing trends, and staying committed to their creative individuality. Posdnuos also references his and other rappers' experiences with being pushed to the margins of rap after dropping classic albums. "Everyone cools off from being hot. It's about if you can handle being cold or not." This was not only prescient for rap artists who successfully pursued decades-long careers in a genre typically seen as a playground for the young, but it was a road map for long-term relevance—stay true to your creative ethos, even in times of change. Does this mean that one should not innovate but always have a North Star? De La Soul followed theirs through every artistic endeavor, musically or not.

Dave caps the track by mocking the idea that rappers in their thirties were too old to perform. As Jake One's hard track descends into its chopping piano and drumbeat, Dave robotically spells out his birthday—September 21, 1968—and the two-line syllables sit on each chop, "Too old to rhyme. Too bad. Too late."

LIVING IN A D.A.I.S.Y. AGE

Dilla

Almost two years following the release of *The Grind Date*, J Dilla, one of De La Soul's most trusted collaborators, passed away. I had read about some of Dilla's health struggles, but I had not fully understood the severity. Those who attended his concerts saw him perform while sitting in a wheelchair. Dilla died of complications of TTP (thrombotic thrombocytopenic purpura) and lupus. Dilla experienced incredible and excruciating bad luck since TTP was a rare blood disease and proved even more debilitating when combined with lupus. But as I learned soon after Dilla's death, African Americans were statistically more likely to develop lupus because of one's genetic disposition and triggers such as stress and UV radiation. Also, socioeconomic factors shaping many Black Americans' lives, such as the lack of access to adequate health care, can affect chances of survival. I had not heard of either disease until the producer's death. While many rappers died from gun violence, Dilla was one of the few rappers who died too young from more "natural" causes. This became a theme in hip-hop culture in the 2010s, touching many of our favorite acts, even De La Soul.

Dilla had been instrumental in helping the group redefine their sound. His tracks "Stakes Is High" and "Much More" set the tone for their respective albums, *Stakes Is High* and *The Grind Date*. The producer provided the group with bangers on the AOI series as well. According to Maseo, De La Soul owed some of their longevity to Dilla's contributions. Maseo said in his Red Bull Music Academy lecture that Dilla "definitely helped carry De La Soul past the tradition of, by the time you make your third album, your career will be over. Well, he helped us beat the odds."

Feel Good

De La Soul offered another outside-the-box contribution a couple of months after Dilla's death. British rockers Damon Albarn and Jamie

Hewlett formed a "virtual" rock band, Gorillaz, featuring animated members 2-D, Murdoc Niccals, Noodle, and Russel Hobbs. Existing in animation, the group recorded their self-titled debut album in 2001. They returned in 2005 with *Demon Days*, which featured the De La Soul–assisted first single, "Feel Good Inc." The groovy track features Maseo laughing in its introduction and two verses by Dave.

Thinking about the Gorillaz concept, the song, and the video, one can see how such a collaboration was unsurprising. The concept of creating and performing as a fictional band existing in animation probably appealed to De La Soul's sense of artistic imagination, even Posdnuos's love of comic books. With their lyrics boasting the title, "Feel Good Inc.," 2-D and Dave offer a bleak picture of corporate capitalism producing a conformist culture. Ironically, De La Soul represents Feel Good Inc. in this case, the corporation seeking to trap everyone in a prison of conformity. In the song, Dave spits a haunting verse bookended by sinister laughs. It is hard to say whether Dave was thinking of the history of corporative divestment in cities like Detroit, but his reference to how companies would ghost Motown references not only Berry Gordy moving Motown Records to Los Angeles in the early 1970s but also how corporations divesting from cities like Detroit after World War II fueled population decline. If we go back to De La Soul's critiques of commercial and corporate rap on *Buhloone Mindstate* and *Stakes Is High*, we recognize how the themes in songs by Gorillaz and De La Soul converge.

If "Feel Good Inc." is about producing a corporatist and cultural prison, it is also about pursuing freedom. The music video demonstrates the binary of stifling conformity and freedom as 2-D performs in a narrow high-rise tower called "Feel Good Inc." During the chorus, viewers see Noodle playing her guitar while sitting on the edge of a floating landmass powered by a giant windmill. The windmill is a metaphor for love, partnership, and community. Powered by wind, of course, a windmill could turn forever, like love. Love can power partnership. And, in an optimistic reading of humanity, it can power community, society, and country (embodied in territory or land) infinitely. While 2-D hypnotically repeats "feel good," the listener might notice that the seeds of liberation lay within the contradictions of the system. In his verse, Dave admits that 2-D could kill the Feel Good corporation. 2-D's bridge, on the other hand, suggests love might also represent the key to freedom. If everyone focused on love rather than serving Feel Good Inc., which suggests short-term gratification, then maybe the windmill might power everyone toward liberation. Love is an infinite power. I can imagine De La Soul, especially Dave, believing in such a notion considering the lamentations about love he articulated on songs like "Itzsoweezee."

"Feel Good Inc." represented an unlikely return to the pop music mainstream for De La Soul. The song helped power *Demon Days* to number 41 on the *Billboard* 200 chart. The video earned two MTV Music Video Awards. Also, the Gorillaz and De La Soul earned a Grammy Award in 2006 for Best Pop Collaboration with Vocals. "Feel Good Inc.," with its ironic title, illustrated that veteran groups like De La Soul could retain mainstream appeal without compromising their ethos.

Building a neoliberal society emphasizing extreme commitments to individualism, market fundamentalism, and global capitalism after the Cold War, or during the Reagan-Bush-Clinton-Bush era, underscored the construction of a one-dimensional society that "Feel Good Inc." critiques. The height of neoconservative foreign policy and the near uniformity of support for the wars in Afghanistan and Iraq stifled popular dissent and contrary views on US foreign policy. The Bush administration went so far as to suggest that if one opposed the war, they were "un-American." While the war in Iraq generated the largest antiwar protests since the Vietnam War, they failed to generate the type of news coverage we would eventually see amid the Movement for Black Lives, the Women's March, the March for Our Lives, as well as the pro-Palestinian protests. Instead, we saw laws passing and adopting policies curtailing our civil liberties, such as the Patriot Act, and establishing "free speech zones" wherever President Bush visited.

GUIDANCE FOR CHANGE

The failed occupation of Iraq and a series of racist incidents pierced the one-dimensional society that the president and his allies tried to build. As many of us protested what we believed was an illegal war based upon fabricated charges, we learned that exporting American-style "liberty and democracy" was more difficult than the pro-war conservatives and liberals had imagined. And incidents like the Jena Six case and Don Imus calling Black Rutgers women basketball players "nappy-headed hoes" reminded us that colorblindness was a lie. The racism and classism embedded in the Bush administration's botched response to Hurricane Katrina, as well as the mainstream media's coverage of the event, reminded us of the farcical nature of colorblindness. But it would be Chicago rapper Kanye West, one of hip-hop's brightest lights in the aughts, who pierced this colorblindness when he said during a televised benefit for Katrina survivors that "George Bush doesn't care about Black people." While West's frank words left actor Mike Myers and many other white Americans stunned, the Chicago rapper had said what many Black Americans were thinking.

The economy did not seem great, at least in my hometown. Businesses and factories continued to shutter. The latter reflected a larger trend in industrial job loss as the United States lost close to six million manufacturing jobs. This led Robert Atkinson to call the 2000s "a lost decade of manufacturing" in a March 2013 *IndustryWeek* article. Then, as Bush touted the "ownership society," mortgage lenders took advantage of Americans' desires to achieve their dreams of homeownership by extending subprime mortgages during the mid-2000s. This scheme blew up in financiers' faces in 2007 as the housing bubble burst and sent the global economy reeling.

While rappers adopted 50 Cent's "Get rich or die tryin'" ethos in the 2000s, De La Soul stayed the course—they found a semblance of independence within the industry and produced music true to their creative ethos. Yet, unlike their first three albums, no one called *Mosaic Thump*, *Bionix*, and *The Grind Date* all-time great classics. Neither did the group revolutionize the sound of rap music. De La

Soul, unlike many of their predecessors, just remained consistent. The three albums indeed contained missteps. But the group made up for their creative imperfections by producing music that confronted their imperfections and anxieties. Rather than allowing themselves to get lost in the shuffle like many of their peers from the 1980s and 1990s, the group stayed relevant by becoming some of hip-hop's best live performers, mentoring and teaming up with newer rappers and producers, forging strategic collaborations with Nike, and working with like-minded artists outside of rap.

I learned to adapt to change and, as Dad used to say, "keep pushing," during the 2000s. I endured a lengthy hospital stay and finally found my calling as a historian and activist. I graduated college three times—earning my BA in history and an MA in African and African American Studies from Ohio State. I finally left my parents' house permanently and went to Kent State University to pursue another MA in history. Our dad, Brandenn, and I focused on Mom's recovery as she lost movement on the right side of her body and was forced to learn to live with her disabilities. Mom no longer moved and functioned with her usual intensity but worked to regain as much of herself as possible. She learned to write with her off-hand; adopted new hobbies to keep her mind sharp, like assembling puzzles; and spent much time watching Ohio State football and basketball with Dad. Like De La Soul and the rest of us, she was "trying people," and life became more about staying the course.

CHAPTER 6

We're Still Here

"People say all the time, 'Well, nobody, nobody can do this no more. Nobody makes music like you. You can't do this like nobody can save hip-hop.' And it's like, yeah, we're that nobody."

—Posdnuos

You're not growing if you've never experienced an existential crisis. It forces us to look back, examine ourselves in the present, and look forward. It is part of the human process of enduring and embracing change. Traumatic events like an unfortunate medical diagnosis, a once-in-a-generation pandemic, or the death of a loved one could spark an existential crisis that leads us to inquire—"What are my priorities?" "Am I on the right path emotionally and spiritually?" "How much time do I have left?"

Like many musicians, rap artists have used their art to tackle such fundamental questions. De La Soul's *Stakes Is High* explored rap's crisis as Dave, Maseo, and Posdnuos questioned the direction of rap music in the 1990s. When it comes to rappers considering their life at a crossroads, one of my favorite albums is Gang Starr's *Moment of Truth*. Guru and DJ Premier dropped their fifth album two years after *Stakes Is High*. At the time of recording, Guru faced a multi-year jail sentence and the breakup of their heralded group. *Moment of Truth* was a make-or-break album for him, professionally and personally. He responded by channeling all of his angst, revelations, and personal struggles into the project, which is often considered one of the group's best.

After three decades in the rap game, De La Soul encountered their moment of truth.

And the Anonymous Nobody is the group's most existential album. Posdnuos, Dave, and Maseo articulated complicated feelings about their work, aging, and mortality. Sadly, the group's ruminations on these issues in documentaries, interviews, and on their last album foreshadowed the untimely passing of one of its members.

The past fifteen years of De La Soul's journey had been marked by their tenacious campaign to reclaim the rights to their first six albums. This was a time when streaming services were revolutionizing the music industry landscape. Their struggle with Tommy Boy Records and Warner Music over ownership of their catalog not only shed light on the efforts of major pop artists like Taylor Swift to safeguard their creative output but also raised pertinent questions about musicians' role in a rapidly evolving industry now dominated by tech giants.

The group's work during the 2010s represents the logical outcome of De La Soul's creative ethos—they embraced personal growth and change. They doubled down on their vulnerability as Black men and leaned further into exploring their limitations and anxieties. This emotional depth in their music allows us to connect with their personal journey on a deeper level.

"Post-Racial"

If De La Soul spent the 2000s charting an independent course in the industry and solidifying their legacy, the group entered the 2010s with the same defiance and quirkiness they displayed in decades past. It was the Obama era. In November 2008, tens of millions of Americans did the unthinkable and voted for an African American for president. I watched the historic moment on TV in my apartment in Kent, Ohio, where I lived while I pursued another MA degree in History at Kent State University. As the networks called the election for Barack Obama, I phoned Mom to talk with her.

"He won!" she said excitedly. "Yes! We have a Black president."

All I could say was, "I know," and think about one of my first political memories: hearing Mom and Dad complaining about how Reverend Jesse Jackson would have been president if more white folks had supported him. Now, my parents, especially Mom, had lived long enough to see white people help elect an African American. Obama supporters erupted in elation across the United States. Kenyans celebrated.

Hip-hop rallied around Obama's presidential campaign, sounding more hopeful than it ever had. Nas and Common praised Obama in songs like "Election Night" and "The People." Atlanta rapper Young Jeezy released another celebratory song with Nas, "My President Is Black." Obama's election also diverted rappers, who were historically critical toward elected officials, into politics. Jay-Z urged his listeners to vote for Obama at concerts. He also organized events and appeared at rallies for the president-elect. Later, President Obama invited many other artists to the White House, as performers and as discussants of policies.

Some white commentators and politicians declared that the United States had finally shaken off its racist past and had become "post-racial." I was skeptical of the idea that the United States had become colorblind or anything of the sort. I never believed that Obama's victory would erase racism and the historical legacies of enslavement and Jim Crow. But, no one living in the 1950s could have fathomed a Black person accomplishing such a feat. We had taken a step. Little did we know what was in store in the coming years, namely the persistence of structural racial and economic inequities. These events reminded us of Dr. King's adage that progress never ran straight. The growing polarization, the racist backlash within the

Tea Party movement, the "birther" attacks, and vigilante and police killings of Black people underscored how the empire struck back.

I entered the doctoral program in history at the University of Michigan nearly nine months after Obama's inauguration. I planned to continue my studies of US and African American history. While I continued to listen to and follow rap music, I probably grew more intellectually distant from hip-hop culture than ever in the few years following my arrival in Ann Arbor. I also gave up doing activist work, at least for the first few years because I was too busy to focus on anything else with my classes, papers, events, and other happenings on campus. I wanted to become the best historian and teacher I could be.

Like many who enter doctoral programs, I encountered growing pains. The first couple of years felt like an existential crisis. I had to get used to working alongside other students who'd achieved at a much earlier age than I did. I also had to continue to navigate being one of the few Black graduate students in the department. I was one of three Black men (a fact about which some other Black graduate students expressed astonishment) in my cohort, but I was often one of the few, if not the only Black graduate student in most of my classes. Unfortunately, I had to navigate microaggressions from white and non-Black students and professors, one of which liked to point out the fact that I was Black and that she thought I only studied race. After helping organize a recruitment lunch for prospective graduate students, I wrote an email to the coordinator suggesting that the students enjoyed the lunch and that we should continue to have such events to show we valued diversity, and the professor responded by saying the department had already done a good job when it came to issues of difference. Still, neither I nor many students of color I spoke to shared the same view as him. Then there were the times when I had to remind non-Black classmates that we did not share the same cultural references because I was Black. I didn't come from the middle class. I might have been a PhD student, but my family was working class and I was still hip-hop.

WE'RE STILL HERE

"Get Away from Here"

In 2012, Posdnuos and Dave returned to music, but not as De La Soul. They linked with French DJs and producers Chokolate and Khalid for a concept album, De La Soul's *Plug 1 & Plug 2 Present . . . First Serve*. By then, I'd learned to expect the unexpected from De La Soul, and *First Serve* was no different. Recording under their longstanding monikers "Plug 1" and "Plug 2," Posdnuos and Dave use the album to tell a well-worn hip-hop story about two aspiring rappers, Jacob "Pop Life" Barrow (Posdnuos) and Deen Witter (Dave), who try to strike it big in the music industry.

But the 2013 boom bap single "Get Away (The Spirit of Wu-Tang)" marked De La Soul's comeback in the 2010s. The group returned to some of the themes on "Stakes Is High" on this comeback single. Built around a sample of the Wu-Tang Clan's introduction to the second disc of *Wu-Tang Forever*, Posdnuos and Dave issue lyrical warnings to rap's newcomers. De La Soul wasn't going anywhere. Posdnuos reminded listeners of the group's legacy by reciting a refrain referencing the group's classic discography.

I was excited to hear some new De La Soul, and I understood the subtitle and the sample's reference to the Wu-Tang Clan. "Get Away" took me back to 1996 and 1997, when I was tired of Diddy and his production team, the Hitmen, sampling 1980s hits. My friends and I celebrated RZA's speech kicking off the second disc of Wu-Tang Clan's second double album, *Wu-Tang Forever*, calling out popified rap. We wanted more innovative art and music that we could relate to.

"Get Away (The Spirit of Wu-Tang)" was a twenty-first–century "Stakes Is High" as Posdnuos and Dave continued their critique of superficial mainstream rap. The music video was simple, yet abstract. Posdnuos, Dave, and Maseo performed lyrics and antics while contained in a Rubik's Cube. Posdnuos's and Dave's battle lyrics and the song's refrain, "Get away from here," were not necessarily complex, but the Rubik's Cube symbolized how few could fully understand the group's art. Some rap artists are three-dimensional. Three dimensions, though, were not enough for De La Soul. They worked in six.

On "Get Away," it was clear the group took aim at commercial rappers, but it was not as clear which ones. I doubt they were talking about anyone specifically. But I do not think it is coincidental that Drake was, at that time, one of the genre's most celebrated new artists. By the time De La Soul released the song and video for "Get Away," Drake had dropped his first two full-length albums, *Thank Me Later* (2010) and *Take Care* (2011). Drake fit RZA's description of rappers who tried to "take hip-hop and make that shit R&B." Drake even included a song named after Wu-Tang Clan's screed against "rap and bullshit" on his third album, *Nothing Was the Same*, called "Wu-Tang Forever."

On the surface, De La Soul seemed to go from "Potholes in My Lawn" to get off my lawn, especially with their refrain, "Get away from here!" Ironically, De La Soul acted not solely as rap's gatekeepers. Maseo, Posdnuos, and Dave were among the most accepting "old-school" groups. But De La Soul's acceptance of new artists does not mean the group believes that rap and hip-hop should not have standards, such as putting in the work, creativity, thoughtful lyricism, and embracing change. Adhering to those principles allowed De La Soul to, as Dave raps on "Get Away," continue "baking works of art" well into the twenty-first century.

"Even More Disruptive"

De La Soul planned "Get Away" to appear on their next album, *You're Welcome*. In the meantime, the music industry had yet to recover from its losses in the 2000s. While digital music stores like iTunes Music and streaming services such as Pandora first appeared in the early 2000s, the ability to listen to music exclusively on these platforms had not entirely caught on. It was not as though we still bought and listened to CDs, but in the early 2010s, there remained a sense that music consumers would still "own" their music.

Our relationship with music consumption shifted in a few short years. In the late 2000s and early 2010s, more Americans continued to purchase their music digitally. However, this changed in 2015 as streaming numbers doubled and this form of consumption overtook digital sales in the music marketplace. The ability of listeners to access vast music libraries for the monthly cost of a CD, or two, powered the music industry's recovery. "The engine that fueled the recovery was not the sales of downloaded songs, however—it was an even more disruptive technology, music streaming," music scholar Larry Wayte writes.

I have always been slow to change how I listen to music. I've always enjoyed its physicality—hunting for and buying CDs and the process of creating my mixtapes, mix CDs, and eventually playlists. While I had downloaded plenty of music, I still believed in buying hard or digital copies of albums by my favorite artists. I kept spindles of mix CDs at my parents' house and in my apartments until 2009.

Being able to access hundreds of thousands of songs on my phone blew my mind. But one initial flaw of the streaming services was that some platforms still did not include all artists' songs and albums. Initially, many major artists like Taylor Swift, Prince, Garth Brooks, and The Beatles refused to allow their music on streaming platforms like Spotify and YouTube. Some streamers like Tidal featured certain artists exclusively. One of the reasons why I subscribed to Tidal was so I could access Prince's catalog. And then there were the artists like De La Soul, whose music seemed conspicuously and mysteriously absent.

A byproduct of the rise of streaming, according to Rebecca Giblin and Cory Doctorow, authors of *Chokepoint Capitalism: How Big Tech and Big Content Captured Creative Labor Markets and How We'll Win Them Back*, is the newfound worth of artists' catalogs. Like those listeners who bought CDs to replace their vinyl and cassette tapes in the 1980s and 1990s, listeners now streamed music, their interests spurred on by this new medium. Sadly, copyright laws and old contracts trapped groups like De La Soul in legal limbo. Streaming did not necessarily render De La Soul invisible, as their post–Tommy Boy music did appear on services. Still, the digitization of music distribution and consumption threatened to erase their most celebrated contributions. Streaming became so dominant among new generations of listeners that if one could not find an artists' catalog on Apple Music, Tidal, or Spotify, it was as if they did not exist.

"Hearing the Music Is More Important than Paying for It"

On Valentine's Day in 2014, De La Soul announced they would make their whole catalog available for free—all fans had to do was sign up for the group's email list. I promptly did so. The group had found a way to reintroduce themselves to new generations of music fans near the twenty-fifth anniversary of their classic album *3 Feet High and Rising*. In typical fashion, Posdnuos, Dave, and Maseo described their gesture as an act of "love." De La Soul gave away their music because copyright laws prevented Apple from selling it on iTunes. Posdnuos told *Rolling Stone*, "We've been blessed to be in the Library of Congress, but we can't even have our music on iTunes."

This was not the first time artists encouraged their fans to bootleg their music. Bob Dylan, Bruce Springsteen, and Pearl Jam famously allowed their fans to bootleg their live shows. So many Grateful Dead fans have recorded the band's shows that the Internet Archive hosts a page containing over 17,000 concerts uploaded by the band's enthusiasts. While some artists like Adele and Taylor Swift refused to allow their music onto streaming platforms because they (and their record labels) were not making enough revenue, De La Soul preferred to give away their music for the love of their fans.

I was happy for fans to have access to De La Soul's music and to be able to understand why they were so beloved. I had not known the group's streaming situation until then. It never occured to me that De La Soul's albums weren't available on iTunes; I already owned all of their Tommy Boy Records albums on CD. And, of course, I had ripped digital copies and stored many of them on various hard drives. But like any good fan, I signed up for De La Soul's email list, twice—once under my first name and again under my middle name, Charles—and received two emails with the album links. I cannot remember whether I downloaded the albums. I signed up because I wanted to support the group.

As one can imagine, few people will pass on free music, unless it is the U2 album that iTunes forced on all of us who bought iPhones (*Songs of Innocence*, in case you forgot). Unlike U2's and Apple's misguided release, De La Soul's offer generated so much demand for the downloads of their catalog that it genuinely broke servers.

In the age of internet criticism, some thought De La Soul's giveaway was a wrong move. Journalist Laurent Fintoni criticized the group for offering what he considered an ill-conceived marketing gimmick, underestimating the high demand that led to crashing their servers, and, ironically, uploading presumably pirated copies of their albums for distribution. Fintoni pointed to a blog post written by web developer Matthew McVickar, who checked the MP3 tags and determined two of the albums De La Soul offered, *AOI: Bionix* and *De La Soul Is Dead*, originated from music blogs. And, in a serious case of snitching, McVickar linked to the blogs that offered those De La Soul records. Fintoni concluded, "Hip-hop is now in its 40s and while we continue to celebrate the anniversaries of various classic albums from the late 80s and early 90s, it would be good if the artists and those around them acted with more technical savvy, some genuine respect for audiences and less impersonal marketing impetus."

Fintoni's criticism of De La Soul's lack of "technological savvy" and "respect for audiences" seems to miss a point about the group and their efforts to get their music out to listeners. One thing that Fintoni and anyone who is familiar with De La Soul should know is that we should not always take them seriously. As communications scholar Kembrew McLeod told Geeta Dayal, who wrote about De La Soul's caper for *Slate*, "Given De La Soul's sense of humor, I think it would be entirely possible that it's an inside joke, a meta-commentary on the craziness that is today's music industry, when they can't even make their own music available through legitimate channels."

Also, Fintoni glossed over the real point of the giveaway. McLeod explained, "Perhaps the issue is as simple as De La or those around them not having access to all their masters, which is a likely but surely not insurmountable problem. Or perhaps someone wanted to make a statement about the complexities facing the music industry today and how consumption has changed." Again, I do not know what the group thought about how they would execute their marketing ploy. Maybe some could call it lazy. But the idea of a group that does possess control over the distribution of their music offering others copies of their content drips with a late capitalist irony that could only transpire amid the transformation from physical to digital media. De La Soul's willingness to grab their music from other blog websites also exemplified their understanding of music ownership—the music they produced was theirs, not another record label's. And, if they were aware they were taking the music from other "owners," they did not care. And, really, how many fans were checking the metadata anyway? I did not care.

Fintoni, McVickar, and other critics of De La Soul's giveaway failed to see the forest for the trees. The giveaway was a shot across the bow at Warner Music. De La Soul intended to gain control over their catalog in a campaign against Warner Music and Tommy Boy Entertainment. Like many political campaigns before and after, the group utilized one of the most essential organizing tools—an email mailing list. By convincing people to exchange their emails for access to the group's music, they created a tool to communicate directly with their fans and to mobilize them. Even if the servers broke, or the music was not CD or vinyl quality, De La Soul had accomplished something ingenious. They introduced themselves to a new generation of hip-hoppers. They also started a public conversation about sampling and the meaning of music ownership in the age of digital music.

Naturally, De La Soul's move caught the attention of Warner Music, and the corporation contacted the group to stop the caper. But the damage was done. An untold number of people downloaded De La Soul's music for free.

De La Soul's "botched" giveaway garnered some positive recognition. Two months later, Maseo, Dave, and Posdnuos earned the Best Artist Webby for their deed. The Webbys are awards presented by the International Academy of Digital Arts and Sciences (IADAS). Starting in 1996, the IADAS extended awards for the best websites and other internet-based ventures. The academy clearly understood the meaning of the group's caper. "But with a long stretch of Twitter trending, De La Soul showed its fans that hearing the music is more important than paying for it," the IADAS stated on their website. The Roots' drummer and pop culture historian, Questlove, presented Posdnuos and Dave with the award, informing the audience, "So *3 Feet High and Rising* has been preserved by the Library of Congress, but it's not available for sale. And this hurts the band, but it also hurts consumers, and it hurts history." Upon acceptance, Pos gave a concise speech—a five-word microphone check. "Check, check, testing, one, two." Dave offered a slight wave and the two exited the stage.

Freedom + Collaboration = Success or *We're Still Here (Now)* or "We're That Nobody"

I learned De La Soul was working on another album after reading a *Rolling Stone* story about the group launching a Kickstarter. It wasn't the *You're Welcome* album they'd announced at the release of "Get Away." Instead, Posdnuos, Maseo, and Dave were producing something altogether different. As per their creative ethos, they decided to change again—they were not relying on traditional sampling techniques used for their first several albums for this record. Rather, they recorded hours of jam sessions and then decided to sample those.

De La Soul's shift away from sampling past music was not the most revelatory news. It would be how they funded and executed their project. Rather than sign with a record label to release the album, De La Soul organized a Kickstarter campaign to raise funds to subsidize production, marketing, and distribution. Dave told DeMarco Williams, writing for *Billboard* in May 2015, "We didn't feel comfortable getting back in bed with a label and anybody sticking their fingers in. We felt like the people who have faith in our product without any questions would be fans. People are believing in us—you can't beat that."

In a time when many Americans turned to crowdsourcing sites like GoFundMe to cover medical bills, funerals, down payments, and to settle debt, the idea of musicians using the same method to cover the costs of recording was not surprising. TLC, another legendary group caught up in label and financial troubles, had successfully launched a Kickstarter campaign earlier that year, raising $430,000 after asking for $150,000. Since its launch in 2009, creatives have raised over eight million dollars via Kickstarter.

By turning to crowdfunding, Maseo, Posdnuos, and Dave wagered their twenty-plus years of good music and goodwill with their fans. Would the fans come through? Or would their Kickstarter fail?

De La Soul framed their campaign as one for creative freedom. De La Soul would bypass their struggles with record labels and the labels' dictates for radio-friendly music. Rather than relying on their sample-based production process, the group worked with a Los Angeles–based band, Rhythm Roots All-Stars, to avoid the "sample police." Their willingness to target the "sample police" represented a continuation of the group's populist ethos that defined their previous albums. The group stated on their Kickstarter page:

Here's the interesting part. We are now in the process of going back to that 200+ hours of music, listening, enjoying and discovering those special moments where, musically, something magical happens, where interesting sounds and layers were forgotten, where new sounds can be sampled, looped, chopped, filtered and arranged, freely, without the intrusive presence of publishing politics and the infamous "sample police." What we've done is created our own crates of records; album upon albums to mine and sample from. In our world, what we've created is freedom, freedom to make the art you believe in without having to compromise your vision. That's what we've always wanted most, that's what we've always believed in, that's what we've fought for, and that's why we're doing this Kickstarter with you.

The group elaborated on how Kickstarter fit into its anti-corporate philosophy in a wide-ranging interview on VladTV in April 2015. Dave pushed back after the host, Vladislav Lyubovny, also known as DJ Vlad, compared De La Soul's Kickstarter to Koch Records, another independent record company. "Fans invest in the Kickstarter for the group to record the album, but unlike Koch or any corporation, the fans don't expect a profit. The difference is a company, [or] corporation who's lending you money to profit from, [as] opposed to a . . . fanbase who just wants to hear your music," Dave argued. The group likened the corporate record label system to slavery, as Prince had done with Warner Music in the 1990s.

In the interview, De La Soul offered an astute analysis of the twenty-first-century music industry. They discussed how the digitization of music distribution and consumption enabled piracy, which conditioned listeners like me to devalue music's worth. Dave critiqued those of us who believed in "free music," explaining to Lyubovny, "A big part of it is cheap people and people who think everything's supposed to be for free." Instead, Dave, Maseo, and Posdnuos argued for a return to the public investment in art. De La Soul was, in essence, a private entity. However, they argued in their Kickstarter for a partnership with their fans that cut out the label and, ostensibly, minimized the record label's ability to advance demands on artists that might compromise their art. De La Soul confirmed their long-held belief that the profit motive represented one of the main driving forces constraining creative freedom. The answer was to bring the public, or the fans, on board as investors. As their Kickstarter stated: "Freedom + Collaboration = Success."

Some of the group's associates questioned De La Soul's Kickstarter campaign. Marketer Brandon Hixon told music journalist Shawn Setaro, "Kickstarter was weird to me, based on the fact that you could lose." He explained, "There's a huge downside to it if it doesn't work. So, I was afraid to put their careers on the line for this service." Group members also went out of their way to explain to journalists and interviewers that they were not "begging." Dave told DeMarco Williams, "There were reservations. It's not that we're broke—these things cost money. The fans aren't looking to loan it to you or get anything back. They want the album. It was the best thing to do."

De La Soul offered a smorgasbord of incentives to invest in their project—flash drives loaded with music; personal emails; CDs for contributing fifteen dollars or more; vinyl; apparel, including autographed pairs of the group's Nike Dunks; as well as experiences like shoe shopping with Posdnuos, toy shopping with Dave, record shopping with Maseo, and dinner with the group. When De La Soul launched its Kickstarter page on March 30, 2015, it hoped to raise $100,000. In hours, it raised more than that, and by May, it had raised more than $600,000.

The group released two documentaries as part of their rollout for the new album, *And the Anonymous Nobody*. *De La Soul Is Not Dead*, produced by Mass Appeal, introduces the group to a new generation. It takes viewers through De La Soul's history—growing up in Amityville, working with Prince Paul, working with Tommy

Boy Records, and recording their first four albums. *We're Still Here (Now) . . . A Documentary about nobody* featured various guests, including Common, Tom Silverman, and the Gorillaz's David Albarn. *We're Still Here (Now)* was the most intimate display of the group's album production, marketing, and selling. The documentary illustrates the fundraising process through Kickstarter. Scenes like the group discussing options for the rock solo toward the end of "Lord Intended," where some kicked around the idea of getting Zack de la Rocha or Chris Cornell, also demonstrate the collaborative nature of the production and recording of *And the Anonymous Nobody*.

The documentary focuses on De La Soul as working-class rappers decades into their careers. In a scene showing their "frickin" two a.m. show in Seville, Spain, Maseo discusses the physical and emotional toll of the constant traveling. "Traveling is tough," Maseo told Ed Lover in an interview. He continues, "One thing I just realized is . . . you're not going to like everything about what you love. There's going to be some warranted challenges." Maseo then admits that he was not the most present as a father due to the travel. "You got your real happy moments and you got your real sad moments. When you're away from home too long, you can get homesick. But then you know your reasons for your sacrifice. . . . Here it is. My childhood dream became my profession, but I had no idea the sacrifices that was going to come with it, you know, especially behind getting married, developing a family, and the times I'm missing from them just to be able to provide and to be able to do something so great, as well. It becomes a bit tough; it's an arduous process to try to sustain both profession and family. And to be perfectly honest, you have temptations of what we do that exist around this."

The documentary concludes with the group discussing longevity and reiterating the ethos they developed since they first started recording *3 Feet High and Rising* with Prince Paul. Dave explains, "It's the process. It's the vision of what we're trying to do here [as] opposed to who the stars are on the record. We're just people doing something cool here, man. We're not concerned about everything else. We're just trying to really do something impressive, innovative, and just different." Posdnuos returns to the record's title, "As well where you know you will have people say all the time, 'Well, nobody, nobody can do this no more. Nobody makes music like you. You can't do this, like, nobody can save hip-hop.' And it's like, yeah, we're that nobody."

The group demonstrates this sentiment on the album cover. In a cartoon illustration, a person holding a mic stands before an angry group. As people in the crowd throw objects, raise a middle finger, scowl, and yell their disapproval, the person states, "I am Nobody." To the left, someone is running away from the crowd, pleading, "What are you doing? Nobody can control them!" The visual really encapsulates De La Soul's careers as rap iconoclasts; their desire to not go with the crowd, whether this crowd comprises popular artists, certain fans, trends within the genre, or the rap industry. Also, the statement "Nobody can control them" is another double entendre. Throughout their careers, De La Soul has proven that nothing and no one—record executives, labels, or the market—could control them. But De La Soul, as "Nobody," have proven they could control any crowd at a show.

De La Soul's *And the Anonymous Nobody* arrived on August 26, 2016. The latest album boasted a guest list unimaginable during the pretentious era of the early and mid-1990s—Jill Scott, Snoop Dogg, Roc Marciano, Pete Rock, Estelle, Usher, 2Chainz, Little Dragon, and David Byrne; their album continues more of the mature themes that appeared on *Mosaic Thump*, *Bionix*, and *The Grind Date*. De La Soul also returned to a soundscape that mixed genres and songwriting structures. *And the Anonymous Nobody* mixed rap, R&B, funk, and rock music. (De La Soul said they tried to get Willie Nelson onto a track called "Unfold," but he declined.) The album featured five-and-a-half-minute-long songs with De La Soul rapping in the last thirty seconds, tracks with three-and-a-half-minute-long rock solos ("Lord Intended"), and a beat-switching track featuring Talking Heads vocalist David Byrne.

The album captures the group discussing topics related to their labor as artists and reckoning with personal pain, mistakes, and death. Following an album intro, "Genesis," featuring Jill Scott, the group presents its industry-critical side on the triumphant and jazzy "Royalty Capes." After hearing poetry serving as a reading of De La Soul's titles, as if we were listening to a scene from *Game of Thrones*, Dave and Posdnuos remind listeners of the group's contributions to rap lyricism. De La Soul not only uses "Royalty Capes" to claim their place among hip-hop sovereigns, but their reference to "royalty" also denotes the group's desire to get paid for their artistic labor. Posdnuos demands recognition as a rap sovereign and for record labels to pay them their royalty checks. Posdnuos explained the meaning of "Royalty Capes" in *We're Still Here (Now)*: "I mean, like, it just means that we've put in a lot of work, we've been blessed to be here to delegate and try things and learn, and we're considered royalty in a lot of people's eyes. We're royalty, but I also pay attention to my royalties."

On "Pain," De La Soul was able to pull Snoop Dogg into a moment of vulnerability, as well. Snoop reminisces about his gangbanging days and the early years of his rap career. He also acknowledges his transformation from Death Row gangsta to the pop culture icon who can be seen next to Martha Stewart. And Snoop admits that he now seeks to keep more of a clean image when he raps, "I'm into public relations." "Pain" is a song one can only feel once they are no longer in their twenties. This is not to say we do not experience adversity when we're younger, but one has to mature enough to develop the ability to turn pain into something productive.

Snoop Dogg and De La Soul would have been an unlikely pairing in the mid-1990s, especially at the height of the east coast/west coast rivalry. Yet, by 2016, both were considered legends who had survived much strife in and outside of rap—Snoop Dogg's acquittal in a murder case, leaving Death Row after Tupac Shakur's death, and beef with Suge Knight; De La Soul's struggles with fan and label expectations, the fracturing of the Native Tongues, Tommy Boy folding, and professional and personal relationships falling apart. Both were bound together by the pain they'd experienced and still turned into art. Also, of course, the collaboration came together because Snoop Dogg wanted to work with De La Soul. Posdnuos told the UK magazine *LeftLion*, "He'd mentioned . . . that we were one of the few hip-hop groups who'd come before him that he liked and he still hadn't worked with. We sent him the track and once he'd heard it then he told us he loved it and wanted to be a part of it."

Posdnuos returned to his struggles with infidelity on the unorthodox "Drawn." De La Soul demonstrates its willingness to continue to push the boundaries of songwriting on the track, which seems more like a five-minute-long Little Dragon tune than a De La Soul song. Of course, that is what the group wants listeners to think. The beat builds for five minutes and then De La Soul finally joins in, rapping about the necessity of moving on. Posdnuos punctuates his verse with an admission of infidelity much like he did on "Trying People." He then acknowledges how fame and fan adulation create a false sense of security and grandiosity. He concludes his verse by playing with the words "I'm mortal." If you take out the apostrophe and combine the words, one gets "immortal." Posdnuos is talking about how his fans deify him when referencing "I'm mortal." But, the rapper reminds everyone that an apostrophe should remain between the two "m"s. Posdnuos is a mortal person, or a broken vessel, like the rest of us. Any of us can succumb to temptation, depending upon the circumstances. Posdnuos's use of "I'm mortal" also brings listeners back to *Buhloone Mindstate* in that it highlights how fans' adulation can blow up their egos and make them unaccountable.

De La Soul earned its first number one on *Billboard*'s Rap Albums chart with *And the Anonymous Nobody*. The group now operated in a world where commercial success was defined, in part, by streaming statistics rather than sales. Listeners streamed *And the Anonymous Nobody* two million times in its first week.

De La Soul's eighth album earned mostly good reviews. In his review of the record for *XXL*, Riley Wallace acknowledged De La Soul's populist purpose for the record, "The 18-song project is everything fans could have hoped for—a real album for the people." The writer called the record "a refreshing listen, ripe with equal amounts of growth and consistency." *SPIN* magazine gave the album an eight out of ten and called it "one of their most ambitious and consistently rewarding albums." Conversely, journalist Kyle Eustice argued that the featured artists weighed down the album. "The album is bursting at the seams with high profile names, making it nearly impossible not to wonder if that's where most of the money went . . . this one feels more crowded, more complicated." Nate Petrin, writing in *Pitchfork* magazine's 6.4 review, saw *And the Anonymous Nobody* as a dour effort for a group presenting its first official project in more than a decade. "If your impression of 'old man rap' is short on energy and long on reflection, this album won't change that. . . . When it sounds tired and bummerish, it's more in keeping with the hazy enervation of contemporary Drake-casualty rap than the proto-backpacker energy of their old joints."

While Petrin's and Eustice's reviews suggest that *And the Anonymous Nobody* was a lesser effort, the reviewers do seek to address an interesting question: How do we assess growth and aging in hip-hop? This query appears weird on the surface because what other genre is there where its artists are not expected to age, or at least produce, perform, and release new music into middle age? I believe this question, the dearth of music where middle-aged rappers deal with surviving into middle age, and the notion that hip-hop is "a young man's sport," have hindered our ability to understand the meanings of rap as an art, and age, or experience.

Despite the critiques of *And the Anonymous Nobody*, De La Soul's eighth record initiated a wave of "grown man rap" albums in the

2010s. Jay-Z dropped *4:44* in 2017; Kendrick Lamar's *Mr. Morale & The Big Steppers*, released in 2022, feels like a direct descendant of De La Soul's *And the Anonymous Nobody*. While Lamar's record might be more vulnerable than *And the Anonymous Nobody*, De La Soul, along with other artists like Phonte and Open Mike Eagle, helped create a permission structure for Black men to rap about extremely personal topics, dealing with their limitations and anxieties and reckoning with their mistakes and the ways they hurt others.

For the fourth time in their careers, De La Soul and A Tribe Called Quest dropped albums in the same year. It would be the last time both groups released records with their full rosters. Three days after Donald Trump won the electoral college vote to clinch the US presidency, A Tribe Called Quest unveiled presumably their last album, *We Got It from Here . . . Thank You 4 Your Service*, the last Tribe album recorded while Phife Dawg was still alive. Like De La Soul returning to their punk sensibility on *And the Anonymous Nobody*, A Tribe Called Quest also presented a fresh interpretation of their aesthetic—clever rhymes over cleverly sampled beats. *We Got It from Here . . .* tapped into afrofuturism on "The Space Program," a critique of structural racism and anti-immigrant sentiment on "We the People," and grief on "Lost Somebody." The record, however, functions as a send-off for, and a tribute to, Phife Dawg, who had passed away due to complications from diabetes eight months before the album's release. Phife Dawg's voice urges listeners to "get it together forever . . . let's make something happen" on "The Space Program" and addresses the political situation on the Kendrick Lamar–featured "Conrad Tokyo." Q-Tip and longtime Tribe collaborator Busta Rhymes praise Phife's lyrical prowess on what essentially functions as a Phife song concluding the album, "The Donald."

The release of these two records by Native Tongues brethren illustrated that both groups could produce quality music thirty years into their careers and remained principal contributors to hip-hop well into the twenty-first century. A Tribe Called Quest dropped a stellar Grammy-nominated album without compromising their sound. De La Soul rallied their fans and peers in rap and rock and produced a svelte album, complete with tracks challenging how rappers approached songwriting and construction. Both demonstrated that their creative ethos and process were keys to longevity, not just chasing trends and loading up their albums with features by the hottest artists.

Two of my favorite groups dropping albums touching on existential topics before and after Trump's election felt appropriate considering how radical his politics were around issues such as immigration. De La Soul and A Tribe Called Quest were clearly at a crossroads in their life phases, as were we as a country. Both albums demonstrated a Black confidence that seemed to reflect the Obama moment. On November 8, 2016, I watched the election results on TV alone, and like many Americans, I believed Hillary Clinton would win. I even said so in a radio interview that's probably floating somewhere online by now. However, I felt unconfident after learning Trump won Michigan, and my PhD advisor sent me a text to express his concern about Clinton's chances. I knew that if he was not optimistic, then we were in trouble. Subsequently, I drove to a local bar to attend the local Democratic party's gathering with some of my radical friends who had worked on a campaign to end student debt. I will never forget the nausea I felt after Wisconsin went for Trump, and I heard one of the Democratic party officials get on the microphone and give a paltry speech about needing to come together. I got up and left after they quoted Dr. Martin Luther King, Jr. We were in big trouble if all anyone had to offer were decontextualized MLK quotes.

Don't Press Play

On their 1991 single "Check the Rhime," A Tribe Called Quest's Q-Tip famously informed us of "Industry rule number four thousand and eighty: Record company people are shady." De La Soul became reacquainted with this rule in their dealings with Warner Bros. and Tommy Boy Records, especially its CEO, Tom Silverman, during their fight for their catalog. Like Prince, who fought Warner Bros. for his legal freedom as an artist, and Taylor Swift, who reclaimed the rights to her music from record executive Scooter Braun, De La Soul launched a campaign to get their music to listeners and fans. For Posdnuos, Maseo, and Dave, the struggle for ownership and for the ability to reap the financial and cultural rewards from their legendary albums underscored the group's populist, anti-corporate orientation in hip-hop culture. As De La Soul saw it, the fight against Silverman and Tommy Boy was not just for their livelihoods, it was also for the people.

De La Soul's giveaway on Kickstarter and the release of their eighth studio album had an added benefit—they provoked a conversation about the unavailability of the group's old music. A week before the album dropped, the *New York Times* published an article publicizing the upcoming release and documenting the disappearance of the group's music. Regarding De La Soul's 2014 Valentine's Day giveaway, journalist Finn Cohen wrote, "The attention wasn't just because the group was giving its catalog away. It was because those six albums have never been available to buy digitally or to stream." De La Soul, one of hip-hop's most original and transformative groups, had been lost to rap and cultural history. They had also lost a lot of money due to their music being absent from streaming services and had obviously lost out on song placements in commercials, TV, and movies. They even missed out on the ringtone trend, as it is possible that many fans would have bought many of their catchy songs and used them for their ringtones.

In addition to the untold financial losses De La Soul incurred from their music's absence on digital music stores and streaming services, the group suffered a blow to their legacy and their place in not just hip-hop history but also Black and US cultural history. Questlove told Cohen, "I mean, *3 Feet High and Rising* is very much in danger of being the classic tree that fell in the forest that was once given high praise and now is just a stump." De La Soul's digital absence has deprived them of new and younger fans who probably would be drawn to their music considering the success of their descendants like Odd Future, Childish Gambino, and Black Hippy, a group comprised of Top Dawg Entertainment artists Kendrick Lamar, ScHoolboy Q, Jay Rock, and Ab-Soul.

Finn Cohen reported that legal complications around contract clauses and sample rules created a potential minefield for Warner and the group. Their catalog's owners, managers, and sample lawyers were unsure whether contract terms struck in the late 1980s and through the 1990s applied to streaming. Would Warner Music Group have to secure more sample clearances? Then, there's the obvious question of who would pay for the process. Tom Silverman thought it would not be difficult for Warner to get the job done. According to Silverman, Warner Music probably knew who held the copyrights and should have been able to strike deals. Silverman's arguments would prove ironic when he reacquired the rights to much of Tommy Boy's catalog in 2017.

Tom Silverman reacquired the rights because Warner had to let go of assets to buy a British label, Parlophone. Two years later, to my astonishment, De La Soul announced their music would be available on streaming services. Nonetheless, the group expressed dissatisfaction with their shares. It appeared that Silverman sought to hold De La Soul to the terms of their 1988 contract while, according to the band, imposing untenable terms. In February 2019, the group posted on their Instagram page that Tommy Boy wanted a ninety/ten split of their royalties, partly to cover what the group called a "phantom" two-million-dollar debt. The group labeled signing with a corporation as "slavery."

The negotiations between De La Soul and Silverman's Tommy Boy Records for a fair contract touched off a seven-month dispute. De La Soul, again, called for collective action. First, they asked fans to boycott the release of their music onto streaming platforms because there was no sense in allowing Tommy Boy to profit if they could not. To support the boycott, De La Soul contacted Tidal Music, partly owned by Jay-Z at the time, and convinced the streamer not to make their music available. Then, in August 2019, almost three years after the release of *And the Anonymous Nobody*, De La Soul announced they had ended the relationship with Tommy Boy, their label of thirty years. Still maintaining that their issue with the label was a matter of respecting and compensating the group fairly for their labor, De La Soul said of the severance of their relationship with Silverman and their old label in an Instagram post,

> Just to put the nail in the coffin. We wish Tommy Boy no ills but we do call for a boycott of anything bearing the name. . . . That old enslaved record label contract dinosaur is long dead and gone, but unfortunately still stinks.

The end of the group's legal relationship with Tommy Boy was not a defeat for De La Soul. In the following year, the label appeared to be willing to negotiate. However, in April 2020, Rostrum Records founder Benjy Grinberg expressed interest in buying Tommy Boy's catalog to return De La Soul's master recordings.

The movement for De La Soul to reacquire their music picked up steam in 2021. In one of those "only De La Soul . . ." moments, the group appeared on a February episode of the TV series *Teen Titans GO!* called "Don't Press Play." In the episode, Maseo, Posdnuos, and Dave joined forces with the Teen Titans to fight a villainous cartoon representation of Tom Silverman (or Tommy Boy Records). This large, red, octopus-like monster had taken control over their music, which turns out to be the group's superpower. Initially, the monster traps the Teen Titans and De La Soul in a crater, places a cage on top of them, and fills it with water. The Titans reference *3 Feet High and*

Rising as the water fills the crater, and then all of them warn that "De La Soul Is Dead" if they do not get out of their predicament. Then, Posdnuos, Maseo, and Dave deploy the "buhloone mindstate"—they inflate themselves, and the pressure from becoming human balloons bursts the cage. Upon confronting Tommy Boy, the monster, Posdnuos offers to negotiate, and the monster slaps all of them into a mountain after declaring the music his. "There's no getting through to this dude," Dave complains. The Titans then spring into action to help De La Soul reacquire their superpowers—their music—in order to defeat the monster. The story ends with Wonder Woman and other members of the Justice League flying by and inviting De La Soul to join their team of superheroes.

De La Soul's guest appearance on *Teen Titans GO!* is yet another example of the group responding to adversity in a creative manner. The episode not only framed the conflict between themselves and Tommy Boy as a battle between good and evil, but it also introduced the group to a younger generation of fans. Additionally, the show's illustrators tapped into a longer history of anti-capitalist politics. During the Gilded Age, critics of corporate capitalism and labor unions like the Industrial Workers of the World (IWW) often depicted this system as an octopus wreaking havoc on society's workers. One such IWW poster depicts the capitalist octopus ensnaring workers in the grip of "wage slavery," poverty, and war. In the case of "Don't Press Play," the octopus-like monster, or Tommy Boy, threatened to kill De La Soul and take their music for itself.

Four months later, De La Soul received a real-life assist. On June 4, 2021, Reservoir Media acquired Tommy Boy for 100 million dollars, paving the way for the group to obtain the rights to their music. Two months later, to my excitement, rapper and De La Soul collaborator Talib Kweli announced the group had prevailed. The monster had been vanquished and De La Soul stood at the precipice of victory, or so I thought.

What I did not know was that the group still had a mountain

to climb to make their music available. Now that they had control over their recordings, they would have to go through the legal process to get all the samples cleared so they would not get hit with any lawsuits. The group hired one of the music industry's leading legal firms, Deborah Mannis-Gardner's DMG Clearances, Inc., to handle the clearances—hunt down copyright owners and negotiate fair terms. Mannis-Gardner explained to *Okayplayer* that many owners hesitated to involve themselves when Tommy Boy still owned the master recordings due to the acrimony between the artists and the label. Yet, according to Mannis-Gardner, various copyright owners changed their minds when Reservoir Media acquired De La Soul's masters and decided to work with the group to release their old music.

As Mannis-Gardner's group handled the legalities around sample clearances, De La Soul enlisted the services of none other than DJ Prince Paul. It had become clear that the group would not be able to convince all copyright holders to allow them to keep the samples on their records. They had a choice—cut samples from certain songs completely, or remaster some of the records with new samples that could be obtained. In August 2022, in a full-circle moment, DJ Prince Paul announced he was working on a "secret project" for the group. He helped lead the effort to refurbish the first four De La Soul records. This took several months.

On January 3, 2023, Reservoir announced they would offer De La Soul's albums for streaming. I was elated. De La Soul had finally won. With the help of many industry allies—including Jay-Z—and fans, the group could finally return their music to the world. We could celebrate the history we'd made by listening to their art.

It also seemed right that we all could listen to their albums in hip-hop's fiftieth year. A younger generation looking to learn more about the culture's history gained access to some of its most treasured albums.

Unfortunately, neither I nor many of us knew that the clock was ticking for one of De La Soul's members.

"Buddy"

I rarely watch The Grammy Awards, but I was curious about how the show would acknowledge the fiftieth anniversary of the creation of hip-hop culture. As many hip-hop fans understand, The Grammys has a complicated, if not checkered, relationship with the genre. The Grammys and Questlove, who organized and curated the set, tried to cram as many rap acts into a thirteen-minute segment as possible. The performance featured several rap luminaries, including Grandmaster Flash, Run-D.M.C., and Queen Latifah. However, I was struck by De La Soul's appearance. Posdnuos, wearing a white suit, appeared in front of a screen filled with daisies and began to perform "Buddy."

"Where are Dave and Maseo?" I wondered.

It was great to see Posdnuos, but his performance appeared somewhat muted. It was weird to see him perform the song alone. I also found the song choice curious. However, watching Posdnuos perform an ode to friendship without two of his best friends seemed ironic, at best.

In a *New York Times* article published weeks later, Posdnuos confirmed my interpretation of his performance. He told Ben Sisario that Dave and Maseo were unavailable due to experiencing health issues. "It was a bittersweet performance for me . . . because I was looking so forward to having my brothers there for this amazing moment," Posdnuos admitted.

February 12 was a pretty ordinary day here in Morgantown, West Virginia—very gray and cloudy. (The skies are usually gray during the winter months here.) I woke up, prepared my classes for the following week, watched a little football, and then went for a run late that afternoon.

Then, as I returned to my house after the run, I got a ping from *The New York Times* on my phone. It was 6:30 p.m. "David Jolicoeur of De La Soul, a rap trio that expanded hip-hop's stylistic vocabulary in the 80s and 90s, has died at 54."

"Oh no."

My heart felt like it jumped out of me.

I was devastated.

Then, I started listening to "Let, Let Me In," one of my favorite songs on *De La Soul Is Dead*.

I had planned to continue prepping for class that night, but I couldn't. There was no way I could do anything else but process Dave's death. I knew of Dave's health issues, but of course, I had not thought about it until that evening when I saw the news trickling out onto social media.

I spent the rest of the evening and that night reflecting on Dave's life and career with others on social media, but mostly within myself. "We lost so many rappers in the last several years, and now Dave. Really?" I sat down in a state of shock, and I let the nostalgia of the somber "Pass the Plugs" just wash over me.

Unfortunately, David Jolicoeur's death transpired amid a terrible trend in hip-hop—Black artists dying entirely too young. We have grown accustomed to the history of young Black artists dying because of gun violence. But, in the last several years, we've watched many of our luminaries die due to natural causes in their forties and early fifties, around fifteen to twenty years earlier than the life expectancy of most African Americans. Phife Dawg and Biz Markie both died from diabetes complications. COVID-19 claimed Fred the Godson's and DJ Kay Slay's lives. Shock G, Coolio, Gangsta Boo, and Mac Miller died from accidental drug overdoses. DOOM died from negligence as hospital staff mishandled his care during treatment for a negative reaction to high blood pressure medication. People Under the Stairs's Double K passed away from alcohol poisoning in 2021 at the age of 43. As journalist and scholar Jelani Cobb observed in *The New Yorker*: "There's a sense that we have reached the far side of some cruel distribution curve. The memories of those who were culled are increasingly paired with those who have simply succumbed."

Out of De La Soul's members, Dave confronted his mortality

through his art most often. He first broached it on "Trying People" on *AOI: Bionix*. One of the most affecting scenes of *We're Still Here (Now)* is Dave's discussion of mortality and how the deaths of his cousin and close friends inspired the next-to-last song on *And the Anonymous Nobody*, "Here in After." Dave explained, "I thought about it [would] be cool . . . if I write a song about, you know, both sides—a person dealing with someone being gone as well as what it would feel like in which I believe in the here and after, a person who's dead, how do they deal with being gone." Dave, in the documentary and in an interview with *SPIN*, insinuates that the song came together through divine intervention. Dave told *SPIN*:

> But Damon [Albarn], not knowing what the song title was and not knowing any lyrics of mine, started writing in a similar way as well. He was talking about reflecting and people not being around, and I was like, 'Well, that's it. That's what the song is about.' This song was brought to us by something.

Then Dave explained Albarn's verses: "I kinda consider his portion of the record the afterlife. So it worked out perfectly." Dave continues, "It's not something I think we're choosing to. It's just where we at in life. Grown men who are dealing with so much, and I want to face it." Dave proceeds to perform his verse, and while doing so, we see old pictures of those presumed gone and a picture of the Apollo Theater's marquee, recognizing the passing of another Native Tongues member, Phife Dawg.

Death is the great equalizer. We all will experience loss, and we will all be carried to a morgue. This is one lesson of aging that the group, especially Dave, tried to articulate on *And the Anonymous Nobody*—we had or would have to reckon with the deaths of our loved ones and ourselves.

LIVING IN A D.A.I.S.Y. AGE

"You're Going to Be Fine"

It was Thanksgiving 2017, and I prepared to drive home to Mansfield. I'd spent the night before protesting the potential visit of a well-known white nationalist to Ann Arbor, Michigan, but I was ready to go home and spend time with family. Then I got the dreaded call.

"Mom is sick. We had to take her to the hospital."

I quickly gathered my stuff and got on the road.

When I arrived at the hospital, Mom was alert and appeared to be in good spirits. Dad explained that Mom seemed unusually sick, and he grew so concerned that he decided to take her to the emergency room. Soon, we learned she had a urinary tract infection, but then, later, the doctor gave Dad some concerning news—she had developed sepsis. They would need to transfer her to the intensive care unit.

Unfortunately, the sepsis progressed, and the hospital decided to transfer Mom to a hospital in Columbus. Her health soon deteriorated.

Mom had spent much of her time in the hospital in the ICU, heavily sedated. But, luckily, she awakened a few days before Dad decided to move her to hospice. I was relieved to see her watching football and hear her talk. Mom was more engaging and talkative. Little did I know we would have our last conversation that day. I just listened to her talking to me. It is possible she was experiencing the type of delirium that many face toward the end of life. She thought I was still dating someone two years after our relationship ended. In her confusion, Mom told me, "Y'all will be all right. You're going to be fine." I was still in shock about the fact that Mom's days were truly numbered. It was hard to accept that she was telling me and all of us goodbye. Mom's goodbye reflects one of Albarn's questions from the afterlife on "Here in After"—Can we let our loved ones go when it's time?

December 16 was Mom's last full day on Earth. We decided to drive down to Columbus to be with her. Time does weird things when death approaches. We knew that she didn't have much time, but we also acted as if she had more time. As we drove, Dad suggested we bring our grandmother because we needed to ensure she saw Mom. When we arrived, we hung out in Mom's room. My older brother Jeff came and picked up Brandenn because we were sleeping at his place that night. I went to hang out with one of my high school friends. It had been a while since we had hung out. Still, time and space felt thick. My brain was foggy. I can barely remember what we discussed.

I was relieved to return to the hospital to see Dad and Mom. Dad told me that her breathing had grown fainter. I kissed her forehead and drove to my brother's to get some rest. Watching TV, I saw "Dad" pop up on my phone. It was around one a.m. I knew—she was gone. I woke Brandenn, and we drove with our older brother to the hospital. We got to see her for the last time, and my sister, Dad, and I drove back to Mansfield in the middle of the night. The way Mom went was fitting—she left while she and Dad watched one of her favorite shows.

Dad lived nearly four more years after Mom died. His passing was sudden. That Saturday in September 2021 seemed like another normal day. It was a beautiful morning, and I decided to shoot basketball at the court in the apartment complex where I lived.

I returned to my apartment around eleven a.m. and received a call from my sister. She told me that, upon returning home from the store, she found Dad on the couch, his chest heaving. His phone was in his hand. He had called 911 before he became unresponsive. It turned out his call for help was his last act.

Maybe forty-five minutes later, I received a call from a doctor at the hospital. He asked, "Was your dad sick?"

I said, "Besides his COPD, I do not believe anything else was wrong."

He said, "I'm sorry to tell you this, but we tried to do everything we could to save him. But your father has expired."

Wow. Now both of our parents were gone.

Our father did not die of COVID. Although he had developed

a skepticism of doctors, believing that he had experienced microaggressions and mistreatment from his physician and terrible side effects from medicine prescribed to treat his eczema, he remained very careful. He lived with COPD, so he did not venture out into the world once the pandemic began. Brandenn diligently wore her masks when she went to the grocery store for him. They even washed the bed sheets I slept on after my visits. One time, when our brother, sister-in-law, niece, and nephew visited for the holiday, Dad stayed inside while my sister and I talked with them on the porch. He did not want to risk any potential exposure.

So while he did not die from COVID, his death must be interpreted within this context. He counted among the "excess deaths" of the pandemic. He was virtually isolated and was probably stressed due to worrying about his and our well-being. He could not see doctors in person, which deepened his skepticism of medical professionals. When one adds the grief he experienced with Mom to the fear and stress brought on by the COVID pandemic, it amounts to his body, his lungs, and his heart giving out.

I hated to watch Mom die slowly and to learn of my Dad dying suddenly. But I can admit that death is clarifying. Watching Dad care for Mom in her last days reminded me of the power of love. I had only seen him that broken two other times: a few years before when Mom was hospitalized, and in the course of her last two weeks. I am unsure if I had ever seen two people that emotionally in sync—when Mom improved, I could tell in Dad's voice that his spirits were up; when she was low in energy, he was somber. I hurt, but I could not imagine his hurt. I'll never forget watching him look out of the window helplessly. The image of Mom watching football while Dad sat, looking outside, was so stark that I took a picture.

Dad's passing intensified the existential crisis that accompanied all the changes in my life—Mom's passing, getting a new job and moving to Alabama, and the isolation of living in a culturally hostile place during the COVID-19 pandemic. However, while packing up my parents' house with Brandenn, I realized that I needed to tend to my mental and emotional health more deliberately. I finally fulfilled a promise that I made to myself in 2019—I would go see a therapist.

Dave's death and his thoughts about the passage of time and death on "Trying People" and "Here in After" take me back to a December 2021 therapy session. My therapist kept asking me what I wanted in life, as it had drastically changed. I knew I felt extremely unmoored after losing both parents and living in a state I hated. I sought happiness, but I was not exactly sure what that would look like. I told her about how alone I felt while attending the department holiday party at work. She then posed a question that stuck with me:

"Where do you want to be when you're sixty? Do you want to be alone at another one of those department parties?"

"Oof," I thought. That scared me.

I finally accepted that I needed to readjust my priorities. The time we have in our physical form is not unlimited, and I could not let my academic or organizing work dominate my life. I had to care for my mental and emotional health and allow myself to find some happiness. I needed to get to living the rest of my life because, as Posdnuos intimated at the end of "Drawn," time keeps moving. Don't waste it.

D.A.I.S.Y.

De La Soul kept pushing forward after Dave's death in hip-hop's fiftieth year. They organized an event, The D.A.I.S.Y. Experience, to celebrate Dave's life and the group's first six albums finally being available for streaming. Hundreds gathered in Webster Hall in New York City, where De La Soul performed their first big concert in 1989. The event reflected the group's embrace of the D.A.I.S.Y. Decades after complaining about flowers being everywhere, they flanked the stage with huge flower decorations. Above the water fountain read a message, "Like a Daisy, I need water."

LIVING IN A D.A.I.S.Y. AGE

Variety's Jem Aswad called the event "a musical wake" for Jolicoeur. (In a sign of the times, Amazon Music and Twitch livestreamed the event.) The event demonstrated De La Soul's rap legacy as many mentees and collaborators like Common, The Roots' Black Thought, Talib Kweli, Chuck D, and Busta Rhymes attended in support of Posdnuos and Maseo. Original Native Tongues members Mike Gee, Prince Paul, Queen Latifah, Dres, Monie Love, Q-Tip, and DJ Red Alert were also in the house. The celebration featured many performances. Latifah and Monie Love performed their hit, "Ladies First," Dres performed Black Sheep's "The Choice Is Yours," and Common performed a freestyled verse recognizing his Native Tongues connection and Dave's influence on his Dilla-produced classic, "The Light," while surrounded by many from the rap community on stage. Driven by the emotions brought on by Dave's death and adrenaline, artists punctuated their performances by giving each other hugs. Love flowed throughout the building.

Emotionally shaken, Posdnuos and Maseo appeared as a testament to the group carrying on their legacy. Posdnuos told the crowd, "You best believe my nigga Dave is looking down right now on everybody." As one does in the wake of loss, Posdnuos and Maseo reflected on the group's origins—moving from the boroughs to Long Island and then linking up. They then explained that Dave would want them to keep going. The event culminated with a countdown to midnight, when the group's music would become available. It was like counting down to a new year as flower-shaped balloons fell from the ceiling, and the beat of "Rock Co.Kane Flow" dropped.

As the balloon-shaped daisy petals fell on everyone at Webster Hall in the early hours of March 3, 2023, De La Soul's first six albums, a testament to their creative genius, finally made their way onto streaming platforms. This was a moment of celebration for all, as it marked the restoration of De La Soul's control of their music and the opportunity for us to appreciate their musical legacy fully.

M.A.S.A.

While De La Soul had won back their rights, the group members understood they'd entered a music economy transformed and still incredibly unfair to many artists. In the months following the rerelease of their Tommy Boy catalog, Maseo used a historical metaphor of enslaved people's transition from emancipation to Jim Crow to explain his complicated feelings about the struggle to acquire control of their music. "It was like freeing the slaves but adding vagrancy laws." He continued, "[The initial ninety/ten split with Tommy Boy Records] was almost like giving me a house I couldn't do nothing with. . . . I have a house I can live in, but I can't sell it. I can't control nothing [in it], but I can live inside of it. . . . It was another form of slavery, in my opinion."

It is true that artists still rely on sales of physical copies of albums (especially vinyl), touring, merchandise, and endorsements. Yet, streaming constitutes around eighty-four percent of music consumption. This leaves many artists fighting for crumbs in the streaming market. The paltry earnings from streaming sources are well reported at this point. Artists earn fractions of a penny from streamers like Spotify, around $0.0033, to be exact. They must be one of the major artists—Taylor Swift, Beyoncé, Drake, Kendrick Lamar, Billie Eilish—to build wealth through music. This arrangement reflects the drastic power imbalance between major record companies and artists. The "Big Three" music labels—Sony Music, Warner Music Group, and Universal Music Group—used their control over music catalogs to negotiate deals that were more favorable for them than they were for their artists.

This arrangement reinforces economic inequality among artists, as well. Artists need to generate tens of millions of streams across all the platforms—Spotify, Apple Music, Tidal, Pandora, YouTube, Deezer, and others—to generate wealth from digital plays. For instance, it took nearly 150 million listens across all platforms for Kendrick Lamar to earn six figures from his Drake diss tracks. Of course, Lamar's case is extreme, like with Swift, Beyoncé, and Eilish. Most artists are not able to garner as many listens. They scrape by.

This structural inequality in the streaming economy drives Alphonse Pierre's reservations with De La Soul's arrival onto music platforms. He writes in his response to De La Soul's arrival for *Pitchfork*:

> In the week since De La Soul finally got around all the music-industry greed and bogus-ass copyright laws that have long kept their first six albums off streaming services, I've been spinning their catalog like it's new. But diving in has left me conflicted, because while I love having their classic material at my fingertips, it feels grim to think about the role of tech companies in preserving important musical legacies. If anything, the entire saga bolsters the power of platforms like Spotify and Apple Music, because it has been treated as if this music wouldn't exist without them.

Pierre's critique did not elaborate on the Big Three's role in creating the new music economy. But Pierre offers an important reminder—one consistent with De La Soul's anti-corporate politics—that big corporations still control music distribution and consumption. And none of these corporations are our friends. As Posdnuos outlined in the group's 2019 *Drink Champs* interview, "It's like saying everyone makes such a big deal about this red MAGA hat. It's like . . . a MASA hat—Make Artists Slaves Again. It's like you gotta get rid of that whole mentality for the entire record company [and] business." And as we have learned about Cassie's allegations that Sean Combs kept her in an abusive and exploitative relationship (although he was subsequently acquitted), some hip-hop music executives are willing to resort to physical violence and terrible contracts to maintain control.

However, De La Soul's history fighting for their catalog before the streaming industry's growth belies Pierre's contention that the group's music is available because of the popularity of Spotify, Pandora, Apple Music, and Tidal. One need only listen to *Buhloone Mindstate* and *Stakes Is High*, visit their Kickstarter page for *And the Anonymous Nobody*, and hear their interviews to know that De La Soul is among the most erudite rap artists when it comes to thinking about conflicts between art and commerce and artists', especially Black artists', struggles with the music industry. They have premised much of their careers on advocating for better work conditions on behalf of other artists and criticizing inequalities in the industry.

The transformation in music distribution indeed accelerated their struggle since it is the main way people engage with music now. Also, it makes sense for artists to fight for their music to become available in a new medium. Ultimately, though, it is reasonable to suggest that De La Soul desired to own their recordings no matter the circumstances—they are the product of their labor, and their catalog serves as a source of income and wealth.

Several key lessons emerge from the streaming wars fought by De La Soul. First, they underscore the crucial need for artists to control not just the means of production but also the means of distributing their music. This would require artists to wage fights like De La Soul's and Taylor Swift's against the owners of their music. It's a call for more collective organization through established unions and labor organizations and for artists to recruit their fan bases for help in their fight for control over their music distribution.

Second, artists need more legal means to protect the fruits of their labor. Dave suggested this much in the 2019 *Drink Champs* interview. "I see the opportunity to make legislation . . . to help new artists and future artists coming. . . . We have to also think that the power is greater than just dollars and cents. I would love to see what comes out of our madness is legislation change. . . . Hopefully this will inspire an attorney . . . or someone who is in the game right now who feels like we need to just change the rules a little bit." Representative Rashida Tlaib and former congressman Jamaal Bowman introduced the Living Wage for Musicians Act in 2024 to address the great disparity in artists' earnings from streaming platforms. The bill would establish a more artist-centered model. It would tax streamers' non-subscription revenues and add a small fee to the subscription price. These revenues would flow to a nonprofit, distributing royalties to artists commensurate with their streams. The bill establishes a cap on each track to distribute more money to more artists.

Ironically, despite these inequalities, De La Soul could not have reappeared at a better time (although their music should always have been available for them to earn revenue from). More listeners have been engaging older music. In 2022, music industry analytics company MRC data reported that streams of older music constituted nearly seventy percent of the market. The trend led jazz historian and culture critic Ted Gioia to ask, "Is Old Music Killing New Music?"

However, as Gioia asserts, this tendency for listeners to consume more old music poses challenges for new artists seeking to break into the music industry. De La Soul spent 2023 capitalizing on this trend as they rereleased their entire Tommy Boy catalog on streaming, cassette tape, CD, and vinyl. They also celebrated *Buhloone Mindstate*'s thirtieth anniversary that year by dropping an extended version of their third record. De La Soul can also take advantage of the interconnectivity of cultural technologies. People can listen to old songs in movies, like "The Magic Number" playing during the closing credits of *Spider-Man: No Way Home*, or "Say No Go" used in the 2024 film about the crack-up of the United States, *Civil War*. Interested listeners could use the Shazam app when they hear "Ring Ring Ring (Ha Ha Hey)" while sitting in the coffee shop, and then go to Apple Music to listen to all of *De La Soul Is Dead*.

Ultimately, though, De La Soul's fight for the rights to its catalog in the streaming era underscores the importance of going to concerts and buying physical and digital media and merchandise directly from the artists. A subscription to a streaming service is a lease—you do not own a copy of the music. You pay for access to the music you love. But, if you own a vinyl record or CD or buy digital copies from artists themselves or through a more artist-friendly platform like Bandcamp, you will always be able to access the music you love. This is why keeping my De La Soul CDs was one of the best fan-related decisions I ever made. I never lost their music.

Music Is Also Technology

With De La Soul rereleasing their catalog in 2023, I also got my wish to teach their first album, *3 Feet High and Rising*, in my History of Hip-Hop in America course at West Virginia University. Rather than asking students to listen to playlists I composed, I asked them to listen to full albums, because I sought to demonstrate the importance of the album form as complete works of art, especially at a time when many of them admitted to engaging music through playlists. I asked students to listen closely to the full album and its construction, especially the skits and production. I also asked them to place songs like "Say No Go" in their historical context.

Several students were astonished by the album's production, relating it to some of the beatmakers they were more familiar with, like Conductor Williams and The Alchemist. Like my previous class, many expressed dismay about how and why De La Soul's music had been missing from streaming platforms. One student responded, "I think all artists should be able to sample music. They aren't copying anyone if they are making something completely new and different." Others in the class concurred.

Students in my Auburn class articulated similar views and concerns about sampling. Yet they also felt the loss of De La Soul's music more acutely after I showed them the Native Tongues segment of the *Hip-hop Evolution* documentary. It is one thing to never know about great music because it is unavailable. But younger generations have come of age as music listeners in an era where sampling is the norm in all genres of music, not just rap but also rock, pop, and country music. Many of them even have greater access to music production tools nowadays. Now some Apple products come with music production software already installed. This was unheard of when I was in college, although my friends and I downloaded pirated copies of FL Studio, also known as Fruity Loops. Of course, as journalist Jeff Chang argued in his *Pitchfork* review of *3 Feet High and Rising*, the debates around sampling are complicated, and they often serve as proxies to cover up historical theft from Black artists. We know sampling did not begin with hip-hop, as white artists in all genres have copied elements of Black music without giving Black musicians credit. Yet, even with Kanye West's emergence in the twenty-first century, some listeners continue to believe that sampling is creative theft.

My students' views on sampling and their ability to think about musical connections across genres illustrate how the return of De La Soul's Tommy Boy discography is tailor-made for a new generation. Younger listeners might be willing to sit down with the group's one-of-a-kind records because of De La Soul's ability to construct musical worlds that remain novel today. While albums like *3 Feet High and Rising*, *De La Soul Is Dead*, and *Buhloone Mindstate* have engendered the creation of other cinematic, genre- and mind-bending records, not many artists have successfully constructed such universe-expanding albums.

Also, this new generation of listeners possesses something my friends and I did not—access to a wealth of recorded music and information about the artists at their fingertips. They can look up lyrics, samples, interviews, reviews, and retrospectives to understand more of the context of De La Soul's albums. Maybe all this access could take away some of the joy of discovery. But I could not have listened to one of my favorite De La Soul songs, "Bitties in the BK Lounge," without being able to locate Taana Gardner's 1981 post-disco hit, "No Frills." Like Chuck D says, music is also technology, and how we engage in culture and how we enjoy it change over time.

EPILOGUE

The Future

"Three black men sticking together, that's beautiful and it's important."

—Maseo

De La Soul has produced one of rap's best discographies. They have revolutionary albums, classics, conscious anthems, and mature records. The group released scores of singles and B-sides and appeared on numerous songs from artists in various genres, from grunge to electronic to pop. *De La Soul Is Dead* is a five-mic classic. *3 Feet High and Rising* is in the Library of Congress, the Grammy Hall of Fame, and appears on countless "best of" albums lists.

Of course, group members often offer an even more authentic answer about their legacy in hip-hop history. Dave, Maseo, and Posdnuos valued their ability to remain De La Soul for more than three decades despite their industry and legal troubles. In their 2019 *Drink Champs* episode, Dave explained, "I think when you can show that we could come together sometimes, worlds apart, and keep going and build from it and make better and create new things, that's important. That's what I would want to embody as 'What did De La do.' Just the idea of staying together through thick and thin and making things work. And giving that example to others to let them know that is possible for them, as well."

Maseo put a finer point on Dave's comments a few years later. He told John Earls, "Three black men sticking together, that's beautiful and it's important." Maseo elaborated on this in another interview after Dave's passing. He said to journalist Lyndsey Parker, "I think sticking together actually says a lot, as simple as that may seem. It says a lot to our genre. It says a lot to our culture. And it says a lot to the music business in general, for bands who couldn't really hold it together." Chuck D often talks of the power of rap groups, yet De La Soul's bond goes deeper. They adapted to revolutionary changes within the music industry and society while retaining their commitment to their artistry, community, and each other. Maseo, Posdnuos, and Dave did not allow the industry to box them into a category. To paraphrase Posdnuos on "Rock Co.Kane Flow," they added a little hardness to survive. Like any group of creatives, I'm sure they fought among themselves. We never heard nor knew about it. De La Soul survived. They personified Chuck D's argument about why rap groups are so important to the culture.

Of course, some might wonder if continuing as De La Soul is worth it without Dave. How many times have we seen record labels try to force highly manufactured, disjointed, and inferior posthumous albums onto grieving fan bases? Also, few rap groups continue after a member's death—the Lost Boyz faded after Freaky Tah was killed. Run-D.M.C. quit after Jam Master Jay's murder, as did the Beastie Boys after MCA passed away from cancer. Gang Starr does not exist without Guru, and it is difficult to see Mobb Deep continuing without Prodigy. Even though A Tribe Called Quest dropped a stellar record, *We Got It from Here . . . Thank You 4 Your Service*, they might be done after Phife's death. Slum Village might be the best example for a rap group carrying on, as T3 has conceived of the collective as one that rotates members after the deaths of Dilla and Baatin and ELZhi's departure.

For a moment, I wondered about De La Soul, too, but then, as I was wrapping up this book, I got to see them perform in concert. A friend and colleague sent me an Instagram message telling me he was flying to Washington, DC, to see Robert Glasper and De La

THE FUTURE

Soul perform at the Kennedy Center. He knew I was working on this book, so he offered to take notes. I responded to the news:

"That's awesome Glasper is playing in DC and having De La as one of his special guests!"

Then I sent the link to my partner with the only response that was appropriate for such news:

"OMG"

She encouraged me to go, but I balked, as I tend to do at many of these opportunities. I do not know why I balked at the possibility of seeing my favorites in concert. I might have thought it was too much for my schedule, since I was trying to write this book while teaching a full class load. Even so, I was more concerned about how I would feel watching them perform without Dave. I was unsure if I could handle it, and if I could not, then would I want to be around anyone?

So I let the next several weeks pass without thinking about the show. My partner asked occasionally, "Are you going to that show?" I'd reply, "I don't know. I'm thinking about it."

Of course, she asked again the week before the show, and I finally admitted to myself that I wanted to and needed to go. Due to untimely deaths, I'd missed opportunities to see many of my favorite groups and artists—A Tribe Called Quest, the Beastie Boys, and Prince are the main acts I regret missing. So, I relented and bought one of the few expensive tickets left.

Robert Glasper did not disappoint with the show's production. The *Black Radio* Orchestra played immaculately. All the guest performances of Dilla-produced songs stirred my feelings of nostalgia. However, I got the sense we were all there to see one act—De La Soul.

LIVING IN A D.A.I.S.Y. AGE

I wondered what kind of routine Maseo and Posdnuos would perform without Dave? Then, two-thirds into the show, Posdnuos and Maseo walked onto the stage and performed a song from their fifth album, *Art Official Intelligence: Mosaic Thump*—"Thru Ya City," a perfect Dilla-produced choice because any travel-related song can illustrate the life of working and touring artists.

"Hell, yeah, they can still do this," I thought, nodding vigorously.

Of course, we all waited for Posdnuos and Maseo to perform the songs we knew would excite everyone, like "Much More." While I could imagine Dave standing opposite Posdnuos at times, he and Maseo mostly replicated the group's usual routine with each standing on opposite sides of the stage and encouraging crowd participation. Although it was exciting to see the living members perform songs in tribute to Dilla and Dave, I also felt comforted. If any rap group could survive and thrive as performers without a key member, De La Soul could.

Naturally, De La Soul's energy set the stage for the only song that deserved to close out the whole show—"Stakes Is High." Rap artist Talib Kweli wrote about how De La Soul's performance of the song has become a spiritual staple in their concert sets. "So to introduce the song, all of us on the tour would join De La onstage and tell the crowd that when we said, 'Vibe,' we wanted them to say, 'Vibration.' We would reply, 'Stakes Is High.' I saw the effect our 'mantra' had on the crowd. Every night, we got them to vibrate harder."

It is little surprise that "Stakes Is High" got the biggest response from the crowd. I saw its effect as all the concertgoers around me shot up from their seats and began reciting the song's lyrics. I saw De La Soul's legacy in the crowd's reaction. The crowd was diverse in race, ethnicity, and age, illustrating that hip-hop had aged a half-century, and De La Soul was there much of the time. Some folks wore full heads of gray hair and were approaching retirement age, and the parents who brought their younger kids recited Posdnuos's lines.

THE FUTURE

The concert also reminded me of how we'd all grown up with De La Soul. The group, broadly speaking, created albums for every stage of life. For many of us, *3 Feet High and Rising* captured our youthful innocence; *De La Soul Is Dead* reflected our teenage angst, *Buhloone Mindstate* might have shown off our early adulthood cynicism and sarcastic sense of humor, while *Stakes Is High* pushed us to take the world around us more seriously. As De La Soul dropped the Art Official Intelligence series, they encouraged us to appreciate life a little more while teaching us the importance of accountability to ourselves, our loved ones, and our community. Finally, as some of us reached midlife, De La Soul released *And the Anonymous Nobody* to remind us to be ourselves and take stock of life honestly so that we don't waste more time.

De La Soul's legacy lies in the group's lifelong commitment to each other as comrades and complicated Black men. Maseo, Posdnuos, and Dave were sure of themselves without putting on a façade or allowing their egos to burst their buhloones. Their legacy also lies in De La Soul being one of the most inviting hip-hop groups ever. They embrace younger artists who seek to pave their own creative lane like Tyler, The Creator and Odd Future; Rapsody; and Westside Gunn. Most importantly, De La Soul invites anyone who feels they cannot be themselves into their community. The group's response to MSNBC's Ari Melber's question about feeling marginalized encapsulates their ethos of creative individualism and inclusiveness perfectly:

Maseo says, "Welcome to the family. C'mon in. Let's hang out."

Then Posdnuos adds: "This world is open to view and partake in all ideas. Let's all just have fun together, man."

Maseo then punctuates, "Don't be afraid to be yourself."

I saw De La Soul's considerable legacy in all the folks at the concert. They had built a multicultural and intergenerational fanbase who fell in love with De La Soul's creative individuality, eccentricity, and playfulness.

LIVING IN A D.A.I.S.Y. AGE

As I walked out of the Kennedy Center, I saw and heard an older guy and, presumably, his son, repeating the "vibe, vibrations" refrain from "Stakes Is High" and thought, hip-hop and De La Soul had come far from Amityville. Now, De La Soul is rap royalty.

APPENDIX

De La Soul: A Listening Guide

De La Soul has produced one of hip-hop's largest catalogs when one considers all of their B-sides, guest appearances, and singles. Here are some lists to help guide you through your De La Soul journey, or to spark some debate. "Feat." is short for "featuring."

PLAYLISTS:

Featuring De La Soul
- "Fallin'" with Teenage Fanclub
- "B-Side to Hollywood" with Camp Lo
- "Gettin' Down at the Amphitheater" with Common
- "The Projects (PJays)" with Handsome Boy Modeling School (Prince Paul and Dan the Automator)
- "If It Wasn't for You" with Handsome Boy Modeling School
- "Soul Rebels" with Reflection Eternal (Talib Kweli and Hi-Tek)
- "Cobbs Creek (Great Skate Remix)" with King Britt
- "What's That? [¿Que Eso?]" with Tony Touch and Mos Def

DE LA SOUL: A LISTENING GUIDE

- "Feel Good Inc." with Gorillaz
- "SUPERVILLAINZ" with DOOM
- "Navajo Rugs" with Stalley
- "Rocket Fuel" with DJ Shadow
- "Turning Me Off" with Slum Village
- "Mr. Big Mouf Pt. II" with Khrysis
- "The Upgrade" with J-Live and Oddisee
- "Flying High" with Diamond D
- "My Year" with Da Beatminerz, Pharoahe Monch, Corey Glover, and Rasheed Chappell

De La Soul and the Native Tongues

- "Buddy (Native Tongue Decision)" Feat. Jungle Brothers, Q-Tip, Monie Love, and Queen Latifah
- Jungle Brothers, "Doin' Our Own Dang" Feat. A Tribe Called Quest, Queen Latifah, and Monie Love
- "A Roller Skating Jam Named 'Saturdays'" Feat. Q-Tip and Vinia Mojica
- "Fanatic of the B Word" Feat. Dres and Mike Gee
- "Mama Gave Birth to the Soul Children" with Queen Latifah
- "What Yo Life Can Truly Be" Feat. Dres, A Tribe Called Quest, and The Chosen Few
- "Sh.Fe.MC's" Feat. A Tribe Called Quest
- "Award Tour" with A Tribe Called Quest
- "How Ya Want It (Native Tongues Remix)" with Jungle Brothers and Q-Tip
- "More Than U Know" with Prince Paul
- "Excursions (J.PERIOD Tribute Remix)"
- "Scheming" with Slum Village, J Dilla, and Phife Dawg

DE LA SOUL: A LISTENING GUIDE

- "Wow Factor" with Phife Dawg
- "2 Live Forever" with Phife Dawg

Songs about Work
- "Oodles of O's"
- "Pass the Plugs"
- "En Focus" Feat. Dres and Shortie No Mas(s)
- "Patti Dooke" Feat. Guru, Maceo Parker, Fred Wesley, and Pee Wee Ellis
- "The Bizness" Feat. Common
- "Long Island Degrees"
- "Dog Eat Dog"
- "The Grind Date"
- "Royalty Capes"
- "Greyhounds" Feat. Usher

Songs about Life
- "Pass the Plugs"
- "I Am I Be"
- "Trouble in the Water" Feat. DJ Honda
- "U Can Do (Life)"
- "Trying People"
- "Held Down" Feat. CeeLo Green
- "The Future"
- "Church"
- "Days of Our Lives" Feat. Common
- "Pain" Feat. Snoop Dogg
- "Memory of . . . (Us)" Feat. Estelle and Pete Rock
- "Drawn" Feat. Little Dragon
- "Here in After" Feat. Damon Albarn
- "Round Trip (For Dave)" with Statik Selektah

DE LA SOUL: A LISTENING GUIDE

All Skits
- "Can U Keep a Secret"
- "Take It Off"
- "Transmitting Live From Mars"
- "Talkin' Bout Hey Love"
- "Who Do U Worship?"
- "Kicked Out the House"
- "Who's Skatin' Promo"
- "Paul's Revenge"
- Skit after "Pony Ride" and before "Stakes Is High"
- Ghost Weed skits

Songs about Being Yourself
- "Change in Speak"
- "The Magic Number"
- "Ain't Hip to Be Labeled a Hippie"
- "I Can Do Anything (Delacratic)"
- "Me Myself and I"
- "Description"
- "Pass the Plugs"
- "Sunshine"

Songs about Politics and Social Issues
- "Ghetto Thang"
- "Say No Go"
- "Tread Water"
- "My Brother's a Basehead"
- "Millie Pulled a Pistol on Santa"
- "Patti Dooke" Feat. Guru, Maceo Parker, Fred Wesley, and Pee Wee Ellis

DE LA SOUL: A LISTENING GUIDE

- "The Hustle" Feat. Da Beatminerz
- "Brakes"
- "Stakes Is High"
- "One Four Love Pt. 1" Feat. Kool G Rap, Talib Kweli, Mos Def, Sporty Thieves, Rah Digga, Common, and Pharoahe Monch
- "The People" Feat. Chuck D
- "Remove 45" Feat. Talib Kweli, Pharoahe Monch, Mysonne, Chuck D, and Styles P

Songs about Hip-Hop
- "Plug Tunin' (Last Chance to Comprehend)"
- "Potholes in My Lawn"
- "Afro Connections at a Hi 5 (In the Eyes of the Hoodlum)"
- "Ego Trippin' (Part Two)"
- "Itzsoweezee (Hot)"
- "Declaration"
- "Verbal Clap"
- "Much More"
- "Rock Co.Kane Flow" Feat. MF DOOM
- "Freedom Train"
- "Get Away (The Spirit of Wu-Tang)"
- "The Return of DST"

Party Songs
- "Me Myself and I"
- "Buddy (Native Tongue Decision)" Feat. A Tribe Called Quest, Jungle Brothers, Monie Love, and Queen Latifah

DE LA SOUL: A LISTENING GUIDE

- "A Roller Skating Jam Named 'Saturdays'" Feat. Q-Tip and Vinia Mojica
- "Ring Ring Ring (Ha Ha Hey)"
- "Breakadawn"
- "4 More" Feat. Zhané
- "U Can Do (Life)"
- "Oooh" Feat. Redman
- "Copa (Cabanga)"
- "Baby Phat" Feat. Devin the Dude and Yummy Bingham
- "Simply Havin'"
- "Simply"
- "Shopping Bags (She Got from You)"

Songs about Love and Sex

- "Jenifa Taught Me (Derwin's Revenge)"
- "Eye Know"
- "Let, Let Me In"
- "Keepin' the Faith"
- "Baby, Baby, Baby, Baby, Ooh Baby" Feat. Jazzyfatnastees
- "Betta Listen"
- "4 More" Feat. Zhané
- "Baby Phat" Feat. Devin the Dude and Yummy Bingham
- "Memory of . . . (Us)" Feat. Estelle and Pete Rock
- "Trainwreck"
- "Drawn" Feat. Little Dragon

My De La Soul Album Rankings (not including mixtapes)

1. *De La Soul Is Dead*
2. *Stakes Is High*

DE LA SOUL: A LISTENING GUIDE

3. *3 Feet High and Rising*
4. *Buhloone Mindstate*
5. *The Grind Date*
6. *Art Official Intelligence: Mosaic Thump*
7. *And the Anonymous Nobody*
8. *Art Official Intelligence: Bionix*
9. *First Serve*

DE LA SOUL'S "COUSINS"

A random encounter at a Cleveland record store in the summer of 2023 inspired this list. Like many record store owners, the owner was gregarious, greeting everyone as they walked in, conversing with customers, and commenting on people's purchases. As I laid vinyl copies of Herbie Hancock's *Sextant,* Flying Lotus's instrumental version of *Flamagra,* Donald Byrd's *Places and Spaces,* and a Madlib album onto his desk, he exclaimed, "Oh these are great selections! You know they are all cousins, right?" He did not explain in depth why, but I understood—all of these albums extended from branches of the jazz family tree.

The owner's question inspired me to ask my students to listen to some of *3 Feet High and Rising*'s "cousins"—Public Enemy's *It Takes a Nation of Millions to Hold Us Back,* the Beastie Boys' *Paul's Boutique,* Queen Latifah's *All Hail the Queen,* and A Tribe Called Quest's *People's Instinctive Travels and the Paths of Rhythm.*

What follows is a list of "cousins," or albums that one should listen to as one goes through De La Soul's catalog.

3 Feet High and Rising
1. The Beatles, *Sgt. Pepper's Lonely Hearts Club Band*
2. Parliament, *Osmium*
3. Ultramagnetic MC's, *Critical Beatdown*

DE LA SOUL: A LISTENING GUIDE

4. Public Enemy, *It Takes a Nation of Millions to Hold Us Back*
5. Beastie Boys, *Paul's Boutique*
6. A Tribe Called Quest, *People's Instinctive Travels and the Paths of Rhythm*
7. Queen Latifah, *All Hail the Queen*
8. Jungle Brothers, *Straight Out the Jungle* and *Done By the Forces of Nature*
9. Digital Underground, *Sex Packets*
10. N.W.A, *Efil4zaggin (Niggaz4Life)*
11. OutKast, *ATLiens* and *Aquemini*
12. Dr. Octagon, *Dr. Octagonecologyst* (Kool Keith, Dan the Automator, and DJ Qbert)
13. MF DOOM, *MM..FOOD*

De La Soul Is Dead

1. Gravediggaz, *6 Feet Deep*
2. Prince Paul, *Psychoanalysis: What Is It?!*
3. Prince Paul, *A Prince Among Thieves*
4. Raekwon, *Only Built 4 Cuban Linx*
5. Dr. Dre, *The Chronic*
6. Wu-Tang Clan, *Enter the Wu-Tang (36 Chambers)*
7. Madvillain (Madlib and MF DOOM), *Madvillainy*
8. MF DOOM, *Operation: Doomsday*
9. Kendrick Lamar, *good kid, m.A.A.d city*
10. Little Brother, *May the Lord Watch*

Buhloone Mindstate

1. Parliament, *Mothership Connection*
2. Guru, *Jazzmatazz, Vol. 1*
3. A Tribe Called Quest, *The Low End Theory*

4. Digable Planets, *Reachin' (A New Refutation of Time and Space)* and *Blowout Comb*
5. Freestyle Fellowship, *Innercity Griots*
6. The Pharcyde, *Bizarre Ride II the Pharcyde*
7. Company Flow, *Funcrusher Plus*
8. The Roots, *Do You Want More?!!!??!* and *Things Fall Apart*
9. Pan Amsterdam and Damu the Fudgemunk, *EAT*
10. Kendrick Lamar, *To Pimp a Butterfly*
11. André 3000, *New Blue Sun*
12. Armand Hammer, *We Buy Diabetic Test Strips*
13. Robert Glasper, *Black Radio* series
14. Jazz Liberatorz, *Fruit of the Past*

Stakes Is High

1. Marvin Gaye, *What's Going On*
2. Prince, *Sign o' the Times*
3. Sly & the Family Stone, *There's a Riot Goin' On*
4. Black Star, *Mos Def & Talib Kweli Are Black Star*
5. Mos Def, *Black on Both Sides*
6. Reflection Eternal, *Train of Thought*
7. A Tribe Called Quest, *Beats, Rhymes and Life*
8. Fugees, *The Score*
9. The Roots, *Illadelph Halflife*
10. Lauryn Hill, *The Miseducation of Lauryn Hill*
11. Bumpy Knuckles, *Industry Shakedown*
12. Gorillaz, *Demon Days*
13. Kendrick Lamar, *To Pimp a Butterfly*
14. Rapsody, *Eve*
15. Nas, *Hip Hop Is Dead*

DE LA SOUL: A LISTENING GUIDE

Art Official Intelligence Series
1. Slum Village, *Fantastic, Vol. 2*
2. Common, *Like Water for Chocolate*, *Electric Circus*, and *Be*
3. Erykah Badu, *Mama's Gun*
4. The Roots, *Phrenology*
5. Kanye West, *The College Dropout*
6. Little Brother, *The Listening*
7. Guru, *Guru's Jazzmatazz, Vol. 3: Streetsoul*

The Grind Date
1. Dilated Peoples, *The Release Party*
2. Pharoahe Monch, *Desire*
3. Phonte, *Charity Starts at Home*
4. The Roots, *The Tipping Point*
5. Zion I, *True & Livin'*

And the Anonymous Nobody
1. Organized Konfusion, *Stress: The Extinction Agenda*
2. Gang Starr, *Moment of Truth*
3. Nas, *Life Is Good* and *King's Disease* series
4. Jay-Z, *4:44*
5. Tyler, The Creator, *Flower Boy*
6. Phonte, *No News Is Good News*
7. A Tribe Called Quest, *We Got It from Here . . . Thank You 4 Your Service*

ACKNOWLEDGMENTS

It is still difficult to believe that I've received the opportunity to spend the last couple of years researching, thinking, reminiscing, and writing about one of my all-time favorite rap groups. Thanks to Julia Chieffetz for offering me the life-changing opportunity to scratch this creative itch. Working on this manuscript provided a much-needed refuge from the tumult taking place where I live and work. To my agent, Sarah Khalil, thank you for guiding me steadily through the journey of publishing this project. Writing this book has been educational, and I do not know what I would have done without your willingness to teach me. I've also appreciated your helping me to keep perspective when I felt insecure about this process. I could not ask for anything more. Thanks to my editor, Nicholas Ciani, for all your work and for challenging me to take this book to another level.

To Mom and Dad, I wish you were here so I could show you how central both of you were in this project. This is not the book you thought I would write when both of you were alive, but I know y'all would be happy and proud of your "college boy." Thank you both for all of your sacrifices—performing manual labor, often more than forty hours a week, and keeping us fed, clothed, housed, and educated. Also, I could not have accomplished this without you teaching me critical thinking skills, instilling confidence in me,

ACKNOWLEDGMENTS

encouraging me to pursue professional training, and introducing me to your love of music. Mom and Dad, I look forward to reading this book to you.

Brandenn, Jeff, Amy, KC, Shae, Malik, Dryden, Lennon, and Jerrick "Terrell" Feagin—thank you for your encouragement and understanding as I hunkered down and wrote this book. Johanna Mellis, I do not have the words to capture my appreciation for your support while writing this project. Thanks for being my number one sounding board and keeping me motivated through a tough year.

This book would not exist if I didn't have the support of my friends, particularly my fellow hip-hop and music enthusiasts from Mansfield, Ohio, especially the CD Jungle crew—Dave McKean, Pete Kyrou, Jason Carrico, Jillian McLaughlin Kyrou, Michael "Bollfrog" LaFlamme, and Chanh Le. Your material support, especially the CDs, enriched my knowledge of music. I am also grateful to my friends who have influenced my social, political, and musical perspectives—Ronald Remark, Eli Osorio, Durrell Black, Jason Jones, Ethan Johnson, Demming Miller, Ryan Donaldson, Kevin Wharton, Storm Daly (RIP), and Darrick Jackson. I will always cherish our collective listening sessions and our long conversations about what we thought was "real" hip-hop. My experiences with you all also offered me foundational knowledge as I acquired a "degree" in hip-hop education in addition to my high school diploma.

Also, a heartfelt thank-you to Desiree Weber, Anne Gray Fischer, Stephen Ward, Garrett Felber, Simon Balto, Guy Emerson Mount, Sarah Myers, Tiffany Ng, Lauren Gottesdiener, and Jessie Wilkerson for your unwavering emotional and intellectual support throughout this project. Your contributions have significantly shaped the direction of this book. I am grateful to Katherine Jewell for your early-stage feedback on chapter drafts, which has been invaluable. Renée Nicholson, our manuscript discussions over lunches helped me flesh out many of the ideas appearing in

ACKNOWLEDGMENTS

this book. And to my department chair, Kate Staples, your efforts to free up my schedule on short notice for this project are deeply appreciated.

Thank you to all of my professors for teaching me the historical and theoretical methods I used in writing this book, especially Matthew Countryman, Matthew Lassiter, Hasan Kwame Jeffries, Zach Williams, Elizabeth Smith-Pryor, Scopas Poggo, James Upton, Christopher Phelps, Howard Brick, and Gina Morantz-Sanchez.

I am grateful to the students who took my The History of Hip-Hop in America classes at Auburn and West Virginia University. Your insights about De La Soul and the Native Tongues have enriched our discussions, helped me frame questions about hip-hop culture, and sharpened my analysis of the group's work. Also, thank you to my Auburn and West Virginia University colleagues who encouraged me to teach my hip-hop history courses.

Lastly, thanks to Kelvin Mercer, David Jolicoeur, Vincent Mason, and Paul Huston for inspiring my intellectual and political development in unexpected ways. You provided the soundtrack to my life. Schwingalokate.

NOTES

Preface

3   *De La Soul's incorporation of comical skits*: Open Mike Eagle, *What Had Happened Was*, season 1, episode 2, "3ft High and Rising: The Origins of De La Soul," Stony Island Audio, Spotify, July 2020, 1:13:30, https://open.spotify.com/episode/68TfpxwLetWlunMr5ZasD9?si=1eb c0f1b454741df.

7   *Francis Fukuyama wrote an analysis of the Cold War*: Francis Fukuyama, *The End of History and the Last Man* (New York: Free Press, 1992).

Chapter 1

9   *Posdnuos told Johnny Dee:* Johnny Dee, "Three Feet High and Yawning," *Record Mirror*, November 4, 1989, 27.

9   *"The idea that we could possibly go somewhere"*: Robin D. G. Kelley, *Freedom Dreams: The Black Radical Imagination* (Boston: Beacon Press, 2022), 2.

10 *"Different was always important"*: Tommy Boy Records, "De La Speaks (1989)," Reelblack One, January 21, 2019, YouTube, https://www.youtube.com/watch?v=wim7wgmhZYc; KEXP, "De La Soul Reflect On Discovering Hip-Hop and The Early Days of the D.A.I.S.Y. Age," November 18, 2021, https://www.kexp.org/read/2021/11/18/de-la-soul-reflect-discovering-hip-hop-and-the-early-days-daisy-age/.

10 *"may well be the 'Sgt. Pepper' of rap"*: Robert Hilburn, "Rap: Striking Tales of Black Frustration and Pride Shake the Pop Mainstream," *Los Angeles Times*, April 2, 1989.

11 *"In those days it was either live with music or die with noise"*: Ralph Ellison, *Living with Music: Ralph Ellison's Jazz Writings* (New York: The Modern Library, 2002), 6–7.

11 *"A fluid style that reduced the chaos of living to form"*: Ellison, *Living with Music*, 6.

12 *"Music called out to me at an early age"*: Posdnuos and Maseo, "De La Soul," in *The Streets Win: 50 Years of Hip-Hop Greatness*, eds. LL Cool J, Vikki Tobak, and Alec Banks (New York: Rizzoli, 2023), 161; "The Influence of Hip-Hop: De La Soul," Rock the Bells, March 29, 2023, YouTube, 58:47, https://www.youtube.com/watch?v=lmLasFX9pwA&t=1290s.

NOTES

12 *[Music is] oxygen*: Posdnuos and Maseo, "De La Soul," 161; Rock the Bells, "The Influence of Hip-Hop."

12 *"I was that kid walking the streets"*: Posdnuos and Maseo, "De La Soul," 161.

12 *"Dave was very colorful with his words"*: Apple Music, "De La Soul: '3 Feet High and Rising,' Dave 'Trugoy the Dove,' & Sampling," posted March 5, 2024, by Apple Music, YouTube, 1:03:03, https://www.youtube.com/watch?v=DxoZiNVOEZ0.

13 *"Long Island was a bit more multicultural"*: Kyle Eustice, "The Right Stuff," *Wax Poetics* 55 (2013), 80.

13 *"In LI you had your own four walls"*: Brian Coleman, *Check the Technique: Liner Notes for Hip-hop Junkies* (New York: Villard, 2007), 144.

13 *"I was going to block parties and backyard parties"*: Ethan Brown, "My Name Is Prince and I Make Beats," *The Source*, No. 115 (April 1999), 138.

13 *He worked with fellow Long Island rapper Biz Markie*: Brown, "My Name Is Prince and I Make Beats," 139.

13 *Maseo says he saw Paul at a party he attended*: "De La Soul," 161.

14 *Rakim grew up in mostly Black Wyandanch*: Rakim and Bakari Kitwana, *Sweat the Technique: Revelations on Creativity from the Lyrical Genius* (New York: Amistad, 2019), 7.

14 *Posdnuos and Trugoy grew up*: Rock the Bells, "The Influence of Hip-Hop: De La Soul."

14 *"This is where it all starts"*: Mass Appeal, prod., *De La Soul Is Not Dead*, September 8, 2016, YouTube, 29:09, https://www.youtube.com/watch?v=8i346sS-_8Q.

15 *"Everyone in the neighborhood"*: Rock the Bells, "The Influence of De La Soul."

15 *"Pos and I really clicked personally"*: Coleman, *Check the Technique*, 145.

15 *"I feel like we do everything"*: Sway's Universe, "DE LA SOUL Paying Homage to David 'Trugoy' Jolicoeur & Speaks on Their Catalogue Finally Streaming," March 3, 2023, YouTube, 58:50, https://www.youtube.com/watch?v=V46EiHI-TdU&list=PLaDbLcNgvWC943BgQT48RPavAT0kLUFbh&index=1.

15 *"My family are Haitian"*: Amir "Questlove" Thompson, "Questlove Q&A: De La Soul," *The Tonight Show Starring Jimmy Fallon*, September 28, 2016, YouTube, 9:07, https://www.youtube.com/watch?v=qA3L2ZzheBc.

15 *"People thought we were Spanish"*: Sway's Universe, "DE LA SOUL Paying Homage to David 'Trugoy' Jolicoeur."

16 *"One of the names I wanted to call Easy Street"*: Thompson, "Questlove Q&A: De La Soul."

16 *"Indeed, to go back in any historical (or emotional) line"*: LeRoi Jones (Amiri Baraka), *Black Music: Essays* (New York: Akashic Books, 2010), 176–7.

NOTES

17 *"Soul brothers and sisters"*: De La Soul, "Ain't Hip to Be Labeled a Hippie," 1989, track 26 on *3 Feet High and Rising (35th Anniversary)*, AOI, LLC, Tidal app.

18 *"We were just the average high schoolers"*: Eustice, "The Right Stuff," 80.

19 *"When I heard De La Soul the first time"*: Mass Appeal, *De La Soul Is Not Dead*.

19 *"And they had, you know, these unusual haircuts"*: Mass Appeal, *De La Soul Is Not Dead*.

19 *"When I first met them"*: Dante Ross, *Son of the City: A Memoir* (Los Angeles: Rare Bird Books, 2023), 119.

21 *"Of the average formulation"*: Ultramagnetic MC's, "Ego Trippin'," 1988, 2004, track 3 on *Critical Beatdown (Re-Issue)*, Roadrunner Records, Tidal app.

21 *"It was really Ultramagnetic that was the catalyst"*: Red Bull Music Academy, "Maseo Talks De La Soul, Sampling and Dilla," posted April 18, 2018, by Red Bull Music Academy, YouTube, 1:04:29, https://www.youtube.com/watch?v=7w3vkUWzGq4&list=PLaDbLcNgvWC943BgQT48RPavAT0kLUFbh&index=30.

21 *"Dave would be like, 'Let's take our fathers' old pants'"*: Russ Bengston, "How De La Soul Revolutionized Hip-Hop Fashion," *Complex*, August 27, 2016, https://www.complex.com/style/a/russ-bengtson/de-la-soul-revolutionized-hip-hop-fashion.

22 *He then connected his nephew, Mike G*: Coleman, *Check the Technique*, 156.

22 *De La Soul recorded* 3 Feet High and Rising: Coleman, *Check the Technique*, 147.

22 *"Whatever idea was brought to the table"*: Coleman, *Check the Technique*, 148.

22 *"It was just a process of all our separate lives"*: Ben Sisario, "De La Soul's Music Is Finally Back. It's a Bittersweet Victory," *New York Times*, March 1, 2024, https://www.nytimes.com/2023/03/01/arts/music/de-la-soul-catalog-streaming.html.

23 *"If you have a creative mind"*: Tommy Boy Records, "De La Speaks (1989)."

24 *"If PE advanced the art of sampling-and-stitching"*: Greg Tate, *Flyboy in the Buttermilk: Essays on Contemporary America* (New York: Simon & Schuster, 1992), 139–40.

24 *Although the album still contained the brash*: Critical appreciation for the Beastie Boys' Paul's Boutique has grown since its release in 1989.

25 *As one reads a comic book-style fictionalized origin story*: De La Soul, *3 Feet High and Rising*, Tommy Boy, 1989, booklet.

25 *"An inevitable development in the class history of rap"*: Robert Christgau, "3 Feet High and Rising," *Village Voice Consumer Guide*, March 28, 1989, https://robertchristgau.com/xg/cg/cgv389-89.php.

NOTES

25   *"One of the most original rap records"*: Michael Azerrad, "3 Feet High and Rising," *Rolling Stone*, January 21, 1997, https://www.rollingstone.com/music/music-album-reviews/3-feet-high-and-rising-95814/, accessed March 24, 2024.

25   *"The music they're doing is not like anything out right now"*: Tommy Boy Records, "De La Speaks (1989)."

26   *"I think De La Soul is some of the freshest music"*: Tommy Boy Records, "De La speaks."

26   *The latter means "to change"*: You can find the group's "Delacratic Dictionary" in Frank151's issue dedicated to De La Soul. The group's dictionary defines "buddy" as "like-minds and people coming together." People, of course, can assemble in many ways, so "buddy" still has multiple meanings. Frank151, "The Delacratic Dictionary," in *Frank151 Chapter 37: De La Soul* (Frank151 Media Group, LLC, 2009), 68–69.

26   *"That was the album version of 'Freedom of Speak'"*: Coleman, *Check the Technique*, 152.

27   *"True to the soul"*: De La Soul, "Change in Speak," 1989, track 3 on *3 Feet High and Rising*, Tommy Boy Records, CD.

27   *Cash's "Five Feet High and Rising"*: Michael Stressguth, *Johnny Cash: The Biography* (Da Capo Press, 2006), 96.

27   *"De La Soul took their abstract song crafting"*: Ross, *Son of the City*, 122.

28   *"A battle rhyme refracted through the brutal status consciousness"*: Jeff Chang, "3 Feet High and Rising," *Pitchfork*, September 23, 2018, https://pitchfork.com/reviews/albums/de-la-soul-3-feet-high-and-rising/.

28   *"The musical chorus of 'Potholes in My Lawn'"*: Chang, "3 Feet High and Rising."

28   *This conclusion should not come as a surprise*: Joseph Stanhope Ciadella, *Motor City Green: A Century of Landscapes and Environmentalism in Detroit* (University of Pittsburgh Press, 2020).

29   *De La Soul's dense lyricism on* 3 Feet High and Rising: William L. Van Deburg, *New Day in Babylon: The Black Power Movement and American Culture, 1965–1975* (University of Chicago Press, 1992), 216.

29   *"Dissident political culture"*: Robin D. G. Kelley, *Race Rebels: Culture, Politics, and the Black Working Class* (Free Press, 1994), 8.

29   *"Alternative" Black masculinity*: Jon Caramanica, "Celebrating De La Soul, with Questlove," *Popcast*, March 8, 2023, 13:55, https://www.nytimes.com/2023/03/08/arts/music/popcast-de-la-soul.html.

30   *"The Jungle Brothers' album* Straight Out the Jungle *was a blueprint*: *Hip-Hop Evolution*, Season 2, Episode 3, "Do the Knowledge," Darby Wheeler, director, aired October 19, 2018, Netflix.

31   *"'Buddy' is either a euphemism for womens or the P word"*: Tate, *Flyboy in the Buttermilk*, 140.

32   *"'Buddy' doesn't mean girl, or sex"*: De La Soul, "Buddy (Native Tongue

NOTES

32   Decision)," 1989, posted August 4, 2023 by WeAreDeLaSoul, You Tube, 4:50, https://www.youtube.com/watch?v=z8mfaAodcXU.

32   *"What the song really gets deep into"*: Tate, *Flyboy in the Buttermilk*, 140.

32   *Q-Tip, who raps about sticking out*: De La Soul, "Buddy (Native Tongue Decision)."

32   *This heterosexual clarity in hip-hop culture*: The latest trend in this homophobic clarity in the rap community is the use of the term "pause" any time a man says anything that might sound sexually "suspect."

32   *In a short verse preceding Q-Tip's and Queen Latifah's*: De La Soul, "Buddy (Native Tongue Decision)."

33   *While Ice Cube says he did not direct "Jackin' for Beats" at anyone*: Ice Cube, "Jackin' for Beats," 1990, track 2 on *Kill at Will*, Priority Records, CD.

33   *"That was another one of those moments where there were 25 people in the studio"*: Evan Serpick, "'3 Feet High and Rising': De La Soul's Track by Track Guide to Groundbreaking 1989 LP," *Rolling Stone*, June 3, 2009, https://www.rollingstone.com/feature/de-la-soul-1989-lp-3-feet-high-rising-track-by-track-guide-69292/.

34   *Lamar commands everyone to discard the "weird ass jewelry"*: Kendrick Lamar, "N95," Track 2 on *Mr. Morale & the Big Steppers*, Interscope Records, 2022, Tidal app. Hip-hop artists and podcasters Blueprint and Illogic also referenced Lamar's "N95" as a descendant of "Take It Off" on an episode of their podcast. See Blueprint and Illogic, "306: The Genius of De La Soul," *Super Duty Tough Work*, Stony Island Audio, March 2023, https://open.spotify.com/episode/36PVoGBRkbKdRX4xLvBHYM?si=5102432d098746ea.

35   *"Crime is a national-defense problem"*: Elizabeth Hinton, *From the War on Poverty to the War on Crime: The Making of Mass Incarceration in America* (Harvard University Press, 2016), 310.

35   *First Lady Nancy Reagan served as the leading spokesperson*: Clint Eastwood, "Just Say No," posted October 12, 2015, by The Oscars, YouTube, 1:32, https://www.youtube.com/watch?v=L-0OeOFuNXs.

35   *Ultimately, the federal government, local law enforcement, and local news media*: Max Felker-Kantor, "Dare to Report," *Inquest*, March 26, 2024, https://inquest.org/dare-to-report/.

36   *"Most-danceable anti-drug song"*: Havelock Nelson and Michael A. Gonzales, *Bring the Noise: A Guide to Rap Music and Hip-Hop Culture* (Harmony Books, 1991), 55.

36   *"A child is born with no state of mind"*: Grandmaster Flash & the Furious Five, "The Message," 1982 and 2004, Track 7 on *The Message*, Sugar Hill Records, Tidal app.

36   *"A baby is born into a world of pits"*: De La Soul, "Say No Go," 1989, track 14 on *3 Feet High and Rising*, Tommy Boy Records, CD.

36   *"By the time we were with Tommy Boy"*: Serpick, "'3 Feet High and Rising.'"

NOTES

37 *However, as journalist Donovan X. Ramsey illustrates*: Donovan X. Ramsey, *When Crack Was King: A People's History of a Misunderstood Era* (One World, 2023).

37 *He cites neonatologist Hallam Hurt's 2015 study*: Ramsey, *When Crack Was King*, 10; Donovan X. Ramsey, "How Dr. Dre and Hip-Hop Helped End the Crack Era," *GQ.com*, July 14, 2023, https://www.gq.com/story/when-crack-was-king-excerpt.

38 *The crocodile warns Trugoy of the "villains"*: De La Soul, "Tread Water," 1989, track 12 on *3 Feet High and Rising*, Tommy Boy Records, CD.

38 *"There's a very deep tradition in many African cultures"*: Harry Allen quoted in Rob Kenner, "De La Soul Picks Their Favorite (and/or Most Hated) Tracks," *GQ*, February 27, 2023, https://www.gq.com/story/de-la-soul-albums-streaming-favorite-songs-dave-jolicoeur-trugoy-the-dove?utm_medium=social.

38 *Posdnuos reiterates the group's commitment to their D.A.I.S.Y. ethos*: De La Soul, "Tread Water."

38 *"'Cause it's just about keeping your head and trudging on"*: Kenner, "De La Soul Picks Their Favorite (and/or Most Hated) Tracks."

39 *Unlike the straightforwardly political music of KRS-One's and Nelson George's Stop the Violence Movement's*: Ian Brennan, *Muse Sick: a Music Manifesto in Fifty-Nine Notes* (PM Press, 2021), 33.

39 *Music scholar and funk expert Rickey Vincent contends*: Rickey Vincent, *Funk: the Music, the People, and The Rhythm of The One* (St. Martin's Griffin, 1996), 26.

39 *According to Prince Paul, they thought recording a commercial single*: Open Mike Eagle, "3 Feet High and Rising."

39 *"Intending to try to identify and isolate the essence of p-funk"*: George Clinton, with Ben Greenman, *Brothas Be, Yo Like George, Ain't That Funkin' Kinda Hard on You?: A Memoir* (Atria, 2017), 214.

40 *"The crowd went bananas"*: "Do the Knowledge," *Hip-Hop Evolution*.

40 *"Mirror, mirror on the wall"*: De La Soul, "Me Myself and I," 1989, posted March 3, 2023, by WeAreDeLaSoul, YouTube, https://www.youtube.com/watch?v=jdtKT5q-CW8.

41 *The video's ending*: Tommy Boy Records, "De La Speaks (1989)."

41 *"They tried to take that song and make it the worst record possible"*: "Do the Knowledge," *Hip-Hop Evolution*.

42 *"We hate this song"*: Rob Harvilla, "A Roller Skating Jam Named 'Saturdays'—De La Soul," February 22, 2023, in *60 Songs that Explain the '90s*, 1:26, https://open.spotify.com/episode/1XIsiHbZLPvE0RpynaAzzE?si=b5eb84c7f4304784.

42 *"We consider our production 'Da Inner Sound, Y'all'"*: Tommy Boy Records, "De La Speaks (1989)."

NOTES

43   *"Random people would come up to me and [be] like"*: Mass Appeal, *De La Soul Is Not Dead*.

43   *Tom Silverman expressed disappointment in De La Soul's reaction*: Mass Appeal, *De La Soul Is Not Dead*.

43   *P.M. Dawn were were never thought of in the same way*: Jake Paine, "Kid Capri Details Exactly How B.D.P. Hijacked the Stage From P.M. Dawn (Video)," *Ambrosia for Heads*, April 24, 2017, https://ambrosiaforheads.com/2017/04/kid-capri-krs-one-pm-dawn-bdp-stage-video/.

43   *Even Questlove admits that he almost got into trouble*: Questlove, "QLS Classic: Tom Silverman," Questlove Supreme, May 2022, 3:15:56, https://open.spotify.com/episode/6bVQNcoBXNaEU5VZHEtfmw?si=10993a1af1784259; Questlove, "Monica Lynch, Pt. 1" Questlove Supreme, March 22, 1:37:31, https://open.spotify.com/episode/1XG40QgXkF9xQt3rcev6ET?si=1c5f9eb167e4413e.

43   *"I mean, every damn photo shoot, you can bet there was a florist"*: Mass Appeal, *De La Soul Is Not Dead*.

43   *"I came in for Patti Labelle"*: WeAreDeLaSoul, "The Sergeant Pepper's of the 80's ✾✾✾," Instagram, August 21, 2023, https://www.instagram.com/wearedelasoul/p/CwN0KnoMMOs/.

44   *"Hippies distinguished themselves by donning eclectic . . . bizarre clothing"*: Damon R. Bach, *The American Counterculture: A History of Hippies and Cultural Dissidents* (University Press of Kansas, 2020), xv.

45   *"People consider them as the hippies of hip-hop"*: Tommy Boy Records, "De La Speaks (1989)."

45   *"We were too white for black folks and too black for white folks"*: Clinton, *Brothas Be, Yo Like George, Ain't That Funkin' Kinda Hard on You?*

45   *"Soul brothers and sisters"*: De La Soul, "Ain't Hip to Be Labeled a Hippie."

47   *"It is true that many of the Black artists sampled by hip-hop producers"*: Chang, "3 Feet High and Rising."

47   *"Guidelines for hip-hop"*: Serpick, "'3 Feet High and Rising.'"

49   *"The most radical art is not protest art"*: Kelley, *Freedom Dreams*, 11.

Chapter 2

50   *"They were young Black men"*: Mass Appeal, *De La Soul Is Not Dead*.

50   *"There wasn't really room to go back into the studio"*: John Earls, "De La Soul—3 Feet High and Rising interview," *Classic Pop*, May 6, 2025, https://www.classicpopmag.com/features/de-la-soul-interview/.

50   *"Departure albums are when musicians pull a COMPLETE creative left turn"*: Jaelani Turner-Williams, "Questlove Salutes New Lil Yachty Album: 'I Love When Artists Pull off a Good Departure Record,'" *Okayplayer.com*, January 30, 2023, https://www.okayplayer.com/music/questlove-lil-yachty-lets-start-here.html.

NOTES

51 *The idea that the world was heading*: C-SPAN, "President George H. W. Bush Announces Persian Gulf War," posted January 15, 2016, YouTube, 12:12, https://www.youtube.com/watch?v=KJ6qpFpIFkY.

52 *"died . . . after a long and painful decline"*: Serge Schmemann, "The Soviet State, Born of a Dream, Dies," *New York Times*, December 26, 1991, https://www.nytimes.com/1991/12/26/world/end-of-the-soviet-union-the-soviet-state-born-of-a-dream-dies.html.

52 *"The ever-changing black experience in America"*: Lena Williams, "In a 90's Quest for Black Identity, Intense Doubts and Disagreement," *New York Times*, November 30, 1991, https://www.nytimes.com/1991/11/30/us/in-a-90-s-quest-for-black-identity-intense-doubts-and-disagreement.html.

53 *In what cultural critic Nelson George called "post-soul" America*: Nelson George, *Post-Soul Nation: The Explosive, Contradictory, Triumphant, and Tragic 1980s as Experienced by African Americans (Previously Known as Blacks and Before That Negroes)* (Viking, 2004), ix.

53 *In September 1991,* The Source *magazine published an issue*: Ras Baraka, "Mo' Dialogue," *The Source*, No. 24 (September 1991), 32–34; dream hampton, "Hip-hop Cinema . . . South Central Style," *The Source*, No. 24 (September 1991), 33–35.

55 *Democratic senator Joe Biden*: Edward-Isaac Dovere, "Joe Biden's Anita Hill Problem," *Politico*, September 21, 2005, https://www.politico.com/story/2015/09/biden-anita-hill-women-senate-clarence-thomas-213864.

55 *The statement carried forward the tradition of Black women*: Kimberlé Williams Crenshaw, "Black Women Still in Defense of Ourselves," *The Nation*, October 24, 2011, https://www.thenation.com/article/archive/black-women-still-defense-ourselves/.

56 *"World's most dangerous group"*: N.W.A, "One Less Bitch," track 11 on *Efil4zaggin*, Priority Records, 1991, Tidal app.

56 *To the surprise of critics*: Derek Thompson, "1991: The Most Important Year in Pop-Music History," *The Atlantic*, May 8, 2015, https://www.theatlantic.com/culture/archive/2015/05/1991-the-most-important-year-in-music/392642/.

57 *"They're obviously just corporate puppets"*: Chuck Klosterman, *The Nineties* (Penguin Books, 2023), 43.

59 *Drawing on cultural studies scholar Lawrence Grossberg's argument*: Jeffrey T. Nealon, *I'm Not Like Everybody Else: Biopolitics, Neoliberalism, and American Popular Music* (University of Nebraska Press, 2018), 55–56.

59 *Nealon argues that this negation highlights*: Nealon, *I'm Not Like Everybody Else*, 59.

59 *"We're in hip-hop, and there's a certain amount of bravado"*: Open Mike

NOTES

Eagle, *What Had Happened Was*, season 1, episode 6, "De La Soul Is Dead," Stony Island Audio, Spotify, August 2020, 1:11:50, https://open.spotify.com/episode/1M7QTeQszFFzHiyQeEpPSB?si=d16d422c625448a2.

60 *"De La Soul Is Dead"*: Mass Appeal, *De La Soul Is Not Dead*.

60 *"Death is a way to transitioning to something else*: Sway's Universe, "DE LA SOUL Paying Homage to David 'Trugoy' Jolicoeur."

60 *"He's better than any rapper I have seen"*: De La Soul, *De La Soul Is Dead*, Tommy Boy Records, 1991, CD Booklet.

61 *"The hippies of hip-hop"*: Quoted in Bob Stanley, *Yeah! Yeah! Yeah!: The Story of Pop Music from Bill Haley to Beyoncé* (W. W. Norton & Company, 2014), 501.

61 *"Ridiculous"*: A Tribe Called Quest, with Leaders of the New School and Hood, "Scenario (Remix)," *The Love Movement*, Jive Records, 1998, CD.

61 *"As we were recording the album"*: Open Mike Eagle, "De La Soul Is Dead," 9:26.

63 *Thus, to paraphrase a later Posdnuos lyric*: See Posdnuos's last verse on De La Soul, "Rock Co.Kane Flow," Track 12 on *The Grind Date*, A.O.I./Sanctuary Urban, 2004, CD.

65 *"Country"*: Otis Redding and Carla Thomas, "Tramp," Track 3 on *King & Queen*, Stax/Atlantic, 1967, Tidal app.

65 *"Like reading De La's journal"*: Kenner, "De La Soul Picks Their Favorite (and/or Most Hated) Tracks."

66 *"And while all of this was going on"*: Kelley, *Race Rebels*, 3.

66 *"hidden transcripts"*: Kelley, *Race Rebels*, 8.

67 *The group did not intend to record "Saturdays"*: Miles Marshall Lewis, "De La Soul: Their Incredible Career in 15 Songs," *Rolling Stone*, February 14, 2023, https://www.rollingstone.com/music/music-lists/de-la-soul-best-songs-1234676581/plug-tunin-1988-1234676739/.

68 *As scholars like Robin Kelley and Tera Hunter show us*: Kelley, *Race Rebels*; Tera W. Hunter, *To Joy My Freedom: Southern Black Women's Lives and Labors after the Civil War* (Harvard University Press, 1997).

68 *On "Saturdays," De La Soul is freeing themselves*: The group's "A Roller Skating Jam Named 'Saturdays'" is my favorite single. De La Soul might boast the genre's largest singles catalogs. Many of them resembled EPs (Extended Play) more than singles that featured multiple versions of one or two songs. On the vinyl and CD singles, De La Soul expands on the disco themes with a remix, "What Yo Life Can Truly Be," featuring verses from many in the Native Tongues camp: Posdnuos, Trugoy, Maseo, Q-Tip, Phife, Chosen Few, and Dres from Black Sheep. This song is a true remix as the lyricists spit rhymes about their favorite day of the week over a different beat built around Earth Wind and Fire's "Shining Star" and Tower of Power's "Ebony Jam." The lyricists chanting "Have fun!"

NOTES

reminds me of the hook to The Roots's "The Session (Longest Posse Cut in History, 12:43)," which appears on the group's first album, *Organix* (1993).

68 *"Random people will come up to us . . ."*: Open Mike Eagle, "De La Soul Is Dead."

71 *She "floats" into Macy's "like a zombie"*: De La Soul, "Millie Pulled a Pistol on Santa," 1991, track 15 on *De La Soul Is Dead*, Tommy Boy Records, CD.

71 *After deriving inspiration from seeing a houseless man wearing*: Kenner, "De La Soul Picks Their Favorite (and/or Most Hated) Tracks."

71 *According to the Rape, Abuse & Incest National Network*: RAINN, "Perpetrators of Sexual Violence," *RAINN.com*, https://www.rainn.org/statistics/perpetrators-sexual-violence, accessed October 23, 2023.

72 *"The record revels in hip-hop's eternal commitment"*: Scott Poulson-Bryant, "De La Soul Is Dead," *Rolling Stone*, May 30, 1991, https://www.rollingstone.com/music/music-album-reviews/de-la-soul-is-dead-250816/.

72 *Famed rock critic Robert Christgau gave De La Soul's second effort*: Robert Christgau, "De La Soul," *Robert Christgau: Dean of Rock Critics*, https://www.robertchristgau.com/get_artist.php?name=de+la+soul.

72 *"Closer to the sophomoric high jinks"*: David Browne, "De La Soul Is Dead," *Entertainment Weekly*, May 24, 1991, https://ew.com/article/1991/05/24/de-la-soul-dead/.

73 *Songs on 6 Feet Deep carried the same darkness:* Tyler, The Creator, and the collective he came into hip-hop with, Odd Future, is often seen as a descendant of the Native Tongues. The rapper sampled Gravediggaz's "2 Cups of Blood" on "LUMBERJACK," which appears on his 2021 album, *CALL ME IF YOU GET LOST*.

76 *"Watch me steppin'"*: De La Soul, "Pass the Plugs," 1991, track 19 on *De La Soul Is Dead*, Tommy Boy Records, CD.

Chapter 3

77 *"I am tired of these popcorn radio records that the label is looking for us to do"*: Kenner, "De La Soul Picks Their Favorite (and/or Most Hated) Tracks."

78 *"We could blow up"*: Scott Poulson-Bryant, "Dead Again?," *Vibe*, October 1993, 54.

80 *I did not know Joe Zawinul wrote the song*: Linda Hillshafer, "Stories of Standards—Birdland," *KUVOJazz*, no date, https://www.kuvo.org/stories-of-standards-birdland/#:~:text=%E2%80%9CBirdland%E2%80%9D%2C%20written%20by%20Joe,was%20released%20the%20following%20year.

80 *"The nineties will be the decade of a jazz thing"*: Gang Starr, "Jazz Thing (Video Mix)," 1999, track 8 on Volume 1 of *Full Clip: A Decade of Gang Starr*, Virgin, 1999, Tidal app.

NOTES

81   *"One of the most on-time records we ever did"*: Coleman, *Check the Technique*, 442.

81   *"The time was really experimental for us"*: Lewis, "De La Soul: Their Incredible Career in 15 Songs."

81   *"The process that established jazz rap as a formative rap subgenre"*: Justin A. Williams, *Rhymin' and Stealin': Musical Borrowing in Hip-Hop* (University of Michigan Press, 2013), 48.

82   *"When it came to hip-hop and jazz"*: Coleman, *Check the Technique*, 447.

82   *"The whole so-called jazz hip-hop movement"*: Danyel Smith, "Gang Starr: Jazzy Situation," *Vibe*, May 1994, 88.

82   *"On the jazz tip"*: Greg Watkins, "De La Soul: Still Grinding," Allhiphop.com, January 1, 2005, https://allhiphop.com/features/de-la-soul-still-grinding/.

82   *"Pos and me were both listening"*: Todd Gilchrist, "De La Soul Producer Prince Paul on Trugoy's Passing, Preserving Mistakes on '3 Feet High and Rising,' and the Group's Legacy," *Variety*, March 10, 2023, https://variety.com/2023/music/news/de-la-soul-prince-paul-trugoy-3-feet-high-1235549426/.

83   *Maceo Parker also learned the piano*: Maceo Parker, *98% Funky Stuff: My Life in Music* (Chicago Review Press, 2013), 7–8, 11.

83   *The trio left James Brown in the mid-1970s*: Parker, *98% Funky Stuff*, 148; Larry Rohter, "Godsons of Soul Reunite to Toot Their Horns," *New York Times*, October 5, 2011, https://www.nytimes.com/2011/10/06/arts/music/fred-wesley-pee-wee-ellis-and-maceo-parker-reunite.html.

83   *"The big hit on the record"*: Parker, *98% Funky Stuff*, 173.

84   *"Fred [Wesley] and I were hired to go to the studio"*: Parker, *98% Funky Stuff*, 167.

84   *"I really respect De La Soul"*: Parker, *98% Funky Stuff*, 167.

84   *"I wanted the work to be a manifestation of the music's intellect"*: Morgan Parker, "How Toni Morrison Wrote Her Most Challenging Novel," *New York Times* Magazine, October 20, 2022, https://www.nytimes.com/2022/10/20/t-magazine/toni-morrison-jazz.html, accessed November 27, 2023.

85   *"I use the term 'jazz' here"*: Cornel West, *Race Matters* (Beacon Press, 1993), 150.

85   *"The interplay of individuality and unity"*: West, *Race Matters*, 150.

87   *"Posdnuos said"*: John Morrison, "Philadelphia Rapper Shortie No Mass Introduces Herself to a New Generation on 'Here Goes Nothing,'" *Bandcamp Daily*, January 21, 2022, https://daily.bandcamp.com/features/shortie-no-mass-here-goes-nothing-interview, accessed November 27, 2023.

87   *"Really took the lead on a lot of this"*: Open Mike Eagle, *What Had Happened Was*, season 1, episode 11, "*Buhloone Mindstate*," Stony Island Audio, Spotify, 18:33, https://open.spotify.com/episode/3HETteXwLAJBGlhSwW1U0C?si=33de6f0b137442e2.

NOTES

88   *"And we strayed away from making fifty songs on an album and streamlined it"*: Todd Gilchrist, "De La Soul Producer Prince Paul on Trugoy's Passing."

90   *Even more seriously, racist and misogynist tropes*: Patricia Hill Collins, *Black Feminist Thought: Knowledge, Consciousness, and the Politics of Empowerment* (Routledge, 2000), 71–78.

91   *Duke's story recalls those of other child celebrities*: Duane Byrge and Mike Barnes, "Patty Duke, Oscar Winner and Sitcom Star, Dies at 69," *The Hollywood Reporter*, March 29, 2016, https://www.hollywoodreporter.com/movies/movie-news/patty-duke-dead-miracle-worker-878902/.

91   *The move grew so popular that Cloud One produced*: Electricladylandblog, "10 Things I Love about Patty Duke," *Electric Ladyland*, June 7, 2017, https://eclecticladylandblog.wordpress.com/2017/06/07/ten-things-i-love-about-patty-duke/.

93   *"'Patty Duke' calls out those who purposefully infiltrate hip-hop"*: Jennifer Peery, "De La Soul: Reincarnated," *The Source*, No. 50, November 1993, 41.

93   *"So if you're a gang member"*: David Mills, "From the Archives: Sister Souljah's Call to Arms: The Rapper Says the Riots Were Payback. Are You Paying Attention?" *Washington Post*, May 13, 1992, https://www.washingtonpost.com/wp-dyn/content/article/2010/03/31/AR2010033101709.html?sid=ST2010033101823.

96   *Reflecting the resurgence of Afrocentricity*: Staci Robinson, *Tupac Shakur: The Authorized Biography* (Crown Publishing Group, 2023), 174–75.

97   *"I had mad love for those guys"*: Ahmir "Questlove" Thompson and Ben Greenman, *Mo' Meta Blues: The World According to Questlove* (Grand Central Publishing, 2015), 147.

98   *"We didn't want to act like a bitch"*: Thompson and Greenman, *Mo' Meta Blues*, 147.

98   *"A manifesto where we tried to clearly articulate"*: Thompson and Greenman, *Mo' Meta Blues*, 147–8.

99   *"I am Shorty"*: De La Soul, "I Am I Be," track 11 on *Buhloone Mindstate*, Tommy Boy Records, 1993, Tidal app.

100   *"At the moment in time"*: Lewis, "De La Soul: Their Incredible Career in 15 Songs."

100   *"Jungle didn't fuck with us"*: Moses Reeves, "A Tribe Called Quest's 'The Low End Theory': 10 Things You Didn't Know," *Rolling Stone*, September 24, 2016, https://www.rollingstone.com/feature/a-tribe-called-quests-the-low-end-theory-10-things-you-didnt-know-106475/.

101   *"The boys had a lot of love-hate rivalries"*: Reeves, "A Tribe Called Quest's 'The Low End Theory.'"

NOTES

101 *"I lean more towards talking about what's going on in my life"*: Lewis, "De La Soul: Their Incredible Career in 15 Songs."

101 *"Pos hurt me when he did that"*: Tracii McGregor, "Tribal Scars," *The Source*, No. 78, March 1996, 112.

102 *"The only ones I feel from the Native Tongues is De La"*: "Using the Force," *The Source*, No. 89, February 1997, 92.

102 *"All labor has dignity"*: Martin Luther King, Jr., *"All Labor Has Dignity,"* ed. Michael Honey (Beacon Press, 2011), 171–72.

105 *"For me, 'Breakadawn' almost felt like"*: Kenner, "De La Soul Picks Their Favorite (and/or Most Hated) Tracks."

105 *He'd been listening to "I Can't Help It"*: De La Soul interviewed by Ebro, "De La Soul Reflects on Their Catalog & Legacy," 2018, posted March 3, 2023, by Apple Music, YouTube, 33:10, https://www.youtube.com/watch?v=xOt5SVuDQyk.

108 *"I remember shooting the video was the worst day"*: Kenner, "De La Soul Picks Their Favorite (and/or Most Hated) Tracks."

108 *"It almost felt like a slave record"*: Kenner, "De La Soul Picks Their Favorite (and/or Most Hated) Tracks."

109 *Critics participating in that year's Pazz and Jop poll*: "The 1993 Pazz and Jop Poll," Robert Christgau: Dean of American Rock Critics, https://www.robertchristgau.com/xg/pnj/pjres93.php.

109 *"Stauncher fans may wonder if Buhloone Mind State"*: Greg Tate, "They Go Where Few Rappers Dare to Follow," *New York Times*, October 17, 1993, https://www.nytimes.com/1993/10/17/archives/recordings-view-they-go-where-few-rappers-dare-to-follow.html.

111 *"It actually feels . . . inauthentic for me to rap"*: Zach Baron, "André 3000 on His New Album and Life After Outkast: The *GQ* Video Cover Story," *GQ*, November 16, 2023, https://www.gq.com/story/men-of-the-year-2023-andre-3000-profile.

Chapter 4

114 *"This was going to be our Marvin Gaye* What's Going On": "De La Soul Is Not Dead."

114 *"Patriarchal hip-hop"*: bell hooks, *We Real Cool: Black Men and Masculinity* (Routledge, 2004), 150.

114 *"If every young black male in America"*: hooks, *We Real Cool*, 148.

114 *"Death-defying"*: Aime J. Ellis, *If We Must Die: From Bigger Thomas to Biggie Smalls* (Wayne State University Press, 2011), 91.

116 *The budding superstar executive*: Cheyenne Roundtree and Nancy Dillon, "Bad Boy for Life: Sean Combs' History of Violence," *Rolling Stone*, May 28, 2024, https://www.rollingstone.com/music/music-features/diddy-friends-bad-boy-artists-abuse-violence-1235028178/.

NOTES

117 *"Make or break"*: Kierna Mayo Dawsey, "3 Wise Men," *The Source*, No. 82, July 1996, 67.

117 *"This was the first album where we knew"*: Mass Appeal, *De La Soul Is Not Dead*.

118 *"Transitional period in which the nation shifted"*: Manning Marable, *Race, Reform, and Rebellion: The Second Reconstruction and Beyond in Black America, 1945–2006* (University Press of Mississippi, 2007), 216.

118 *While the 1994 Crime Bill did not create mass incarceration*: Doug Stanglin, "Fact Check: 1994 Crime Bill Did Not Bring Mass Incarceration of Black Americans," *USA Today*, July 3, 2020, https://www.usatoday.com/story/news/factcheck/2020/07/03/fact-check-1994-crime-bill-didnt-bring-mass-incarceration-black-people/3250210001/; Williams Cole, "Against the Giuliani Legacy," *The Brooklyn Rail*, May/June 2001, https://brooklynrail.org/2001/05/local/against-the-giuliani-legacy-part-one.

118 *"In the early 1990s, resistance to the emergence of racialized social control"*: Michelle Alexander, *The New Jim Crow: Mass Incarceration in the Age of Colorblindness* (The New Press, 2020), 70.

118 *"Crisis in Black leadership"*: West, *Race Matters*, 51.

119 *"Farrakhan saw that vacuum"*: Henry Louis Gates, *Thirteen Ways of Looking at a Black Man* (Random House, 1997), 145.

120 *"Had the worst leadership in the black community since slavery"*: Gates, *Thirteen Ways of Looking at a Black Man*, 145.

120 *"Time to get paid"*: The Notorious B.I.G., "Juicy," 1994, track 10 of *Ready to Die*, Bad Boy Records, Tidal app.

121 *"For many African-Americans, the congressional inquiry"*: Donna St. George, "Church Burnings Raise Questions About Racism," *The Oaklahoman*, June 16, 1996, https://www.oklahoman.com/story/news/1996/06/16/church-burnings-raise-questions-about-racism/62352093007/; Quoted in Steve Walker, "The Evidence of Things Not Seen," *The Source*, No. 84, September 1996, 118.

122 *"Any love for Dr. Dre and Snoop Dogg and Death Row"*: XXL Staff, "Suge Knight Disses Diddy at the Source Awards—Today in Hip-Hop," *XXL*, August 3, 2023, https://www.xxlmag.com/suge-knight-disses-puffy-source-awards/.

122 *"The South's got something to say"*: Ben Brasch, "How André 3000's 'The South Got Something to Say' Speech Changed Hip-Hop," *Washington Post*, August 7, 2023, https://www.washingtonpost.com/history/2023/08/07/hip-hop-andre-3000-southern-rap/.

123 *"Washed up"*: Tupac Shakur, "Watch Ya' Mouth," Unreleased, 1996, posted December 12, 2022 by Makaveli Recordz, YouTube https://www.youtube.com/watch?v=_hzthkquD9s.

125 *"Start the revolution"*: Nas, "N.Y. State of Mind," 1994, track 2 on *Illmatic*, Columbia Records, CD.

NOTES

126 *A slew of classic releases in 1996*: Other releases in 1996 include Master P's *Ice Cream Man*, which included a breakout single, "Bout It, Bout It II"; Crucial Conflict's *The Final Tic*; The Roots' *Illadelph Halflife*; Jeru the Damaja's *Wrath of the Math*; Xzibit's *At the Speed of Life*; Westside Connection's *Bow Down*; Ghostface Killah's debut album, *Ironman*; Tupac's posthumous Makaveli release, *The Don Killuminati: The 7 Day Theory*; Lil' Kim's *Hard Core*; Snoop Doggy Dogg's *Tha Doggfather*; DJ Shadow's *Endtroducing. . . .* ; Foxy Brown's *Ill Na Na*; Mobb Deep's *Hell on Earth*; Keith Murray's *Enigma*; and Redman's *Muddy Waters*. Of course, I cannot forget Kool Keith, along with producer Dan the Automator and DJ Qbert, released Dr. Octagon's *Dr. Octagonecologyst*.

126 *"One of those amazing qualities that Paul brings is the zaniness. . . ."*: Mass Appeal, *De La Soul Is Not Dead*.

127 *"Man, it was just reflecting on real people's everyday struggles"*: Okayplayer, "In Their Own Words: De La Soul Reveals the Secret History of 'Stakes Is High,'" Okayplayer.com, January 5, 2023, https://www.okayplayer.com/originals/de-la-soul-stakes-is-high.html.

127 *"Rather than sirens and gunshots"*: Chris Norris, "Funky Fresh Grown-ups," *New York*, September 2, 1996, 50.

127 *"Me, as an individual, I express every level of it"*: "De La Soul *Rap City* Interview '96 Talking *Stakes Is High*," *Rap City*, 1996, posted March 2, 2023, by L. Millionz763, YouTube, https://www.youtube.com/watch?v=CGStQE3Ns3U&list=PLaDbLcNgvWC943BgQT48RPavAT0kLUFbh&index=18.

127 *"Since all of this is happening"*: Bönz Malone, "De La Soul," *Vibe*, August 1996, 86.

131 *"I got questions about your life"*: De La Soul, "Long Island Degrees," 1996, track 9 of *Stakes Is High*, Tommy Boy Records, CD.

131 *"It was heartbreaking because we're talking about Italian mobs"*: Okayplayer, "In Their Own Words."

131 *"This was reality for me"*: Okayplayer, "In Their Own Words."

132 *"They didn't have to be 'down'"*: Synapse, "Behind the Board," in *Frank151 Chapter 37: De La Soul* (Frank151 Media Group, LLC, 2009), 81.

133 *"Gambinos"*: The Fugees, "Red Intro," 1996, *The Score*, Ruffhouse/Columbia, Tidal app.

133 *"Acting like Sicilians"*: EPMD, "U Got Shot," 1999, *Out of Business*, Def Jam Records, Tidal app.

135 *Many women and men have since accused Combs*: Roundtree and Dillon, "Bad Boy for Life."

135 *"It's a dog eat dog competition"*: De La Soul, "Dog Eat Dog," 1996, *Stakes Is High*, Tommy Boy Records, Tidal app.

135 *"If it ends tomorrow, I got my daughter"*: "De La Soul *Rap City* Interview '96."

NOTES

136 *"The change in the business was taking place"*: Okayplayer, "In Their Own Words."

137 *"I don't get a whole lot of good food to eat"*: De La Soul, "Pony Ride," 1996, track 15 on *Stakes Is High*, Tommy Boy Records, CD.

137 *The houseless man's description of his experience*: While the houseless man's description is more haunting than Kanye West's sojourn through his personal struggles, I should note that *My Beautiful Dark Twisted Fantasy* features comments on racism and ends with a remix of Gil Scott-Heron's "Comment #1," which appears on *Small Talk at 125th and Lenox* (1970). West structures the song "Who Will Survive in America" around the question Scott-Heron asks on "Comment #1." Scott-Heron's question "Who will survive in America?" remains apt in the context of De La Soul's *Stakes Is High*.

138 *Q-Tip played some of his beats for Posdnuos*: Dan Charnas and Jeff Peretz, *Dilla Time: The Life and Afterlife of J Dilla, the Hip-Hop Producer Who Reinvented Rhythm* (MCD, Farrar, Straus and Giroux, 2022), 109.

138 *"'Stakes Is High' came up on the beat"*: Okayplayer, "In Their Own Words."

139 *"How does the music dictate real life"*: Mass Appeal, *De La Soul Is Not Dead*.

140 *"However, in an echo of the 1969 moon landing"*: Malcolm W. Browne, "Bright Comet Is Making Its Closest Approach to Earth Tonight," *New York Times*, March 24, 1996, https://www.nytimes.com/1996/03/24/us/bright-comet-is-making-its-closest-approach-to-earth-tonight.html.

142 *"Is it a crime to sex your mind to death?"*: De La Soul, "4 More," 1996, track 12 on *Stakes Is High*, Tommy Boy Records, CD.

145 *As historians Nelson Lichtenstein and Judith Stein write about the telecommunications law*: Nelson Lichtenstein and Judith Stein, *A Fabulous Failure: The Clinton Presidency and the Transformation of American Capitalism* (Princeton University Press, 2023), 412.

145 *According to historian Katherine Rye Jewell, Clear Channel*: Lichtenstein and Stein, *A Fabulous Failure*, 412.

145 *"Whereas saying and doing something original in rap"*: S. Craig Watkins, *Hip Hop Matters: Politics, Pop Culture, and the Struggle for the Soul of a Movement* (Beacon Press, 2005), 138.

145 *The bill generated so much anger within the Clinton administration*: Andrew Glass, "Clinton Signs 'Welfare to Work' Bill, Aug. 22, 1996," *Politico*, August 22, 2018, https://www.politico.com/story/2018/08/22/clinton-signs-welfare-to-work-bill-aug-22-1996-790321#:~:text=22%2C%201996,-. President%20Clinton%20hugs&text=After%20having%20vetoed%20two%20welfare,and%20Work%20Opportunity%20Reconciliation%20Act.

146 *"Superpredator"*: John DiIulio, Jr., "The Coming of the Super-Predators,"

NOTES

Washington Examiner, November 27, 1995, https://www.washingtonexaminer.com/magazine/1558817/the-coming-of-the-super-predators/.

146 *DiIulio helped spark a media panic*: Carroll Bogert and LynNell Hancock, "Analysis: How the Media Created a 'Superpredator' Myth That Harmed a Generation of Black Youth," *NBC News*, November 20, 2020, https://www.nbcnews.com/news/us-news/analysis-how-media-created-superpredator-myth-harmed-generation-black-youth-n1248101.

146 *"Opts to wax old school"*: David Sprague, "Stakes Is High," *Rolling Stone*, August 8, 1996, https://www.rollingstone.com/music/music-album-reviews/stakes-is-high-248757/.

146 *"De La Soul have settled for a series of serviceable, midtempo grooves"*: Jeff Salamon, "De La Soul, 'Stakes Is High,'" *Spin Magazine* (August 1996), 96, https://books.google.com/books?id=ODyv3kH8WPMC&pg=PA98#v=onepage&q&f=false.

146 *"And while they've always had a cynical streak"*: Ethan Smith, "Stakes Is High," *Entertainment Weekly*, July 12, 1996, https://ew.com/article/1996/07/12/stakes-high/.

147 *"It's a relief to have them back"*: Robert Christgau, "Consumer Guide," *Robert Christgau: Dean of American Rock Critics*, https://www.robertchristgau.com/xg/cg/cgv796-96.php.

147 *"Stakes Is High holds a singular place in my heart"*: Jack Hamilton, "When I First Heard *Stakes Is High*," *Slate*, July 20, 2016, https://slate.com/culture/2016/07/de-la-soul-stakes-is-high-and-hip-hops-nostalgia-problem.html.

147 *"A ferociously intelligent record"*: Hamilton, "When I First Heard *Stakes Is High*."

147 *"Seminal"*: Okayplayer, "In Their Own Words."

147 *"Apologies are in order"*: Blake Gillespie, "The Prophecy of *Stakes Is High*," *Vinyl Me Please Blog*, July 1, 2016, https://www.vinylmeplease.com/blogs/magazine/the-prophecy-of-stakes-is-high-which-turns-20-today.

148 *Benjamin, an activist and Black studies professor*: Ruha Benjamin, *Viral Justice: How We Grow the World We Want* (Princeton University Press, 2022), 131.

148 *"The cultural, political, and economic exigencies of the day"*: Marc Lamont Hill, *Beats, Rhymes, and Classroom Life: Hip-Hop Pedagogy and the Politics of Identity* (Teachers College Press, 2009), 3.

149 *"Police at least are reassured that the graffiti does not seem much more"*: Lisa Loeffler, "Neighbors Patrol Against Graffiti," *Mansfield News Journal*, August 20, 1998, 1.

150 *"Violence has been the inseparable twin of materialism"*: Martin Luther King, Jr., *Where Do We Go from Here: Chaos or Community?* (Beacon Press, 2010), 68.

NOTES

Chapter 5

154 *"The art that we do is official"*: Matt Muro, "De La Soul's Spirit Didn't Need City Streets," *New York Times*, August 13, 2000, https://www.nytimes.com/2000/08/13/nyregion/de-la-soul-s-spirit-didn-t-need-city-streets.html.

154 *"I think we did all the complainin' on the last album"*: Letisha Marrero, "Plug Chutin'," *The Source*, No. 132, September 2000, 214.

155 *"Once you're by your third album"*: WeAreDeLaSoul, "De La Soul Remembers Live at Tramps, NYC, 1996," posted April 26, 2024, by WeAreDeLaSoul, YouTube, 10:22, https://www.youtube.com/watch?v=Z7LnJy99YKo.

159 *Sahdeeq then ended his verse*: Hip-hop for Respect, "*Hip-hop for Respect*—'One Four Love (Pt. 1)' [Official Video]," 1999, posted April 15, 2021, by Francesco Marcone, YouTube, 4:07, https://www.youtube.com/watch?v=0N9LDJ04tac.

159 *I nodded my head*: Hip-hop for Respect, "*Hip-hop for Respect*—'One Four Love (Pt. 1)' [Official Video]."

159 *"The idea of doing a three-CD series was a joke at first"*: Rashaun Hall, "De La Soul Bows Triple-CD Project," *Billboard*, July 15, 2000.

160 *"The art that we do is official"*: Muro, "De La Soul's Spirit Didn't Need City Streets."

160 *"Regarding the series title"*: Hall, "De La Soul Bows Triple-CD Project."

169 *"This album isn't what people will expect from De La Soul"*: Hall, "De La Soul Bows Triple-CD Project."

162 *"A full-service company whose online home"*: Brian Coleman, "Public Enemy: Prophets of Rage in the Online Age," *CMJ New Music Monthly*, September 1999, 43.

163 *According to Jonathan Sterne*: Jonathan Sterne, *MP3: The Meaning of a Format* (Duke University Press, 2012), 1–2.

163 *"The [internet] allows a kid who has a .8 percent chance of getting signed"*: Coleman, "Public Enemy: Prophets of Rage in the Online Age," 43.

168 *"Get down to Disney World in Florida"*: George W. Bush, "Excerpts from Bush Speech on Travel," *New York Times*, September 28, 2001, https://www.nytimes.com/2001/09/28/us/a-nation-challenged-excerpts-from-bush-speech-on-travel.html.

168 *"The most patriotic thing we can do . . . is make money"*: David Barstow and Diana B. Henriques, "9/11 Tie-Ins Blur Lines of Charity and Profit," *New York Times*, February 2, 2002, https://www.nytimes.com/2002/02/02/nyregion/9-11-tie-ins-blur-lines-of-charity-and-profit.html; Emily Stewart, "How 9/11 Convinced Americans to Buy, Buy, Buy," *Vox*, Sep-

NOTES

tember 9, 2021, https://www.vox.com/the-goods/22662889/september-11-anniversary-bush-spend-economy.

168 *"Music is a part of everyone's life"*: "Apple Music Event 2001—The First Ever iPod Introduction," 2001, posted April 3, 2006, by JoshuaG, YouTube, 9:12, https://www.youtube.com/watch?v=kN0SVBCJqLs.

170 *"Posdnuos approaches the topic with a sensitivity"*: WeAreDeLaSoul, "'Baby Phat' (Official Music Video) [HD]," 2001, posted July 7, 2023, by WeAre DeLaSoul, YouTube, 3:49, https://www.youtube.com/watch?v=v-s5qNxnEyQ.

171 *"Stabbin'"*: De La Soul, "Held Down," 2001, track 6 on *A.O.I.: Bionix*, Tommy Boy Records, Tidal app.

172 *"It starts with a phone message*: De La Soul, 2001, "Trying People," track 18 on *A.O.I.: Bionix*, Tommy Boy Records, Tidal app.

173 *"For us"*: De La Soul, "Trying People."

176 *"Rome wanted Timbaland to produce"*: Noreaga, host, "De La Soul | *Drink Champs*," posted March 29, 2019, by Revolt, YouTube, 1:50:00, https://www.youtube.com/watch?v=jsv1R3PrGAU.

177 *"[Going independent] was the best thing that ever happened"*: Noreaga, "De La Soul | *Drink Champs*," March 29, 2019.

178 *Artist 50 Cent made news after earning a 100-million-dollar payout*: Zach O'Malley Greenburg, "Cash Kings 2007–2011: Hip-Hop's Top Earners," *Forbes*, December 27, 2011, https://www.forbes.com/sites/zackomalleygreenburg/2011/12/27/hip-hop-cash-kings-2007-2011/?sh=144a37fc369e.

178 *Lyricists like Eminem, Snoop Dogg, and Kanye West soon joined*: "Hip-Hop Cash Kings," *Forbes*, July 17, 2012, https://www.forbes.com/2007/08/15/hip-hop-millionaires-biz-cx_lg_0816hiphop.html?sh=40ae9f7f8547.

179 *"People gotta go out there and bust they, bust they ass for a job"*: De La Soul, "The Grind Date," 2004, track 5 on *The Grind Date*, A.O.I./Sanctuary, Tidal app.

179 *"Keep my John Deere out here plowin' the fields"*: De La Soul, "The Grind Date."

182 *"You know what I mean? Rap outsold crack"*: De La Soul, "Church," 2004, track 6 on *The Grind Date*, A.O.I./Sanctuary, Tidal app.

183 *"Yo! It's been instilled in me since infinite, y'all"*: De La Soul, "Much More," 2004, track 4 on *The Grind Date*, A.O.I./Sanctuary, Tidal app.

184 *Dave steps onto the tour bus like a superhero, wearing an Incredible Hulk arm*: "De La Soul—'Much More' (feat Yummy) *Chappelle Show*," 2004, posted August 13, 2009, by JKW3910, YouTube, 2:33, https://www.youtube.com/watch?v=GKLn53NRjHk.

185 *DOOM deployed his signature flow and his clever use of metaphor*: De La

NOTES

Soul, "Rock Co.Kane Flow," track 12 on *The Grind Date*, A.O.I./Sanctuary, 2004, Tidal app.

185 *"Everyone cools off from being hot"*: De La Soul, "Rock Co.Kane Flow."

185 *"Too old to rhyme. Too bad. Too late"*: De La Soul, "Rock Co.Kane Flow."

186 *Maseo said in his Red Bull Music Academy lecture*: Red Bull Music Academy, "Maseo Talks De La Soul, Sampling and Dilla."

187 *Viewers see Noodle playing her guitar while sitting on the edge of a floating landmass*: Gorillaz, "Feel Good Inc." (Official Video), 2005, posted June 28, 2016, by Gorillaz, YouTube, 4:13, https://www.youtube.com/watch?v=HyHNuVaZJ-k.

189 *But it would be Chicago rapper Kanye West*: Ethan Alter, "Kanye West Said, 'George Bush Doesn't Care about Black People' on This Day in 2005," *Yahoo Entertainment*, September 2, 2023, https://www.yahoo.com/entertainment/kanye-west-said-george-bush-doesnt-care-about-black-people-on-this-day-in-2005-130006321.html.

189 *"A lost decade of manufacturing"*: Robert Atkinson, "Why the 2000s Were a Lost Decade for American Manufacturing," *IndustryWeek*, March 14, 2013, https://www.industryweek.com/the-economy/article/22006840/why-the-2000s-were-a-lost-decade-for-american-manufacturing.

189 *"Ownership society"*: The White House: President George W. Bush, "Fact Sheet: America's Ownership Society: Expanding Opportunities," *The White House: President George W. Bush*, August 9, 2004, https://georgewbush-whitehouse.archives.gov/news/releases/2004/08/20040809-9.html.

Chapter 6

191 *"People say all the time"*: WeAreDeLaSoul, *We're Still Here (Now)*.

191 *He responded by channeling all of his angst*: Peter A. Berry, "DJ Premier Remembers the Fist Fights and Legal Troubles That Birthed Gang Starr's *Moment of Truth* Album," *XXL*, March 30, 2018, https://www.xxlmag.com/dj-premier-interview-gang-starr-moment-of-truth-album/.

195 *"Get away from here"*: De La Soul, "Get Away," Single, A.O.I., 2013.

196 *"take hip-hop and make that shit R&B"*: Wu-Tang Clan, "Intro," track 1, volume 2 on *Wu-Tang Forever*, Loud Records, 1997, CD.

196 *"baking works of art"*: De La Soul, "Get Away."

197 *However, this changed in 2015 as streaming numbers doubled*: Ed Christman, "U.S. Recording Industry 2015: Streams Double, Adele Dominates," *Billboard*, January 6, 2016, https://www.billboard.com/music/music-news/us-recording-industry-2015-streams-double-adele-dominates-nielsen-music-6835216/, accessed June 9, 2024; Victor Luckerson, "Streaming Has Officially Taken Over the Music Business," *Time*, March 22, 2016, https://time.com/4268402/streaming-music-digital-downloads-youtube-spotify/.

NOTES

197 *"The engine that fueled the recovery"*: Larry Wayte, *Pay for Play: How the Music Industry Works, Where the Money Goes, and Why* (University of Oregon, 2023), 115, https://opentext.uoregon.edu/payforplay/.

197 *Initially, many major artists like Taylor Swift, Prince, Garth Brooks, and The Beatles:* Steve Knopper, "Islands in the Stream: The 10 Biggest Holdouts in Digital Music," *Rolling Stone*, January 2, 2015, https://www.rollingstone.com/music/music-news/islands-in-the-stream-the-10-biggest-holdouts-in-digital-music-232923/.

197 *A byproduct of the rise of streaming*: See Chapters 4 and 5 of Rebecca Giblin and Cory Doctorow, *Chokepoint Capitalism: How Big Tech and Big Content Captured Creative Labor Markets and How We'll Win Them Back* (Beacon Press, 2022), Kindle.

198 *"We've been blessed to be in the Library of Congress"*: Jason Newman, "De La Soul to Make Entire Catalog Available for Free," *Rolling Stone*, February 13, 2014, https://www.rollingstone.com/music/music-news/de-la-soul-to-make-entire-catalog-available-for-free-70568/.

198 *So many Grateful Dead fans have recorded the band's shows*: Grateful Dead, Internet Archive, https://archive.org/details/GratefulDead?tab=collection.

198 *While some artists like Adele and Taylor Swift refused*: Luckerson, "Streaming Has Officially Taken Over the Music Business."

199 *Fintoni pointed to a blog post written by web developer Matthew McVickar*: Matthew McVickar, "It Appears De La Soul Themselves Hit the Torrents," *Matthew McVickar*, February 14, 2014, https://matthewmcvickar.tumblr.com/post/76652564304/tumblinerb-as-you-mightve-heard-de-la-soul-are.

199 *"Hip-hop is now in its 40s"*: Laurent Fintoni, "De La Soul Is . . . Dumb? Why the Group's Botched Album Giveaway Leaves Them Looking Bad," *Fact Magazine*, https://www.factmag.com/2014/02/16/de-la-soul-is-dumb-why-the-groups-botched-album-giveaway-leaves-them-looking-bad/.

200 *"Given De La Soul's sense of humor"*: Quoted in Geeta Dayal, "Free Samples," *Slate*, February 25, 2014, https://slate.com/culture/2014/02/de-la-souls-free-downloads-the-bands-long-complicated-copyright-tangle.html.

200 *"Perhaps the issue is as simple as De La or those around them"*: Dayal, "Free Samples."

201 *"But with a long stretch of Twitter trending"*: The Webby Awards, "De La Soul," 2014, https://winners.webbyawards.com/2014/specialachievement/241/de-la-soul.

201 *"So 3 Feet High and Rising has been preserved by the Library of Congress"*: The Webby Awards, "Questlove Presents De La Soul with Artist of the Year at the 18th Annual Webby Awards," posted May 20, 2014, by The Webby Awards, YouTube, 6:48, https://www.youtube.com/watch?v=DlOtvZChu7o.

NOTES

201 *"Check, check, testing, one, two"*: The Webby Awards, "Questlove Presents De La Soul with Artist of the Year at the 18th Annual Webby Awards."

202 *"We didn't feel comfortable getting back in bed with a label"*: DeMarco Williams, "De La Soul on Their Kickstarter-Funded Comeback Album: 'We Didn't Feel Comfortable Getting Back in Bed With a Label,'" *Billboard*, May 18, 2015, https://www.billboard.com/pro/de-la-soul-on-their-kickstarter-funded-comeback-album-we-didnt-feel/.

202 *TLC . . . had successfully launched a Kickstarter campaign*: Zara Golden, "TLC Raised $430,000 on Kickstarter for Their New Album," *The Fader*, February 19, 2015, https://www.thefader.com/2015/02/19/tlc-raised-430000-on-kickstarter-for-their-new-album.

202 *Since its launch in 2009*: Kickstarter.com, "About," https://www.kickstarter.com/about?ref=global-footer.

203 *"Here's the interesting part"*: De La Soul, "De La Soul's NEW ALBUM," *Kickstarter*, March 30, 2015, https://www.kickstarter.com/projects/1519102394/de-la-souls-new-album?ref=discovery.

203 *"Fans invest in the Kickstarter for the group to record the album"*: DJ Vlad, host, "De La Soul: Signing to a Major Label Is Slavery," posted April 27, 2015, by djvlad, YouTube, 14:41, https://www.youtube.com/watch?v=V5VslWglQrM&list=PLaDbLcNgvWC943BgQT48RPavAT-0kLUFbh&index=6.

203 *"A big part of it is cheap people and people who think everything's supposed to be for free"*: DJ Vlad, "De La Soul: Signing to a Major Label Is Slavery."

204 *"Freedom + Collaboration = Success"*: De La Soul, "De La Soul's NEW ALBUM."

204 *"Kickstarter was weird to me"*: Shawn Setaro, "How De La Soul Crowdfunded Their New Album with $600K from Kickstarter," *Forbes*, August 30, 2016, https://www.forbes.com/sites/shawnsetaro/2016/08/30/de-la-souls-kickstarter-success/.

204 *"There were reservations"*: Williams, "De La Soul on Their Kickstarter-Funded Comeback Album."

205 *"Traveling is tough"*: WeAreDeLaSoul, *We're Still Here (Now) . . . A Documentary about nobody*, 2016, posted August 26, 2016, by WeAreDeLaSoul, YouTube, 33:49, https://www.youtube.com/watch?v=tmpGJ7P_xsw.

205 *"You got your real happy moments"*: WeAreDeLaSoul, *We're Still Here (Now)*.

205 *"It's the process"*: WeAreDeLaSoul, *We're Still Here (Now)*.

206 *"As well where you know you will have people"*: WeAreDeLaSoul, *We're Still Here (Now)*.

206 *"Well nobody, nobody can do this no more"*: WeAreDeLaSoul, *We're Still Here (Now)*.

206 *"I am Nobody"*: De La Soul, *And the Anonymous Nobody*, 2016, booklet, AOI, LLC, CD.

NOTES

206 *De La Soul said they tried to get Willie Nelson*: Eric Diep, "De La Soul Talk New Album and Getting Snubbed by Willie Nelson," *Complex*, August 26, 2016, https://www.complex.com/music/a/eric-diep/de-la-soul-talk-new-album-getting-snubbed-by-willie-nelson.

207 *"I mean, like, it just means that we've put in a lot of work"*: WeAreDeLa Soul, *We're Still Here (Now)*.

207 *"I'm into public relations"*: De La Soul and Snoop Dogg, "Pain," 2016, track 3 on *And the Anonymous Nobody*, AOI, LLC, CD.

208 *"He'd mentioned . . . that we were one of the few hip-hop groups"*: Jared Wilson, "De La Soul Talk Crowdfunding Their Latest Release," *LeftLion*, February 23, 2017, https://leftlion.co.uk/features/2017/02/de-la-soul/.

208 *"I'm mortal"*: De La Soul, "Drawn," 2016, track 12 on *And the Anonymous Nobody*, AOI, LLC, CD.

209 *Listeners streamed* And the Anonymous Nobody: Victoria Hernandez, "Hip-hop Album Sales: Young Thug's 'No, My Name Is Jeffrey,' Lands in Top 10 of *Billboard* 200," *Hip-hop DX*, September 5, 2016, https://hiphopdx.com/news/id.40292/title.young-thugs-no-my-name-is-jeffery-lands-in-top-10-of-billboard-200.

209 *"The 18-song project is everything fans could have hoped for"*: Riley Wallace, "De La Soul Make a Strong Return with *And the Anonymous Nobody*," *XXL*, August 26, 2016, https://www.xxlmag.com/de-la-soul-make-a-strong-return-with-and-the-anonymous-nobody/.

209 *"One of their most ambitious and consistently rewarding albums"*: SPIN Staff, "Review: De La Soul, Still Rising After All These Years on *And the Anonymous Nobody*," *SPIN*, August 22, 2016, https://www.spin.com/2016/08/review-de-la-soul-and-the-anonymous-nobody/.

209 *"The album is bursting at the seams with high profile names"*: Kyle Eustice, "Album Review: De La Soul— *And the Anonymous Nobody*," *Consequence*, August 26, 2016, https://consequence.net/2016/08/album-review-de-la-soul-and-the-anonymous-nobody/.

209 *"If your impression of 'old man rap'"*: Nate Petrin, "And the Anonymous Nobody," *Pitchfork*, September 3, 2016, https://pitchfork.com/reviews/albums/22353-and-the-anonymous-nobody/.

210 *"Get it together forever"*: A Tribe Called Quest, "The Space Program," track 1 on *We Got It from Here . . . Thank You 4 Your Service*, Epic Records, 2016, Tidal app.

211 *"Industry Rule number four thousand and eighty"*: A Tribe Called Quest, "Check the Rhime," track 9 on *Low End Theory*, Jive Records, 1991, Tidal app.

212 *"The attention wasn't just because the group was giving its catalog away"*: Finn Cohen, "De La Soul's Legacy Is Trapped in Digital Limbo," *New York Times*, August 9, 2016, https://www.nytimes.com/2016/08/14/arts/music/de-la-soul-digital-albums.html.

NOTES

212 *"I mean, 3 Feet High and Rising is very much in danger"*: Cohen, "De La Soul's Legacy Is Trapped in Digital Limbo."

213 *In February 2019, the group posted on their Instagram page*: WeAreDeLaSoul, "Don't feed the Vultures," Instagram, February 26, 2019, https://www.instagram.com/p/BuWvRLMl6AM/?utm_source=ig_embed&ig_rid=71018951-6565-4bf4-8b7e-a5275c69bf62.

214 *To support the boycott*: Mark Sweeny, "Jay-Z Sells Majority Stake in Tidal Music Streaming Service to Jack Dorsey's Square," *The Guardian*, March 4, 2021, https://www.theguardian.com/business/2021/mar/04/jay-z-sells-majority-stake-in-tidal-music-streaming-service-to-jack-dorseys-square.

214 *"Just to put the nail in the coffin"*: WeAreDeLaSoul, "Thank You Friends and Fans," Instagram, August 9, 2019, https://www.instagram.com/p/B08l_UTFvCh/.

214 *Rostrum Records founder Benjy Grinberg*: Kyle Eustice, "Rostrum's Benjy Grinberg Joins De La Soul in Fight to Get Masters Back from Tommy Boy," *Hip-hop DX*, April 27, 2020, https://hiphopdx.com/news/id.55615/title.rostrums-benjy-grinberg-joins-de-la-soul-in-fight-to-get-masters-back-from-tommy-boy.

215 *"There's no getting through to this dude"*: "Teen Titans and De La Soul—Teen Titans Go! 'Don't Press Play,'" 2021, posted February 22, 2021, by Teen Titans Clips, YouTube, 3:08, https://www.youtube.com/watch?v=B8x-xyA34XQ.

215 *"Wage slavery," poverty, and war*: See copy of the Industrial Workers of the World (IWW) poster at Michael Mark Cohen, "IWW Cartoons," *Cartooning Capitalism*, no date, https://www.cartooningcapitalism.com/iww-cartoons.

215 *Two months later, to my excitement*: Jem Aswad, "Reservoir Acquires Iconic Tommy Boy Music, Groundbreaking Hip-Hop Label, for $100 Million," *Variety*, June 4, 2021, https://variety.com/2021/music/news/reservoir-acquires-tommy-boy-1234988666/; Brad Callas, "Talib Kweli Confirms De La Soul Finally Owns the Rights to Their Masters," *Complex*, August 8, 2021, https://www.complex.com/music/a/brad-callas/talib-kweli-de-la-soul-own-rights-music.

216 *Mannis-Gardner explained to* Okayplayer: Shawn Setaro, "Here's How De La Soul Cleared The Samples for Their Classic Catalog's Streaming Debut," *Okayplayer*, February 9, 2023, https://www.okayplayer.com/originals/de-la-soul-samples-deborah-mannis-gardner-interview.html.

216 *In August 2022, in a full-circle moment, DJ Prince Paul announced*: Bandini, "Prince Paul Confirms He Has Finished His De La Soul Project," *Ambrosia for Heads*, December 10, 2022, https://ambrosiaforheads.com/2022/12/de-la-soul-prince-paul-reunion-news/#:~:text=In%20August%20of%202022%2C%20Prince,and%20music%20engineer%20Scotty%20Hard.

NOTES

216 *On January 3, 2023, Reservoir announced*: Reservoir Media, "Reservoir Brings De La Soul's Iconic Catalog to Streaming Platforms," *Reservoir Media*, January 3, 2023, https://www.reservoir-media.com/reservoir-brings-de-la-souls-iconic-catalog-to-streaming-platforms/.

217 *However, I was struck by De La Soul's appearance*: Joe Coscarelli, "The Grammys Celebrate 50 Years of Hip-Hop in a Joyous Performance," *New York Times*, February 5, 2023, https://www.nytimes.com/2023/02/05/arts/music/grammys-hip-hop-50th-anniversary-performance.html.

217 *"It was a bittersweet performance for me"*: Ben Sisario, "De La Soul's Music Is Finally Back. It's a Bittersweet Victory," *New York Times*, March 1, 2024, https://www.nytimes.com/2023/03/01/arts/music/de-la-soul-catalog-streaming.html.

217 *"David Jolicoeur of De La Soul . . . has died"*: Ben Sisario, "De La Soul's David Jolicoeur, Who Rapped as Trugoy the Dove, Dies at 54," *New York Times*, February 12, 2023, https://www.nytimes.com/2023/02/12/arts/music/trugoy-the-dove-dave-jolicoeur-dead.html.

218 *"There's a sense that we have reached the far side"*: Jelani Cobb, "Hip-Hop at Fifty: An Elegy," *The New Yorker*, March 16, 2023, https://www.newyorker.com/news/daily-comment/hip-hop-at-fifty-an-elegy.

219 *"I thought about it [would] be cool"*: WeAreDeLaSoul, *We're Still Here (Now)*.

219 *"But Damon . . . started writing in a similar way"*: WeAreDeLaSoul, *We're Still Here (Now)*.

219 *"I kinda consider his portion of the record the afterlife"*: WeAreDeLaSoul, *We're Still Here (Now)*.

223 *"Like a Daisy, I need water"*: Jem Aswad, "De La Soul and Trugoy Finally Get Their Flowers at 'D.A.I.S.Y.' Party–Concert with Dave Chappelle, Queen Latifah, Common, More," *Variety*, March 3, 2023, https://variety.com/2023/music/news/de-la-soul-trugoy-daisy-dave-chappelle-queen-latifah-common-1235542305/.

224 *"A musical wake"*: Aswad, "De La Soul and Trugoy Finally Get Their Flowers."

224 *"You best believe my nigga Dave is looking down"*: Digital Hustle Films, "The DAISY Experience—De La Soul Tribute," 2023, posted March 4, 2023, by Digital Hustle Films, YouTube, 1:33:49, https://www.youtube.com/watch?v=cUG85HFwiPQ.

225 *"It was like freeing the slaves but adding vagrancy laws"*: Jaelani Turner-Williams, "De La Soul Talks Fight to Regain Control of Masters," *Okayplayer*, August 28, 2023, https://www.okayplayer.com/de-la-soul-peoples-party.

225 *Artists earn fractions of a penny*: Tidal pays out the most of all of the streaming services. Clare Mulroy, "Spotify Pays Artists (Sort of), but Not Per Stream. Here's How Much It Breaks Down To," *USA Today*, October 22,

NOTES

2022, https://www.usatoday.com/story/life/2022/10/22/how-much-per-spotify-stream/8094437001/.

226 *"In the week since De La Soul finally got around"*: Alphonse Pierre, "De La Soul Is Finally Streaming—But at What Cost?" *Pitchfork*, March 10, 2023, https://pitchfork.com/thepitch/de-la-soul-is-finally-streaming-but-at-what-cost/.

226 *"It's like saying everyone makes such a big deal about this red MAGA hat"*: Noreaga, "De La Soul | *Drink Champs*."

226 *And as we have learned about Cassie's allegations that Sean Combs*: Roundtree and Dillon, "Bad Boy for Life."

227 *"I see the opportunity to make legislation"*: Noreaga, "De La Soul | *Drink Champs*."

228 *Representative Rashida Tlaib and former congressman Jamaal Bowman recently introduced*: Damon Krukowski, "How Are Musicians Supposed to Survive on $0.00173 Per Stream?" *The Guardian*, March 28, 2024, https://www.theguardian.com/commentisfree/2024/mar/28/new-law-how-musicians-make-money-streaming; Congresswoman Rashida Tlaib, "Tlaib Introduces Living Wage for Musicians Act," *Congresswoman Rashida Tlaib*, March 6, 2024, https://tlaib.house.gov/posts/tlaib-introduces-living-wage-for-musicians-act.

228 *"Is Old Music Killing New Music"*: This trend of people listening to older music more makes sense. It is, in a sense, an analog to everyone buying CDs to replace their cassette tapes and vinyl records. Ted Gioia, "Is Old Music Killing New Music?" *The Atlantic*, January 2023, https://www.theatlantic.com/ideas/archive/2022/01/old-music-killing-new-music/621339/, accessed June 9, 2024; Glenn Rowley, "Old Music Now Makes Up Nearly 70% of American Consumption: Report," *Consequence*, January 21, 2022, https://consequence.net/2022/01/old-music-70-percent-share-of-market/.

230 *Of course, as journalist Jeff Chang argued in his* Pitchfork *review*: Chang, "3 Feet High and Rising."

Epilogue

231 *"Three black men sticking together, that's beautiful and it's important"*: John Earls, "De La Soul: 'Three Black Men Staying Together for So Long Is Beautiful and Important,'" *Classic Pop*, June 7, 2022, https://www.classicpopmag.com/2022/06/de-la-soul-interview/.

231 *"I think when you can show that we could come together sometimes"*: Noreaga, "De La Soul | *Drink Champs*."

231 *"Three black men sticking together"*: Earls, "De La Soul: 'Three Black Men Staying Together for So Long Is Beautiful and Important.'"

232 *"I think sticking together actually says a lot"*: Lyndsey Parker, "De La Soul on Carrying On, Honoring Trugoy the Dove's Legacy: 'Every Member

NOTES

Has to Actually Die Before This Thing Can Be Over,'" *Yahoo! Entertainment*, July 25, 2023, https://www.yahoo.com/entertainment/de-la-soul-honoring-trugoy-the-dove-legacy-195729983.html.

234 *"So to introduce the song"*: Talib Kweli, *Vibrate Higher: A Rap Story* (MCD, Farrar, Straus and Giroux, 2021), 5.

235 *"Welcome to the family"*: MSNBC, "Hear De La Soul on Lyrics, Music, Today's Rappers in Ari Melber 2023 MSNBC Interview," MSNBC.com, posted March 24, 2023, by MSNBC, YouTube, 28:04, https://www.youtube.com/watch?v=VTXXsN0GXtY.

INDEX

A
Ab-Soul, 213
Adderley, Julian Edwin "Cannonball," 81
Adele, 198
Ad-Rock, 163–164
Aerosmith, 72
Afghanistan, 67, 188
African Americans. *See also* Black Americans
   in the 1990s, 52–53
   adoption of term, 52
   Clarence Thomas hearings and, 54–55
   crack cocaine epidemic and, 37
   identity politics and, 54–55
   Levittown and, 14
   portrayed in *Boyz N the Hood* (film), 54
   Rodney King beatings (1991), 53–54
Afrika Baby Bam (Nathaniel Hall), 14, 30, 32, 67
Afrika Bambaataa, 19
Afrocentrism, 21, 30, 52, 79, 96
"Afro Connections at Hi 5 (In the Eyes of the Hoodlum"), 62
afro-futurism, 48–49, 210
"Against All Odds" (Tupac Shakur), 123
Aguilera, Christina, 155
Aid to Families with Dependent Children program, 145
"Ain't Hip to Be Labeled a Hippie," 45
Air Force, 4, 5
Albarn, Damon, 186–187, 205
The Alchemist, 3, 48, 229
Alexander, Michelle, 118
Alice in Chains, 57
Ali, Muhammad, 95
Ali Shaheed Muhammad, 14, 30
Allen, Harry, 38
All Eyez on Me (Tupac Shakur), 126
"All Good?," 165
All Hail the Queen (Queen Latifah), 30
alternative hip-hop, 57
Amityville High School, 14
"Am I Worth You?," 165
André 3000, 111, 122
And the Anonymous Nobody, 192, 205–210, 219, 235, 246
And the Anonymous Nobody (documentary), 204

Angles Without Edges (Yesterdays New Quintet), 110
animals, conversing with, 38
animation, 186–187
Anti-Drug Abuse Act (1986), 35
AOI (subsidiary label), 177
Apani B Fly, 144
apartheid/anti-apartheid movement, 6, 30, 52
Apple (company), 168–169, 198
Apple Music, 198, 225
A Prince Among Thieves (Prince Paul), 73, 74
Aquemini (OutKast), 2
Armstrong, Louis, 80, 81
"A Roller Skating Jam Named 'Saturdays,'" 67, 101, 107
The Arsenio Hall Show, 93, 94
Art Official Intelligence series, 45
   AOI: Bionix, 164–165, 169, 179, 199, 219
   AOI: Mosaic Thump, 154, 160, 163–164
   appealing to everyone, 169–170
   "cousins" of, 246
   mature themes on, 182
   name origin, 160
"The Art of Getting Jumped," 164
Aswad, Jem, 224
Atkinson, Robert, 189
Atomic Pop, 162
Auburn University, 1
"Award Tour" (A Tribe Called Quest), 102
Ayers, Roy, 81, 110
AZ, 117, 165
Azerrad, Michael, 25

B
"Baby, Baby, Baby, Baby, Ooh Baby," 142
Baby Bam. *See* Afrika Baby Bam (Nathaniel Hall)
"Baby Phat," 105, 170–171
Back on the Block (Quincy Jones), 79
Bad Boy Records, 116–117, 121, 122, 134–135
Badu, Erykah, 165
Bandcamp, 229
Baraka, Amiri, 16

INDEX

Baraka, Ras, 54, 133
barking dogs, 11
Bartz, Gary, 81
The Beach Boys, 25
Beastie Boys, 3, 20, 23, 46, 47, 163, 232, 233, 243
The Beatles, 25, 45, 170
Beats (company), 178
Beats, Rhymes, and Classroom Life (Hill), 148
Beats, Rhymes & Life: The Travels of A Tribe Called Quest (documentary), 3, 87, 120
"Beautiful Night" (Prince Paul), 73
"being down," 132, 172
Benjamin, Ruha, 148
Bernard, John, 88
Best Artist Webby, 201
"Betta Listen," 141–143
"Between the Sheets" (The Isley Brothers), 135
Beyoncé, 177
Bey, Yasiin (Mos Def), 110, 128, 156, 158
Biden, Joe, 35, 55
Big Daddy Kane, 79–80, 130
"Big Poppa" (The Notorious B.I.G.), 135
Big Sha, 74
Bilal, 165
Billboard, 56, 159, 202, 208
Bionix, 164–165, 169–173
"Birdland" (Quincy Jones), 79, 112
Birdman, 178
"The Bitch in Yoo" (Common), 122
"Bitties in the BK Lounge," 62, 64–65, 67, 69
Bizarre Ride II The Pharcyde (The Pharcyde), 81
Biz Markie, 13, 14, 47, 218
"The Bizness," 134–136
Blackalicious, 157
Black Americans. *See also* African Americans; Black music/artists; Black women
    Clarence Thomas hearings and, 54–55
    country or rural roots of, 28
    Million Man March, 119–120
    political leadership among, 118–119, 192–193
    Reagan era and, 37–38
    search for identity, in 1990s, 52–53
Black Bastards (K.M.D.), 184
Black churches, 121
Black freedom dreaming, 9–10, 48–49
Black Hippy, 213
"Black Is Black" (Jungle Brothers), 30, 40
"Black Korea" (Ice Cube), 107
Black masculine stereotypes, 46
Black masculinity, 10, 22, 25, 29, 30–31
    in albums of Ice Cube, 54
    criticisms of, 114
    "death-defying," 114, 131, 133–134
    De La Soul challenging dominant expressions of, 10
    in *De La Soul Is Dead*, 51, 65
    De La Soul Is Dead providing a model for, 75
    De La Soul's new, 52
    gangsta rap and, 92
    "gangster," 53
    "I Am I Be" and, 98, 102
    Native Tongues and, 30
    rap fame and, 78
    rap jazz and, 81
Black music/artists. *See also* rap music/musicians
    bell hooks on, 114
    "crossing over" to please white audiences, 91–92
    cultural appropriation and, 90–91
    dying young early, 218
    exploited by record labels, 82
    forward-looking, 16–17
    "soul" in, 16
    white artists stealing from, 46–47
Blackness, 53, 54, 61, 63, 91, 92
Black Panthers, 96
Black Power movement, 45, 53
Black Rock Coalition, 17, 26
Black Rutgers basketball players, 189
Black scholarship, Jazz aesthetics and, 85
Black Sheep, 88–89
Black Star, 156
Black Thought, 163
Black women
    hypervisibility/invisibility of, 89, 90
    Tupac Shakur's music and, 96–97
    used as props in gangsta rap party videos, 96
Black Wyandanch, New York, 14
Blakey, Art, 81
body positivity, 170–171
body sizes, 170–171
bombings, 120–121
Bomb Squad, 46
Bone Thugs-N-Harmony, 157
"Bonita Applebaum" (A Tribe Called Quest), 32, 33
Boogie Down Productions, 22, 23, 25–26, 128, 129, 149
Boss, Kenneth, 157, 159
Bow Down (Westside Connection), 122
Bowie, David, 60
Bowman, Jamaal, 228
Boyz N the Hood (film), 54, 92
Branch Davidians, 120, 121
"Breakadawn," 104–108
"Breaking Bells (Take Me to the Mardis Gras)" (Crash Crew), 20
Breezly Brewin', 74
"Brenda's Got a Baby" (Tupac Shakur), 96, 103

INDEX

"The Bridge Is Over" (Boogie Down Productions), 129
"Brooklyn's Finest" (Jay-Z and the Notorious B.I.G.), 123, 126
Brooks, Garth, 197
The Brothers Johnson, 4
Brown, Charlie, 101
Browne, David, 72–73
Brown, Ethan, 13
Brown, James, 83
Brown, Nicole, 119
"Buddy," 20, 30, 31–32
"Buddy (Native Tongue Decision)," 65, 107, 217
Buhloone Mindstate, 77–113, 117, 187, 208, 230, 235. *See also* individual song titles
   album/CD cover for, 86
   "buhloone" metaphor, 77–78
   "cousins" of, 244–245
   new voice on, 86–87
   recording of, 87–88
   reviews, 108–109
   thirtieth anniversary, 228
"Bullshit" (The Pharcyde), 138
Burwell, Sammy. *See* DJ Sammy B
Bush, George H.W., 52
Bush, George W., 166, 167, 168
Busta Rhymes, 14, 101, 107, 126, 182–183, 210, 224
Butta Verses, 177
Butts, Reverend Calvin, 114, 115, 125
By All Means Necessary (Boogie Down Productions), 23
Byrd, Donald, 81
Byrne, David, 206, 207

C

The Cactus Album (3rd Bass), 184
Calloway, Sway, 60
Campbell, Tevin, 79
capitalism, 68, 137, 168, 169, 179, 181, 187, 215
Cardi B, 1
Carne, Jean, 110
Carroll, Sean, 157, 159
Carter, Ron, 80–81, 82
Cash, Johnny, 24, 27
Cash Money Records, 155
Ced Gee, 20
Cee-Lo/Cee-Lo Green, 165, 171, 172
Chaka Khan, 163, 165
"Change in Speak," 26–27
Chang, Jeff, 28, 46, 230
Chapman, Tracy, 17, 64
Chappelle, Dave, 164, 183–184
The Chappelle Show, 183–184
Chappelle's Show (television show), 37

Charnas, Dan, 139
Chaundon, 179, 182–183
"Check the Rhime" (A Tribe Called Quest), 81, 211
Chic, 67
Chicago (band), 67
Childish Gambino, 213
"Children's Story" (Slick Rick), 156
"The Choice Is Yours" (Black Sheep), 224
Chokepoint Capitalism (Giblin and Doctorow), 197
Chokolate, 195
Christgau, Robert, 25, 72, 146, 147
Chuck D., 22, 29, 134, 162, 163, 224, 232
"Church" ("It's Reality"), 182–183
Church Arson Prevention Act (1996), 121
church arsons, 121
Clair, Joe, 136
Clark, Marcia, 119
The Clash, 57
Clear Channel, 145
Cleaver, Eldridge, 119
Clinton, Bill, 93–94, 116, 118, 121, 145, 153
Clinton, George, 17, 25, 39–40, 44–45, 48–49, 84. *See also* Funkadelic; Parliament Funkadelic
Clinton, Hillary, 146, 211
The Clipse, 177–178
Cloud One, 91
Cobain, Kurt, 56–57
Cobb, Jelani, 218
Coca-Cola, 178
Cohen, Finn, 212, 213
Cohen, Lyor, 117
Cold War, 5–6, 7, 49, 52
Coleman, Brian, 13, 22, 26, 162
Coleman, Ornette, 17, 80
College Media Journal New Music Report (magazine), 162
Collins, Phil, 105
colorblindness, 90, 189
Coltrane, John, 17, 80, 81
Combs, Sean "Puff Daddy," 105, 106, 116, 122, 123, 128, 135, 144, 156, 178, 226
"Come Close" (Common), 31
comical skits, 3, 126
The Coming (Busta Rhymes), 126
commercial rap, 139–140, 149, 150, 156, 187
Common, 21, 31, 33, 75, 110, 115, 121–122, 135, 138, 141, 158, 163, 177, 193, 205, 224
Common Sense, 121, 134
Company Flow, 75, 144, 156, 157

INDEX

Comprehensive Crime Control Act (1984), 35
Congressional Black Caucus (CBC), 119
"Conrad Tokyo" (A Tribe Called Quest), 210
Coolio, 218
"Copa (Cabanga)," 165
copyright protection/laws, 198, 213, 216
Cornelius, Don, 75
The Cosby Show (television show), 53
country music, 28
COVID pandemic, 222
"Cowboys" (Fugee), 133
crack cocaine addiction, 35, 36–37
Crash Crew, 20
Crazy Wisdom Masters (Jungle Brothers), 100
Crime Bill (the Violent Crime Control and Law Enforcement Act) (1994), 116, 118, 119
Criminal Minded (Boogie Down Productions), 128–130
Critical Beatdown (Ultramagnetic MC), 20–21
Culkin, Macaulay, 91
Curren$y, 178
Curry, Denzel, 110

D

Daddy-O, 19
"D.A.I.S.Y.," 26
"D.A.I.S.Y. Age," 18
D.A.I.S.Y. Experience, 223–224
D.A.I.S.Y. idea (Da Inner Soul, Y'all), 26, 38, 49
    Black masculinity and, 29
    De La Soul Is Dead and, 50, 51
    "Eye Know" and, 31
    killing off image of, 50, 51
    "Me Myself and I" and, 39
    misinterpretations of, 10, 42–43, 45–46, 88
    as a misinterpreted trend, 50
    negation of, in *De La Soul Is Dead,* 59–60, 62
    3 Feet High and Rising, 10
D'Angelo, 164, 165
Dan the Automator, 48, 176
DARE (Drug Abuse Resistance Education), 35
Daryl Hall & John Oates, 24, 36
Davis, Miles, 79
Dayal, Geeta, 200
Day-Glo D.A.I.S.Y. aesthetic, 10, 24, 49, 59
Dead Prez, 158, 167
death(s)
    of author's parents, 220–223
    of David "Trugoy" Jolicoeur, 217–219
    De La Soul Is Dead album name and, 60
    of the Notorious B.I.G., 143–144
    Tupac Shakur and, 104, 122, 143–144

Death Certificate (Ice Cube), 54, 77, 107
"death-dealing coolness," 114–115
"death-defying" Black masculinity, 114, 131, 133–134
Death Row Records, 116, 121, 122
Deezer, 225
Definitive Jux, 156
Def Jam Records, 20
"De La Game," 18
"De La Orgee," 30–31
De La Soul. *See also* D.A.I.S.Y. idea (Da Inner Soul, Y'all); Maseo (Vincent Mason); Posdnuos (Kelvin Mercer); Trugoy (David Jolicoeur)
    accomplishments of, 231
    after *Stakes Is High,* 154–156
    appearance on *Teen Titans GO!,* 215
    aspiring to be different, 10
    Auburn University students on, 1–2
    authenticity in, 115–116, 127–128
    Blackness of, 92
    catalog ownership, 212–214
    in concert, 232–234
    "cousins" of, 243–246
    creative freedom of, 45–46, 47, 48, 75–76, 176–177
    criticism of rap industry, 10–11, 62, 75–76, 88, 115, 139–140
    dispute with Tommy Boy Records, 211–212, 213–214
    documentaries on, 204–205
    on fame and success, 57, 78–79, 208
    first connecting with Prince Paul, 18–19
    formation of, 15
    futuristic drive, 17, 48–49
    on gangsterism and materialism, 115
    "hippie" image/label of, 10, 39
    hippie label and aesthetic of, 42–45
    invisibility of fall-off, 88–89
    jazz rap and, 85
    Kickstarter campaign of, 201–204
    legacy of, 231–236
    listening guide for, 237–243
    master recordings of, 216
    meaning and origin of group name, 15, 16–17
    message of, 9
    mid-1990s rap industry conflicts and, 123
    Native Tongues and, 100–102
    ownership of their catalog, 192, 211–216
    radio singles of, 104–105
    signing on with Tommy Boy Records (1987), 19
    sticking together, 231–232
    streaming services and, 197, 198, 212–213, 224, 227–228
    style and clothing of, 21
    Tommy Boy Entertainment and, 176

INDEX

Tommy Boy Records and, 179
   as "working" artists, 178–180
De La Soul Is Dead, 3, 4, 43, 50–76, 149, 199, 235. *See also* individual song titles
   as act of negation, 59–60
   album cover and illustrated panels in, 60
   author's identification with, 74–75
   "cousins" of, 244
   criticisms/reviews of, 88
   De La Soul defending themselves in, 63–64
   as departure album, 50–51
   rap musicals and, 73–74
   reframing identity of De La Soul, 61–62
   reviews of, 72–73
De La Soul Is Not Dead (documentary), 19, 126, 204–205
De La Soul music. *See also* individual song and album titles
   demo tape (1986), 17–18
   giving away their, 198–201, 212
   global politics/Black culture and, 6–7
   incorporation of other genres, 3–4
   influences of, 20
   lyricism and language, 20–21, 26–29, 62
   not accessible on streaming services, 2–3
   sampling techniques and approach, 2, 9, 22–24
   Tommy Boy catalog, 2, 3, 225
De La Speaks (documentary), 23
"Deliverance" (Space), 184
Democratic Leadership Conference, 118
Demon Days (Gorillaz), 187, 188
departure albums, 50–51
Descartes, René, 99
Devin the Dude, 170
Diallo, Guinean Amadou, 157, 158, 159
Diddy, 178. *See* Combs, Sean "Puff Daddy"
A Different World (television show), 53
Diff'rent Strokes (television show), 35
Digable Planets, 78, 84–85, 94
digital music, 162–163, 196–198, 212–213, 228–229
Digital Underground, 96, 97
DiIulio, John J. Jr., 146
Dilated Peoples, 144, 157, 178
Dilla Time: The Life and Afterlife of J Dilla (Charnas), 139
Dingilizwe, 184
DJ D-Nice, 129
DJ Kay Slay, 218
DJ Moe Love, 20
DJ Muggs, 48
DJ Premier, 47, 48, 155, 165, 191
DJ Quik, 116
DJ Red Alert, 22, 44–45, 100, 224
DJ Sammy B, 30
DJ Scott La Rock, 129, 130

DJ Screw, 18
DJ Shadow, 48
DJ Sub-Roc, 184
DJ Vlad, 203
DMG Clearances, Inc., 216
Doctorow, Cory, 197
"Dog Eat Dog," 136
Doggystyle, 109
Dolphy, Eric, 81
"The Donald" (A Tribe Called Quest), 210
Donaldson, Lou, 81
Don Cartegena (Fat Joe), 131
Done By the Forces of Nature (Jungle Brothers), 100
The Don Killuminati: The 7 Day Theory (Tupac Shakur), 123
"Don't Press Play," 214
DOOM, 48, 177, 184–185
Dorough, Robert, 27
Do the Right Thing (film), 84
double albums, 159
Double K, 218
"Down Syndrome," 132, 172
Drake, 1, 103, 196, 225
"Drawn," 208, 223
Drayton, William ("Flavor Fav"), 17
Dr. Dre, 73, 77, 92, 97, 109, 116, 122, 124, 155, 178
Dres (Andres "Dres" Titus), 88, 89, 224
Drink Champs podcast, 176, 226, 231
"Drop" (The Pharcyde), 138
drug use and drug control, 34–38, 70, 102
Drumming, Neil, 162
Du Bois, W.E.B., 16
Duke, Anna Marie "Patty," 90–91
Dumile, Daniel. *See* DOOM
The Dust Brothers, 24, 46, 48
Dylan, Bob, 198

E

Earls, John, 231
Earth, Wind & Fire, 4
East Massapequa, New York, 14
Eastwood, Clint, 35
Easy Street (rap group), 15
Eazy-E, 77, 129
Ebonics, 29
Efil4zaggin (N.W.A.), 56, 73
ego(s), 79, 94–95, 171–172
"Ego Trippin' (Part 2)," 87, 88, 94–98, 107, 123, 140
"Ego Trippin'" (Ultramagnetic MC), 21, 94–95
"Ego Tripping (there may be a reason why)" (Giovanni), 95
Electric Lady Studios, 165
"Electric Relaxation" (A Tribe Called Quest), 142
Elektra Records, 176, 184

INDEX

Elie, Lolis Eric, 80
Ellington, Duke, 111
Elliott, Missy, 4, 89, 107, 110, 144, 155
Ellis, Aime J., 114
Ellison, Ralph, 11
Ellis, Pee Wee, 83
El-P, 48, 156
Eminem, 103, 178
"En Focus," 86, 88, 89, 90
Entertainment Weekly, 72–73, 88
Enter the Wu-Tang (36 Chambers) (Wu-Tang Clan), 124
EPMD, 69, 78, 133
Eric B. and Rakim, 22, 23, 129
"Escobar" (persona), 131
Escobar, Pablo, 131
Estelle, 206
E.T. (film), 27
Eustice, Kyle, 209
"Eye Know," 30, 31, 32, 33, 59, 65, 106, 107
"Eye Patch," 81, 88, 130

F

The Fabulous Fleas, 67
"Fallin'," 151
Fanning, Shawn, 162
Fantastic, Vol. 2 (Slum Village), 138
Farrakhan, Louis, 55, 119–120
fashion and clothing, 12, 21, 33, 178
Fat Joe, 128, 131
fat phobia, 171
"Feel Good Inc." (Gorillaz), 187–188
Felker-Kantor, Max, 35
50 Cent, 178, 189
"Fight the Power" (Public Enemy), 39
Fintoni, Laurent, 199, 200
Fitzgerald, Ella, 80
"Five Feet High and Rising" (Cash), 27
The Five Heartbeats (film), 91, 108
Flava Flav, 177
flowers, 21, 31, 42, 43–44, 59–60, 223
flowers, in marketing campaigns, 43–44
Follow the Leader (Eric B. & Rakim), 23
food service, working in, 64–66
Forbes (magazine), 178
4:44 (Jay-Z), 169, 210
"4 More," 141, 142
Foxy Brown, 141
Frank (magazine), 132
Freddie Foxxx, 164
Fred the Godson, 218
"freedom dreaming," 9–10, 48–49
"Freedom of Speak," 18, 26
Freestyle Fellowship, 81, 85
Fresh, Doug E., 20
Frukwan, 73
The Fugees, 126, 133, 144, 146
Fukuyama, Francis, 7

Fulson, Lowell, 64, 65
Funkadelic, 25, 39, 45, 70. *See also* Parliament Funkadelic

G

Gambino crime family, 131
Gangsta B, 18
Gangsta Boo, 218
gangsta rap(pers), 54, 82, 85, 96, 114
   Blackness/Black masculinity and, 79, 92
   Criminal Minded (Boogie Down Productions), 129–130
   criticisms of, 133–134
   east coast, 116
   mid-1990s aesthetic, 117
   Stakes Is High and, 126–127, 129–130
   Tupac Shakur and, 96–97
Gang Starr, 78, 80, 150, 191–192, 232
"gangster" Black masculinity, 53
gangsterism, De La Sou's criticism of, 130–132
"The Gas Face," 184
Gates, Daryl, 35
Gates, Henry Louis, 119–120
Gaye, Marvin, 25, 117
Gee, Mike, 14, 30, 224
Geffen Records, 136
Genesis, 105
George, Nelson, 39, 53
George Westinghouse Career and Technical Education High School, 14
"Georgia on My Mind" (Maceo Parker and band), 83
"Get Away (The Spirit of Wu-Tang)," 195–196
Get Fresh Crew, 20
g-funk, 96, 116
Ghetto Music: The Blueprint of Hip Hop (Boogie Down Productions), 149
"Ghetto Thang," 36, 39, 70
Ghostface Killah, 103, 117, 121, 167, 177
Giblin, Rebecca, 197
Gillespie, Blake, 147
Gioia, Ted, 228
Giovanni, Nikki, 95
Giuliani, Rudolph, 118
Glaceau, 178
Glasper, Robert, 110–111, 232–233
Gnarls Barkley, 171
Goldman, Ronald, 119
Gonzales, Michael, 36
Goode, Wilson, 87
Goodie Mob, 144, 171
good kid (Kendrick Lamar), 74
"Good Ole Country Boy" (Parliament), 28
Gorbachev, Mikhail, 52
Gordy, Berry, 135, 187
Gore, Al, 166
Gorillaz, 186–188

284

INDEX

"Go Stetsa," 18
Gotti, John, 131
GQ (magazine), 38, 65, 105, 107–108
graffiti art, 149
Grammy Awards, 84–85, 111, 188, 210–211, 217
Grandmaster Flash, 3, 217
Grandmaster Flash & the Furious Five, 35–36, 57
Grateful Dead, 198
Gravediggaz, 73
"Grease" (Frankie Valli), 67
The Great Adventures of Slick Rick (Slick Rick), 23
Green, Grant, 81
Grinberg, Benjy, 214
The Grind Date, 177, 178–180, 182, 185, 186, 189, 206, 246
"Grindin'," 177–178
Grossberg, Lawrence, 59
"grown rap," 104
grunge music, 56
guns and gun violence, 71, 129, 130–131, 218
Guru (Gang Staar), 78, 80, 82, 85, 191–192, 232

H

hairstyles/haircuts, 21, 33
Haitian culture, 12, 15, 38, 150, 151
Hall, Arsenio, 61, 75
Hall, Nathaniel. *See* Afrika Baby Bam (Nathaniel Hall)
Hamilton (musical), 73–74
Hamilton, Jack, 147
hampton, dream, 54
Handsome Boy Modeling School, 176
"hard" rap, 54, 79, 82, 92
Hargrove, Roy, 165
Harlem Black Panthers, 96
Harlins, Latasha, 97
Harris, Kamala, 65
"Held Down," 165, 171
"Hell on Earth" (The Notorious B.I.G.), 117
Hendrix, Jimi, 45
"Here in After," 219, 220, 223
Hewlett, Jamie, 186–187
"Hey Ladies" (The Dust Brothers), 24
High Fidelity (magazine), 11
Hilburn, Robert, 10, 25
Hill, Anita, 55
Hill, Lauryn, 89, 144
Hill, Marc Lamont, 148
hip-hop
    battle over what constituted "real," 156–157
    combined with jazz, 82
    deepening an understanding of, 149–150
    De La Soul's contributions to, 183

De La Soul songs about, 241
    grind culture, 177–180
    Long Island and, 13, 14
    "Patty Dooke" and, 91, 93
Hip-Hop Evolution (documentary), 1–2
Hip Hop for Respect (four-song EP), 158–159
hippie aesthetic and label, 10, 39, 42–45, 51, 59, 61
Hi-Tek, 136
Hixon, Brandon, 204
Hobbs, Russel, 187
"Holler if Ya Hear Me" (Tupac Shakur), 97
Holmes, Larry, 123
homophobia, 32, 125, 134, 141
"Hoo Bangin' (WSCG Style)" (Westside connection), 122
hooks, bell, 114, 116, 128, 130
Houghton, Eddie "STATS," 147
houselessness, 137–138
"How Ya Want It We Got It (Native Tongues Remix)," 102, 156
Hubbard, Leonard, 87
Hurricane Katrina, 189
Hurt, Hallam, 37
Hussein, Saddam, 167
Huston, Paul ("Prince Paul"). *See* Prince Paul (Huston, Paul)

I

"I Am I Be," 77, 98–104, 105, 172, 175
"I Be Blowin'," 88, 99, 112–113
"I Can't Go for That" (Daryl Hall & John Oates), 36
"I Can't Help It" (Michael Jackson), 104, 105, 106, 108
Ice Cube, 33, 53–54, 74, 77, 101, 107, 119, 122–123
"Ice Ice Baby" (Vanilla Ice), 60, 61
Ice-T, 29, 79
Iconix International, 178
"I Get Around" (Tupac Shakur), 95–96, 97, 123
Illmatic (Nas), 121, 126
"I'll Stay," 70
"I'm Bad" (LL Cool J), 21
Immortal Technique, 167
Imus, Don, 189
individuality, theme of, 33–34, 171
Industrial Workers of the World (IWW), 215
"I Need Love" (LL Cool J), 32, 173
infidelity, 208
International Academy of Digital Arts and Sciences (IADAS), 201
Internet Archive, 198
"In the Woods," 87, 98, 102
Invincible, 158
The Invitation, 18
Iovine, Jimmy, 178
iPod, 168–169

285

INDEX

Iraq, 52, 167, 188–189
The Isley Brothers, 135
Italian mobs, 131–132
Ito, Judge Lance, 119
It Takes a Nation of Millions to Hold Us Back (Public Enemy), 3, 23, 24, 46, 129, 243
iTunes, 3, 169, 196, 198, 199
"It Was a Good Day" (Ice Cube), 107
It Was Written (Nas), 126, 131
"Itzsoweezee (HOT)," 150–153, 173, 188
"I Used to Love H.E.R." (Common), 75, 121–122, 135

J

"Jackin' for Beats" (Ice Cube), 33
The Jackson 5, 4
Jackson, George, 148
Jackson, Jermaine, 4
Jackson, Jesse, 6, 52, 93, 119, 193
Jackson, Michael, 4, 5, 49, 79, 91, 108
Jackson, Milt, 82
jail population, 118, 145–146
Jake One, 183, 184, 185
Jamal, Ahmad, 138
James, Rick, 60
"Janie's Got a Gun" (Aerosmith), 71
Jarobi (Jarobi White), 30
Jay Dee (J Dilla). *See* J Dilla
Jay-Z, 73, 103, 115, 117, 123, 126, 127, 128, 133, 150, 157, 168, 169, 178, 180, 193, 210, 214
Jazz (Morrison), 84
"Jazz (We've Got)" (A Tribe Called Quest), 81
"Jazz Corner of the World" (Quincy Jones), 79, 80
Jazz Is Dead, 110
Jazz Messengers, 81
jazz music(ians)/jazz rap, 11, 78, 79–85, 110–111
J.B. Horns, 84
J Dilla, 48, 111, 138–139, 156, 163, 165, 170, 177, 183, 186
Jean, Wyclef, 133
Jena Six case, 189
"Jenifa Taught Me (Derwin's Revenge)," 30–31, 64, 65, 141
Jermaine Jackson (Dynamite), 4
Jeru the Damaja, 123
Jewell, Katherine Rye, 145
Jews, Levittown and, 14
Jheri curl, 33
"Jimmy" (Jungle Brothers), 31
J-Live, 157
Jobs, Steve, 168
Jolicoeur, David Jude. *See* Trugoy (David Jolicoeur)
Jones, LeRoi, 16
Jones, Quincy, 79, 110, 112
Juice (film), 97
Juice Crew, 30
Juice WRLD, 1
"Juicy" (The Notorious B.I.G.), 116, 120, 128
Juju, 67
Jungle Brothers, 14, 21, 29, 30, 32, 40, 94, 100, 102, 151, 156
Junior M.A.F.I.A., 141
Jurassic 5, 157
"Just Say No" campaign, 35, 36

K

Kaelin, Kato, 119
Kangol hat, 40
Kanye West. *See* West, Kanye
Karson, Jamie, 168
Kelley, Robin D.G., 9–10, 48, 49, 66, 68
Kent State University, 190, 193
Khalid, 195
"Kick in the Door" (The Notorious B.I.G.), 123
Kickstarter campaign, 201–204
Kid Capri, 151
Killer Mike, 110–111
King, John, 24
King, Martin Luther Jr., 120, 125, 150–151, 193, 211
King of New York (film), 131
"King of New York," 116–117
King, Rodney, 53–54, 119, 157
Kiss FM, 13, 22
Klosterman, Chuck, 57
K.M.D., 184
"Knee Deep" (Parliament), 5, 106
Knight, Suge, 116, 122, 207–208
Knowles, Matthew, 177
Koch Records, 203
Kool G Rap, 116, 158
Kool Keith, 20, 21, 38, 74
Kool Moe Dee, 22, 79–80
Koresh, David, 120, 151
Kravitz, Lenny, 17
KRS-One, 29, 39, 43, 94, 116, 129, 178

L

Labcabincalifornia (The Pharcyde), 138
"La Di Da Di" (Doug E. Fresh), 20
"Ladies First" (Queen Latifah and Monie Love), 1, 32, 224
Ladson-Billings, Gloria, 148
Lamar, Kendrick, 1, 4, 34, 74, 111, 210, 213
Large Professor, 48
La Rock, Scott, 129–130
Latifah. *See* Queen Latifah
Latinx audience, 15
Leaders of the New School, 101, 126
Leary, Denis, 168

INDEX

Lee, Spike, 80, 84, 182
LeftLion, 208
"Let, Let Me In," 64–65
Let's Start Here (Lil Yachty), 50
Levittown suburb, 14
Levitt & Sons, 14
Levitt, William, 14
Lewis, John, 120
Lewis, Mel "Chaos," 87
Lewis, Miles Marshall, 81, 100
Lewis, Ramsey, 81
Licensed to Ill (Beastie Boys), 20
Lichtenstein, Nelson, 145
Life After Death (The Notorious B.I.G.), 131
Life on Planet Groove (Maceo Parker), 83
"The Light" (Common), 224
Like Water for Chocolate (Common), 138
Lil' Kim, 141, 180
Lil Yachty, 50–51
Limp Bizkit, 155
Little Brother, 180
Little Dragon, 206
Living Colour, 17, 26
Living Wage for Musicians Act, 228
LL Cool J, 12, 15, 20, 21, 22, 29, 32, 149
"Long Island Degrees," 130–134, 182
Long Island, New York, 12, 13–14
"Long Island Wildin'," 88
"Lord Intended," 205, 207
Lords of the Underground, 151
Los Angeles Police Department (LAPD), 35, 37
Los Angeles Times, 10, 25
Lost Boyz, 232
"Lost Somebody" (A Tribe Called Quest), 210
Louganis, Greg, 134
The Love Movement (A Tribe Called Quest), 156
Lover, Ed, 205
love songs, 32, 33
The Low End Theory (A Tribe Called Quest), 80–81, 82, 160
Luck (Posdnuos's brother), 14
Lucy Pearl, 156
Lynch, Monica, 19, 22
lyricism and language
  AOI albums, 169–170
  in *De La Soul Is Dead*, 62
  De La Soul's higher level of, 26–29
  De La Soul's inspiration for, 20–21
  misogynist, 141
  Stakes Is High/"Stakes Is High," 130, 140
Lyubovny, Vladislav, 203

M

m.A.A.d city (Kendrick Lamar), 74
Mack 10, 122–123
Mack, Craig, 134, 135
Madden, Steve, 168
The Mad Lads, 26
Madlib, 48, 110, 156, 185
Madvillainy (DOOM and Madlib), 185
Mafioso ideology/personas, 116, 128, 131–132, 133, 139–140, 151
"The Magic Number," 27
Malcolm X, 125
Mandela, Nelson, 6
Mann, Herbie, 81
Mannie Fresh, 155
Mannis-Gardner, Deborah, 216
Mansfield, Ohio, 4
Marable, Manning, 117–118
Marciano, Roc, 206
Marrero, Letisha, 154
Marsalis, Branford, 80
Marshall, Thurgood, 54
Martin, Terrace, 111
MASA hat (Make Artists Slaves Again), 226
Maseo (Vincent Mason)
  birthplace, 13
  choosing stage name, 15–16
  connecting with Prince Paul, 18–19
  desire for freedom, 9
  dress, 1
  early experiences with music, 12
  formation of De La Soul and, 15
  "plug" name of, 16
Mason, Vincent. *See* Maseo (Vincent Mason)
Master P, 155, 157
materialism, 34, 98, 135, 150, 151, 156, 182. *See also* wealth, pursuit and displays of
The Maury Povich Show, 138
MCA, 24, 136, 232
McCoy, Angelith and Melvin, 4, 5–6, 52, 53, 57–58, 79, 157–158, 160–161, 166, 175, 180–182, 190, 193, 220–222
McCoy, Austin
  early music experiences, 4–5
  early political memories of, 6, 193
  education, 160–161, 190, 194
  emotional expression by, 103–104
  high school years of, 124–125
  illness during college, 174–175
  influence of De La Soul on, 5–6
  influence of *Stakes Is High* on, 149–150
  seeing De La Soul in concert, 232–234
  wearing glasses, 58–59
McCoy, Brandenn, 5, 175, 190, 221, 222
MC Hammer, 60–61, 81
McLeod, Kembrew, 200
MC Lyte, 26, 141
McMellon, Edward, 157, 159
McVeigh, Timothy, 120–121
McVickar, Matthew, 199
Melber, Ari, 235

INDEX

Melle Mel, 36, 38, 79, 94
"Me Myself and I," 1, 4–5, 9, 39, 40–42, 59, 67, 88, 94, 105, 107, 151
Menace II Society (film), 92
Mercer, Kelvin. *See* Posdnuos (Kelvin Mercer)
"The Message" (Grandmaster Flash & the Furious Five's), 35–36, 38
Method Man, 165
MF Doom, 184–185
Mighty Ryders, 67
Migos, 1
Mike D, 163–164
Mike Gee (Michael Small), 14, 22, 30
Miller, Mac, 218
"Millie Pulled a Pistol on Santa," 70–71, 73
Million Man March, 55, 119–120
Mills, David, 93
The Mindbenders, 70
"Mind Power" (James Brown), 138
Miranda, Lin Manuel, 74
misogyny, 114, 116, 125, 141
MM..FOOD (DOOM), 185
Mobb Deep, 115, 117, 123, 232
Mo' Better Blues (film), 80, 84
mob-inspired songs and albums, 116–117
Mojica, Vinia, 101
Moment of Truth (Gang Starr), 150, 191–192
Monch, Pharoahe, 136, 144, 157, 163
Monica, Vinia, 68
Monie Love, 1, 29, 30, 32, 151, 224
Monk, Thelonious, 81
Montana, Tony, 131
Morrison, John, 87
Morrison, Toni, 84
Mosaic Thump, 154, 160, 163–164
Mos Def, 33, 75, 115, 136, 144, 157, 158
Mother Emanuel African Methodist Episcopal Church, 121
Motown Records, 135, 187
MP3s, 162–163
MP3: The Meaning of a Format (Sterne), 163
Mr. Morale & The Big Steppers (Kendrick Lamar), 210
MTV Music Video Awards, 188
"Much More," 105, 183–184, 186
Muhammad, Ali Shaheed, 30, 110, 138, 156
Murdoc Niccals, 187
Murphy, Richard, 157, 159
Murry Bergtraum High School, 14
music. *See also* hip-hop; rap music/musicians; streaming services
   author's early experiences with, 4–5
   De La Soul's knowledge of, 128–129
   earnings from streaming, 224–228
   evolving tastes in, 112–113
   iPod/iTunes and, 168–169
   neo-soul, 164–165, 169
   soul, 164–165
   spirituality, Black, 16
   music distribution, 227–228. *See also* digital music; streaming services
My Beautiful Dark Twisted Fantasy (Kanye West), 137
"My Brother's a Basehead," 70, 75

N

"N95" (Kendrick Lamar), 34
Napster, 162, 169
Nas, 115, 117, 121, 123, 124, 126, 127, 128, 131, 141, 167, 169, 180, 193
National of Islam (NOI), 119
Native Tongues, 1, 3, 14, 22, 29, 30, 33, 67, 75, 86–87, 89, 93, 99–100, 101–102, 105, 110, 126, 151, 156, 165, 176, 208, 210, 224, 238
Naughty by Nature, 130, 164
Nealon, Jeffrey T., 59
Nelson, Havelock, 36
neo-soul music, 164–165, 169
The Neptunes, 155
Nevermind (Nirvana), 56
New Blue Sun (André 3000), 111
New Jack City (film), 37, 92
The New Jim Crow (Alexander), 118
"New World Order" speech (Bush), 52
The New Yorker, 218
New York Times, 22, 52, 55, 109, 160, 212, 217
Nichols, Rich, 87
"Night of the Living Baseheads" (Public Enemy), 35–36
Nike Dunks, 204
98% Funky Stuff (Maceo Parker), 83, 84
9th Wonder, 48, 156
Nirvana, 56–58
"(Not Just) Knee Deep" (Parliament Funkadelic), 39–40
No Limit Records, 155
No Malice, 177–178
Noodle, 187
Norris, Chris, 127
"No Strings Attached" (The Mad Lads), 26
The Notorious B.I.G. (Christopher Wallace), 14, 74, 89, 97, 114–115, 116, 121, 124, 131, 135, 155
"Not Over Till the Fat Lady Plays the Demo," 69, 73
nuclear weapons, 6
N.W.A, 23, 29, 54, 73, 101
"N.Y. State of Mind" (Nas), 125

O

Obama, Barack, 192–193
Odd Future, 1, 213, 235
Off the Wall (Michael Jackson), 79, 104, 108
Ohio State University, 160, 180

INDEX

"Oh Mr. Sprinkler, Mr. Sprinkler," 67–68
Okayplayer, 127, 131, 136, 138, 147, 216
Oklahoma City bombing (1995), 120–121
One Day It'll All Make Sense (Common), 75
Only Built 4 Cuban Linx (Raekwon), 121–122, 131
onomatopoeia, 62
"On the Radio" (Crash Crew), 20
"Oodles of O's," 62
"Oooh," 105
Open Mike Eagle, 59, 87, 210
Operation: Doomsday (MF DOOM), 185
Organized Konfusion, 151
Organized Noize, 158
Osmium (Parliament), 28
OutKast, 2, 4, 122, 144, 155
Out of Business (EPMD), 133
Out of Time (R.E.M.), 56

P

Paid in Full (Run-D.M.C.), 24, 129
"Pain," 207
Pandora, 196, 225
P.A. Pasemaster Mase. *See* Maseo (Vincent Mason)
Paris, 167
Parker, Charlie, 79, 80
Parker, Lyndsey, 232
Parker, Maceo, 82–83
Parks, Rosa, 125
Parliament, 5, 28, 39, 40, 45
Parliament Funkadelic, 24, 28, 40, 45, 62, 83, 96. *See also* Clinton, George
Parlophone, 213
"Pass the Peas" (Maceo Parker), 83
"Pass the Plugs," 75, 83
pastiche sampling techniques, 3
patriarchy, 120
Patriot Act, 188
"Patti Dooke," 88, 90–93, 106
"patty duke" move, 91
Paul's Boutique (Beastie Boys), 3
Paul's Boutique (The Dust Brothers), 24
"Pawn Star," 171
peace sign, 21, 31, 43, 49, 62
Pearl Jam, 57, 198
"Pease Porridge," 62–63
"Pease Porridge Hot" (nursery rhyme), 62–63
"Peer Pressure," 170
"Peg" (Steely Dan), 31
Penascola, Florida, 4, 57–58
People Under the Stairs, 157, 180, 218
Perry, Jennifer, 93
Personal Responsibility and Work Opportunity Reconciliation Act (PRWORA), 145
Pete Rock & C.L. Smooth, 94
Petrin, Nate, 209

The Pharcyde, 78, 81, 138
Pharrell, 3, 33, 73
Phife Dawg, 30, 32, 61, 81, 101, 142, 156, 163, 210, 218, 219, 232
Philadelphia, Pennsylvania, 87
Phonte, 169, 210
Pierre, Alphonse, 226
Pitchfork, 28, 47, 209, 226, 230
Please Hammer Don't Hurt 'Em (MC Hammer), 60
Plug 1 & Plug 2 Present . . . First Serve, 195
"Plug Tunin,'" 18, 19, 20, 22, 26
P.M. Dawn, 43
Poetic, 73
police and policing, 53, 118, 157–159
political rap groups, 6, 39
political violence, 120–121
politics
    Black leadership in, 118–119
    Cold War, 5–6, 7, 49, 52
    De La Soul songs about, 240–241
    example of a Patti Dooke in, 93–94
    presidential election (2000), 165–166
    Reagan era, 34–35, 37–38
    September 11th terrorist attacks and, 167
"Pony Ride," 137
Posdnuos (Kelvin Mercer)
    on being different, 10
    birthplace, 12–13
    choosing stage name, 15–16
    desire for freedom, 9
    dress, 2
    early experiences with music, 11–12, 14–15
    in Easy Street, 15
    glasses of, 5
    on *Hip Hop for Respect*, 158, 159
    on inspiration for "Say No Go," 36
    on Long Island, New York, 13
    "plug" name of, 16
    on "The Message," 38
"post-soul" America, 53
"Potholes in My Lawn," 26, 27–28, 140, 180, 196
Poulson-Bryant, Scott, 72, 78
Power, Bob, 132
Poyser, James, 165
Pras, 133
The Predator (Ice Cube), 54, 77
Prince, 4, 17, 197, 203, 212
Prince Paul (Huston, Paul), 6, 9, 224
    birthplace, 13
    on "Buddy," 31–32
    on *Buhloone Mindstate*, 87–88
    Buhloone Mindstate and, 82
    on D.A.I.S.Y, 59–60
    De La Soul Is Dead and, 51
    early music experiences, 13
    first connecting with De La Soul, 18–19

INDEX

Prince Paul (Huston, Paul) *(cont.)*
  in "Itzsoweezee (HOT)" video, 151
  Mosaic Thump and, 164
  recording of *3 Feet High and Rising,* 22
  sample clearances and, 216
  solo albums, 73
  Stakes Is High and, 126, 146
  Stetsasonic and, 18
prison population, 118, 145–146
psychedelic sound/influence, 10, 42
Psychoanalysis (What Is It?) (Prince Paul), 73
Public Enemy, 3, 6, 14, 17, 23–24, 30, 35–36, 39, 46, 47, 93, 129, 134, 162, 163, 243
Puff Daddy. *See* Combs, Sean "Puff Daddy"
Pusha T, 177–178

Q

Q-Tip, 14, 30, 32, 67, 68, 81, 82, 100, 101–102, 110, 138, 156, 210, 224
Quad Studios, Manhattan, 122
Queen Latifah, 1, 21, 29–30, 32, 88, 100, 103, 110, 148, 217, 224
Questlove, 15, 21, 43, 50, 97–98, 165, 201, 212–213, 217
"Quiet Storm" (Smokey Robinson), 105

R

Race Matters (West), 85
Race Rebels: Culture, Politics, and the Black Working Class (Kelley), 66
racial identity, 52–53
racism, 17, 91, 99, 121, 130, 140, 150, 157, 189, 193–194
radio stations, corporate-controlled, 145
Raekwon, 73, 103, 117, 121–122, 128, 131
Rah Digga, 158, 164
Rainbow Coalition, 93, 119
Rakim, 12, 14, 22, 23, 26, 29, 129
Ramsey, Donovan X., 37
Rangel, Charles, 35
Rap City, 124, 127, 136
rap industry. *See also* Tommy Boy Records
  creative freedom in, 78
  criticism of, in "The Bizness," 134–135
  De La Soul's criticism of, 10–11, 62, 75–76, 88, 115, 139–140
  grind culture in, 178–180
  hypervisibility and invisibility in, 88–89
  mid-1990 conflict in, 121–123
  pursuit of wealth and fame in, 78–79
  restructuring of, in late 1990s and early 2000s, 136
  tension and competition within, 100–102
rap musicals, 73–74
rap music/musicians. *See also* gangsta rap(pers)
  adopting non-Black gangster personas, 131–132
  buhloone mindstate in, 78
  changing landscape of (mid-1990s), 128–129
  coming out of New York, mid-1980s, 20
  criticisms of, 114–115
  cultural appropriation in, 90–92
  deaths of, 115, 143–144, 186, 217–219
  emotional expression, 103–104
  gangster rap, 54
  growth in popularity of, 56
  jazz rap, 78, 79, 80–85, 110
  killings of, 129–130
  in the late 1990s, 155–156
  legal clampdown on, 47–48
  Mafioso aesthetic, 116, 128, 131, 133, 139–140, 151
  middle-aged, 111
  move into pop culture's mainstream, 144–145
  success and profit in, 183
  surviving after a member's death, 232
Rapsody, 235
Ras Kass, 158
Raw Deluxe (Jungle Brothers), 102, 156
Rawkus Records, 136, 156, 157, 159
Ready to Die (The Notorious B.I.G.), 116, 121, 134, 137, 148
Reagan era, 34–35, 37–38
Reagan, Nancy, 35, 36
"realness," De La Soul on, 103, 106, 115, 127
Reasonable Doubt (Jay-Z), 126
"Rebirth of Slick (Cool Like Dat)" (Digable Planets), 84–85
Recording Academy, 84
Red Bull Music Academy, 21, 186
Redding, Otis, 31, 65
Redman, 164, 165
Reid, Vernon, 17, 26
R.E.M., 56, 105
Republican Party, 54, 55
Reservoir Media, 215, 216
Resurrection (Common), 75
rhymes/rhyming, 27–28, 62, 140, 184
Rhythm Roots All-Stars, 202
Ridenhour, Carlton "Chuck D," 17
"Ring Ring Ring," 67–70, 105, 107, 140, 142, 165
Robinson, Dawn, 156
Robinson, Smokey, 105
Rocawear, 178
Rock, Charlie, 15
"Rock Co. Kane Flow," 183, 184
Rock, Jay, 213
Rock, Pete, 47, 48, 151, 206
Rockwell, 4
Rockwilder, 163
Rolling Stone, 25, 33, 36, 67, 72, 146, 198

INDEX

Rollins, Sonny, 83
Rome, Sylvia, 176
Roof, Dylann, 121
The Roots, 33, 97, 115, 136, 144, 151, 165, 178, 180
Ross, Dante, 19, 22, 27
Rostrum Records, 214
"Royalty Capes," 207
Rubin, Rick, 20
Ruby Ridge, 121
Ruff Ryders, 155
"Rules" (Wu-Tang Clan), 167
Run-D.M.C., 12, 20, 24, 29, 30, 129, 217, 232
"Runnin'" (The Pharcyde), 138
Rush Management, 100
RZA, 73, 124, 195

S

Saadiq, Raphael, 156
Salamon, Jeff, 146
Salt-n-Pepa, 94
"Same Song" (Tupac Shakur), 96
sampling music, 2, 3, 9
   for *Buhloone Mindstate*, 84
   debates about, 229–230
   in *De La Soul Is Dead*, 61–62
   De La Soul's approach to, 23, 24
   De La Soul shifting away from, 201–202
   jazz music, 79, 81, 82
   "Little Ole Country Boy," 28
   Maceo Parker on, 83–84
   Mos Def mocking Puff Daddy's, 156
   on "Patti Dooke," 108
   by Vanilla Ice and MC Hammer, 60
   by white artists, 46–47
Sanctuary, 177
"Saturdays," 68
"Say It Loud (I'm Black and I'm Proud)" (James Brown), 83
"Say No Go," 35–37, 39, 70, 107, 177, 228, 229
Scarface, 74, 77, 92
Schmemann, Serge, 52
ScHoolboy Q, 213
School Daze (television show), 53
Schoolhouse Rock, 23, 27
Schoolly D, 29, 116
The Score (The Fugees), 126
Scott, James C., 29, 66–67
Scott, Jill, 206, 207
Scott, Travis, 1
"Self-Destruction" (The Stop the Violence Movement), 39
September 11th terrorist attacks (2001), 166–168
Sermon, Erick, 107, 133
Serpick, Evan, 33–34

sex(uality)
   "Buddy"/"Buddy (Native Tongue Decision)" and, 31–32
   in *De La Soul Is Dead*, 62, 64–65
   De La Soul songs about, 242
   "Jenifa Taught Me" and, 30–31
   Stakes Is High songs about, 141–142
sexism, 55, 142
sexual assault and abuse, 70–72, 122, 135
Sgt. Pepper's Lonely Hearts Club Band (The Beatles), 25
Shabaam Sahdeeq, 158–159
Shades of Blue (Madlib), 110
"Shake Everything You've Got" (Maceo Parker and band), 83
Shakur, Afeni, 96
Shakur, Lumumba, 96
Shock G., 218
Shortie No Mas(s), 86–87, 88, 89, 99
"The Show" (Doug E. Fresh), 20
"Shwingalokate," 46
"Sick of Talkin'," 137–141
Silverman, Tom, 19, 23, 43, 159, 176, 205, 212, 213, 214
Simmons, Russell "Rush," 100
Simone, Nina, 17
"Simply," 170
"Simply Havin" (The Beatles), 170
Simpson, Mike, 24
Simpson, O.J., trial of, 119
Singleton, John, 54
Sisario, Ben, 217
6 Feet Deep (Gravediggaz), 73
skits, 3, 24
   Buhloone Mindstate, 88
   "De La Orgee," 30–31
   De La Soul Is Dead, 62
   list of De La Soul's, 240
   "Not Over Till the Fat Lady Plays the Demo," 69
   Stakes Is High, 126–127, 137
   "Take It Off," 33, 139
   "Talkin' Bout Hey Love," 64
   "Transmitting Live from Mars," 23, 46
Slate, 147, 200
Slick Rick, 20, 23, 156, 171
Slum Village, 138, 176, 232
Sly & the Family Stone, 25
Small, Michael. *See* Mike Gee (Michael Small)
Smith, Bessie, 17
Smith, Danyel, 82
Smith, Denzel, 148
Smith, Ethan, 146–147
Smith, Lonnie Liston, 81
Smith, Mychal Denzel, 148
Snoop Dogg, 85, 109, 122, 178, 206, 207–208
Snow White, 40
"Somebody's Watching Me" (Rockwell), 4

INDEX

Sony Music, 225
soul music, 164–165
"Soul Power" (Maceo Parker and band), 83
Soulquarian movement, 165
The Souls of Black Folk (Du Bois), 16
Soul Sonic Force, 19
The Source, 13, 53–54, 72, 81, 88, 108–109, 121, 124, 146, 156
Source Awards (1995), 122
South Africa, 6
"South Bronx" (Boogie Down Productions), 129
southern rap, 155
Space, 184
"The Space Program" (A Tribe Called Quest), 210
"speak," 26–27
SPIN magazine, 146, 209, 219
The Spinners, 4
spiritual traditions, in Black culture, 16
spirit world, Black culture and, 16
Spoonie Gee, 91
"Spoonin' Rap" (Spoonie Gee), 91
Spotify, 3, 197, 198, 225, 227
Springsteen, Bruce, 198
The Square Roots (The Roots), 87
"Squat," 163–164
Stakes Is High, 75, 114–153, 186, 187, 191, 235. See also individual song titles
   "cousins of," 245
   influence on author, 150
   reviews of, 146–148
   serious direction taken in, 126–127
"Stakes Is High," 105, 137, 139, 140, 152, 186, 195, 234, 236
Stakes Is High: Life After the American Dream (Smith), 148
"Stakes Is High" video, 138, 139–140
Star Trek, 105
Steely Dan, 31
Stefani, Gwen, 155
Stein, Judith, 145
Sterne, Jonathan, 163
Stetsasonic, 18, 19
Stop the Violence Movement, 39
Straight Outta Compton (N.W.A), 23
Straight Out the Jungle (Jungle Brothers), 30
streaming services, 2, 192, 196–198, 212–213, 225–229
Strictly 4 My N.I.G.G.A.Z (Tupac Shakur), 97
"Strong Island," 14
Stubblefield, Clyde, 83
suburbia, 14, 27, 28, 61
"Sucker MCs" (Run-D.M.C.), 21
Sugarhill Gang, 105
Sugar Hill Records, 20
"Suicidal Thoughts" (The Notorious B.I.G.), 117
Sun Ra, 48–49

Supa Dave West, 163, 165, 177
"Super Freak" (Rick James), 60
"superpredator," 146
Swift, Taylor, 59, 192, 197, 198, 212, 225, 227
Swizz Beatz, 155

T

T3, 232
Take Care (Drake), 196
"Take It Off," 33–34, 139
Talib Kweli, 33, 75, 136, 144, 157, 158, 215, 224, 234
"Talkin' Bout Hey Love," 64–65
Tate, Greg, 17, 24, 31, 32, 109
Teen Titans GO!, 214–215
Telecommunications Act (1996), 144
The Temptations, 91
Tha Alkaholiks, 163
Thank Me Later (Drake), 196
"(Sittin' On) the Dock of the Bay" (Otis Redding), 31
There's a Poison Goin' On (Public Enemy), 162
There's a Riot Going on (Sly & the Family Stone), 25
3rd Bass, 78, 184
Thomas, Carl, 177
Thomas, Carla, 65
Thomas, Clarence, 54–55
Thompson, Ahmir, 87
Thompson, Terressa. *See* Shortie No Mas(s)
3 Feet High and Rising, 2, 3, 214–215, 229, 235. *See also* individual song titles
   collage approach to sampling in, 9
   countercultural spirit in, 6
   "cousins" of, 243–244
   creative individualism in, 24–25
   "freedom dreaming" on, 9–10
   musician influences on, 20–21
   psychedelic production and vibe on, 10
   recording, 22–23
   reviews and critics on, 25–26
   35th Anniversary edition, 18
"Three Is the Magic Number," 27
Thriller (Michael Jackson), 79
"Thriller" (Michael Jackson), 4
"Thru Ya City," 163, 234
Tidal, 197, 198, 225
Tidal Music, 214
Timbaland, 144, 155, 176
Tlaib, Rashida, 228
Tommy Boy Entertainment, 176
Tommy Boy Records
   De La Soul ending relationship with, 213–214
   De La Soul's catalog and, 2, 3, 192
   De La Soul's criticism of, 75–76, 82, 135, 179

INDEX

De La Soul's dispute/negotiations with, 211–212
demanding a "radio record" for *Buhloone Mindstate,* 104
desire for another hit, 67, 68
ending partnership with Warner Music Group, 176
first impressions of De La Soul, 19
going defunct, 136
marketing strategies, 10, 43
releasing "Plug Tunin' " single, 22
requesting a radio-friendly single, 39
in *Teen Titans* episode, 215
on triple album, 159
Top Dawg Entertainment, 213
To Pimp a Butterfly (Kendrick Lamar), 111
To the East, Blackwards (X Clan), 39, 149
To The Extreme (Vanilla Ice), 60
"Tramp" (Lowell Fulson), 64, 65
"Transmitting Live from Mars" (skit), 23, 46
Treach, 130, 164
"Tread Water," 37–38, 39
A Tribe Called Quest, 1, 14, 21, 29, 30, 31, 32, 78, 80–81, 85, 87, 88–89, 100, 101, 109, 115, 120, 122–123, 144, 156, 160, 210–211, 232
"trife life," 115
TR Love, 20
Trotter, Tariq, 87
Trugoy (David Jolicoeur). *See also* De La Soul
 approach to music, 12
 birthplace, 13
 on "Bitties in the BK Lounge," 65
 on "Breakadawn," 107–108
 choosing stage name, 15–16
 death, 217–219
 desire for freedom, 9
 dress, 2
 in Easy Street, 15
 growing up in East Massapequa, 14
 Haitian background, 12, 15, 38, 150, 151
 on individuality in rap, 33–34
 influencing clothing style of De La Soul, 21
 on Long Island, New York, 13
 "plug" name of, 16
 Stakes Is High and, 150
Trump, Donald, 210, 211
"Trying People," 172–173, 175–176, 219, 223
Tucker, C. Delores, 114, 115, 125
Tupac Shakur, 74, 77, 89, 92, 95–97, 115, 116, 121, 122, 123, 126, 130, 143–144, 157, 180
turntables, 11, 12
The Turtles, 23, 24, 46

21 Savage, 1
2Chainz, 206
2-D, 187, 188
2Pacalypse Now (Tupac Shakur), 96, 138
Tyler, Steven, 71
Tyler, The Creator, 3, 235

U
"U Can Do (Life)," 163, 165
"U Can't Touch This" (MC Hammer), 60
"U Got Shot" (EPMD), 133
Ultramagnetic MC, 20–21, 94–95
Uncle Jam Wants You (Funkadelic), 39
"Under Pressure" (David Bowie and Queen), 60
Universal Music Group, 225
University of Michigan, 194
Usher, 206
utopianism, 9–10, 49

V
Valli, Frankie, 67
Van Deburg, William L., 29
Vanilla Ice, 60–61, 93
Van Winkle, Robert, 61
Variety, 82, 88, 224
Vaughan, Sarah, 80
"Verses from the Abstract" (A Tribe Called Quest), 82, 101
Vibe (magazine), 78, 82, 100, 122, 127, 143
videos
 "Baby Phat," 170–171
 "Breakadawn," 106–108
 D.A.I.S.Y. images in, 44
 "Ego Trippin' (Part Two)" and, 95–96, 130
 "Eye Know," 31
 "Feel Good Inc.," 187–188
 "Get Away," 195–196
 "I Get Around" (Tupac Shakur), 97
 "It Was a Good Day" (Ice Cube), 107
 "Itzsoweezee," 151–153
 "Janie's Got a Gun" (Aerosmith), 71
 "Me Myself and I," 5, 40–41
 "Much More," 183–184
 satirical depiction of, 95–96, 97–98
 Stakes Is High, 138, 139–140
 "What They Do" (The Roots), 97
 The Wizard of Oz, 164
Village Voice, 32
Vincent, Rickey, 39
violence
 De La Soul songs about, 164
 gun, 130–131
 police, 53–54, 157, 158–159
 political, 120–121
 by "superpredators" (Black youth), 145–146
Viral Justice (Benjamin), 148
VladTV, 203

293

INDEX

W
Waco, Texas, 151
Walker, Steve, 121
Wallace, Christopher. *See* The Notorious B.I.G. (Christopher Wallace)
Wallace, Riley, 209
Warner Bros., 100, 135
Warner Music Group, 2, 176, 179, 192, 200, 201, 203, 213, 225
War on Drugs, 34–35
War on Terror, 167
Warren G, 116
Warwick, Dionne, 114, 115
Washington, Denzel, 84
Washington, Kamasi, 111
"Watch Ya' Mouth" (Tupac Shakur), 123
Watkins, Greg, 82
Watkins, S. Craig, 145
Wax Poetics, 13
Wayte, Larry, 197
wealth, pursuit and displays of, 79, 95, 98, 115, 132, 139–140, 157, 178. *See also* materialism
Weather Report, 80, 81
Weaver, Randy, 121
Webby awards, 201
Webster Hall, New York City, 223
We Got It from Here . . . Thank You 4 Your Service (A Tribe Called Quest), 210, 232
Welcome 2 Detroit (J Dilla), 138
welfare reform, 145–146
We Real Cool: Black Men and Masculinity (bell hooks), 114
We're Still Here (Now) . . . A Documentary about nobody (documentary), 205, 219
Wesley, Fred, 83, 84
West, Cornel, 85, 114, 118
West, Kanye, 3, 48, 73, 99, 137, 156, 178, 189
Westside Connection, 122–123
Westside Gunn, 235
"Westside Slaughterhouse" (Mack 10), 122
West Virginia University, 229
"We the People" (A Tribe Called Quest), 210
What's Going On (Marvin Gaye), 117
"What They Do" (The Roots), 97
"What We Do (For Love)," 171
Where Do We Go from Here: Chaos or Community (King), 150
white lyricists, 61
white population
   artists stealing and sampling from Black artists, 46–47
   Beastie Boys and, 20
   Black artists appealing to, 91–92
   De La Soul's Blackness and, 92
   "Patti Dooke" and, 93–94
white supremacists, 120–121
"Who Do You Worship," 73
Williams, Justin A., 81
Williams, Lena, 52
Williamson, Lisa "Sister Souljah," 93–94
Winfrey, Oprah, 146
The Wizard of Oz (movie), 107, 164
A Wolf in Sheep's Clothing (Black Sheep's Dres), 89
women. *See also* Black women
   approach to, in *Stakes Is High*, 141–142
   body sizes and, 170–171
   De La Soul's mixed approach to, 171
   rappers, 89, 141
"Wonce Again Long Island," 141
Wonder, Stevie, 4
work, De La Soul songs about, 64–67, 68
World Trade Center bombing (1993), 120
Wrath of Math (Jeru the Damaja), 123
Wreckx-N-Effect, 81
"Written on the Wall" (The Invitation), 18
"Wu-Gambinos" (Raekwon), 131
Wu-Tang Clan, 3, 109, 117, 120, 121, 123, 124, 139, 150, 152, 157, 167, 195, 196
Wu-Tang Forever (Wu-Tang Clan), 120, 150, 195
"Wu-Tang Forever," 196
Wu-Tang Records, 74

X
X Clan, 39, 149
XXL, 209
Xzibit, 74, 163

Y
Yesterdays New Quintent, 110
"You Don't Wanna B.D.S.," 164
Younge, Adrian, 110
Young, Neil, 49
Young Thug, 1
Young Zee, 151
You're Welcome, 196, 201
"You Showed Me" (The Turtles), 23, 46
YouTube, 197, 225
Yummy Bingham, 177, 184

Z
Zawinul, Joe, 80
Zev Love X, 184
Zion I, 157

ABOUT THE AUTHOR

Austin McCoy is an assistant professor of history at West Virginia University, specializing in African American History, labor history, social movements, and hip-hop culture. His work has appeared in numerous outlets including CNN, the *Baffler*, the *Washington Post*, *Black Perspectives*, *Public Books*, and *Truthout*. He lives in Morgantown, West Virginia.